FOR GOD'S SAKE,
REST!

James L. Anderson

For God's Sake, REST!

DISCOVERING THE PLEASURE OF HIS REST

Pleasant Word (a division of WinePress Publishing, PO Box 428, Enumclaw, WA 98022) functions only as book publisher. As such, the ultimate design, content, editorial accuracy, and views expressed or implied in this work are those of the author.

Unless otherwise indicated, all Scriptures are taken from the Holy Bible, New International Version, Copyright © 1973, 1978, 1984 by the International Bible Society. Used by permission of Zondervan Publishing House. The "NIV" and "New International Version" trademarks are registered in the United States Patent and Trademark Office by International Bible Society.

Scripture references marked NASB are taken from the New American Standard Bible, © 1960, 1963, 1968, 1971, 1972, 1973, 1975, 1977, 1995 by The Lockman Foundation. Used by permission.

Scripture references marked NKJV are taken from the New King James Version, © 1979, 1980, 1982 by Thomas Nelson, Inc., Publishers. Used by permission.

Scripture quotations marked ESV are taken from The Holy Bible: English Standard Version, copyright © 2001, Wheaton: Good News Publishers. Used by permission. All rights reserved.

Scripture references marked MSG are taken from The Message Bible © 1993 by Eugene N. Peterson, NavPress, POB 35001, Colorado Springs, CO 80935, 4th printing in USA 1994. Published in association with the literary agency—Aline Comm. POB 49068, Colorado Springs, CO 80949. Used by permission.

ISBN 13: 978-1-4141-0829-2
ISBN 10: 1-4141-0829-X
Library of Congress Catalog Card Number: 2006908072

DEDICATION

For God's Sake, Rest! Discovering the Pleasure of His Rest is dedicated to my wife, Lois Ann Anderson. Lois has stood with me through ministry journeys, bouts of depression, and my whole Sabbath-rest discovery. More than anyone else she has urged me to take rest, Sabbath-rest. When I was stuck in workaholic ruts and Sabbath resistance, Lois nudged me out the door and on my way to my meeting place with God. We now offer Sabbath-retreats to pastors, missionaries, and church leaders. She is at my side helping me tell my story and tenderly encouraging others as she once encouraged me.

TABLE OF CONTENTS

FOREWORD

I am becoming convinced that we who claim to be followers of Jesus are missing something very basic in our lives in the 21st century. In my current role as a seminary president, I have visited hundreds of churches and met with scores of pastors and church folks. Again and again I find that people tell me they believe their lives are "too busy." Even in their busy-ness they frequently report feeling guilty because they are not doing everything they think they should. In the end, most are just tired. The self-diagnostic terms I hear are stressed out, strung out, worn out, wrung out, or burned out. And the result is that they just want *out*—that is, out of ministry, out of their jobs, out of their marriages, out of the stress.

Hectic, frenetic living fosters a shallowness in the soul. When I observe the life of the contemporary church, I do not see a lack of activity. Indeed, one of my greatest concerns for the American church is that we are so thoroughly program-focused we take little time for the nourishment of our inner lives. We do many things for God, but then we spend little with God. For a long time I've felt that many of us have our lives out of order with no healthy pacing. We become what T.S. Eliot called "hollow men" who, when pressure and temptation come, crumble. I'm quite sure that one reason for the all-too-frequent stories recounting the moral falls of church leaders is that many well-meaning and hard-working Christian workers have an emptiness in their inner beings.

I was talking about this perception several years ago at a conference when I had the chance to meet with Jim Anderson. He and I agreed that most people have established a pattern of living that needs repair. We also agreed that one of the foundational means of healing is found in the fourth commandment: "Observe the Sabbath Day by keeping it holy as the LORD your God has commanded you. Six days you shall labor and do all your work but the seventh day is a Sabbath to the LORD your God..." (Dt. 5:12-14a).

This commandment is ignored by some who say it no longer has any relevance to New Testament Christians. Others who have turned a day of rest into a burdensome and boring set of rules and regulations have distorted it. Certainly there are few who view Sabbath-keeping as refreshing and renewing. In Genesis 1, God worked six days and then ceased that work for one day, a Sabbath. Then he made us in his image. The message: his pattern is to be adopted by those made in his image.

Pastor Jim Anderson reminds us of the ongoing validity and importance of the fourth command—and he provides help in how to live in the light of it. He has convinced me that the Fourth Commandment is still to be obeyed and that, when we obey it, we will live more fully as God has created us to live. I pray that, in reading his message, we will all find our lives to be less busy—more productive—and thoroughly glorifying to God.

Greg Waybright, PhD
President, Trinity Evangelical Divinity School

PREFACE

I sat in a college classroom on a warm summer day. Determined to gradu-
ate from college the following spring, I elected to squeeze in a few more
credits during the summer months. The subject was human psychology.
The professor had stalled out on Maslow's hierarchy of human needs.
I didn't mind, since Maslow's contribution interested me. Psychologist
Abraham Maslow (1908-1970) proposed that people have a hierarchy of
needs ranging from security to self-actualization. Higher needs come into
focus only after lower needs are met. It made perfect sense to me. Maslow
had given me a reason to focus on my needs the rest of my life.

Most books on the shelves of secular and Christian bookstores focus
on human needs. I've found that focusing on my needs is an endless cycle.
Once one need is addressed another emerges from my body, my soul, and
my mind. Each need screams to be satisfied. As a result I could spend my
entire life climbing up Maslow's hierarchy of human needs, seldom peek-
ing beyond myself.

In contrast *For God's Sake, Rest! Discovering the Pleasure of His Rest*
focuses first and foremost on pleasing God. When God is my focus, He
meets essential needs in bunches while higher self-fulfillment needs seemingly melt away.

The book of Genesis states, "In the beginning God...." The Twenty-
Third Psalm begins, "The Lord is my Shepherd...." The Lord's Prayer starts
with, "Our Father who is in Heaven...." Our self-help slant is apt to rewrite
the prayer to begin with, "Give us this day our daily bread" and end with,
"By the way, I'd like tomorrow's bread today as well."

Most books that recognize pleasing God as the answer to satisfying human needs focus on *doing or working* for God. *For God's Sake, Rest!* values *rest* as a means of pleasing God. For years I was told that I had to do something to please God and to use my gifts to serve him. I thought doing things was the only way I could please him. If I didn't do something great, I wasn't of much value to God.

I remember flying home from a pastors conference in southern California, weeping as I peered through the window of the aircraft. I wanted to do something great for God but just didn't seem to have the means to do it. Through a series of life-changing events my eyes were opened to the Scriptures which say that God actually rests and desires that we join him in that rest. As a person at rest in him I am of value.

Furthermore once I learned to appreciate rest, serving God energized me. Rest enabled me to distinguish between God's part and my part of his work on earth. When it comes to service, I have noticed that God won't do my part for me; and I certainly cannot do his part for him. Thus when resting in God precedes working for God, I am better able to rise to the occasion and work as commissioned by him with a much clearer perspective.

Rest has a higher appeal than satisfying my need for it. Rest is about pleasing God by entering it. God takes pleasure in my rest and calls me to rest as a means of pleasing him and enjoying his delight.

This book addresses three questions: How can I rest so as to please God? How can I rest from work? How can I rest while engaged in work and life? These questions are answered consecutively in the three sections of the book. Once we believe and accept that rest is truly pleasing to God and have learned what it means to truly rest, we are ready to rest at work and in all of life.

ACKNOWLEDGEMENTS

Dr. Lareau Lindquist was one of the first persons who encouraged me to take extended time alone with God, time I didn't think I had. Tom Bussard, Navigators staff, prodded me until I finally gave in to the quiet call of Sabbath-rest. Tom has been a mentor, encourager, and close friend ever since. Lois, my wife of thirty-five years, has consistently reminded me to meet with God and reorient my life with His peace in the face of much anxiety. Our sons, Scott and Nate, were a constant reminder to lighten up and take a break during the years they were at home. Now that they are grown they encourage my own faith and scourge my life of pat answers.

I am indebted to the many authors, both living and deceased, whose writings enlightened my understanding of the Sabbath. Gordon MacDonald, David Mains, Eugene Peterson, D.A. Carson, Oswald Chambers, Corrie ten Boom, and Abraham Joshua Heschel are a few of the many who have cleared a trail for me to follow.

I thank my father, the late Harold E. Anderson, for teaching me to value truth, honesty, and hard work. I am confident that my own search for a rhythm of work and rest began by watching Dad struggle to strike a balance between work and rest. I thank my mother, Jeanette Anderson, for being a constant source of stability in my life. Both parents provided a wealth of character, life experience, and opportunities.

The three congregations I served—Grace Evangelical Free Church of Davenport, Iowa, Conover Evangelical Free Church of Conover, Wisconsin, and Grace Fellowship of Overland Park, Kansas—each played a role in my growing understanding and practice of Sabbath-rest. They faithfully granted me a portion of my week for seeking the Lord in solitude that I might experience God deeply and lead them to God freely.

The late Dr. Warren Benson, director of the Doctor of Ministry program at Trinity Evangelical Divinity School, served as my Doctor of Ministry project mentor and guided my final project, *Sabbath Rest for Pastors*. Had I fully heeded his encouragement, this book would have been written long ago, and he would have been alive to read it. Dr. David Larsen, professor of preaching, contributed additional guidance throughout the project. The project proved to be the embryo of this book.

The North Central District of the Evangelical Free Church granted me the time to complete my manuscript. Superintendent Tom Mouw has labeled my writing "a labor of love." Director of Pastoral Care Dean Johnson has served as my mentor for many chapters of pastoral ministry. His modeled humility has inadvertently molded portions of this book.

I must thank the dozens of pastors and their wives who have attended Sabbath-rest retreats and absorbed what I conveyed to them about rest. Their consideration of the Sabbath concept has encouraged me to keep promoting the rest factor as a preventative and cure to ministerial burnout.

Roger Palm, of *Pastor Write*, sharpened my writing skills and encouraged me to publish the work. Friend and church leader Steve Muyskens spent hours proofreading, while his wife, Nancy, encouraged me by writing her own book, *The Curtain Is Torn*. Sue Van Hal and Steve Schwartz enhanced the project with numerous proof readings. I am grateful for the contributions of all of these individuals and others who collectively brought this book to fruition.

Finally, I acknowledge The Lord of the Sabbath as the God of rest. I acknowledge the Bible as a book about rest. God has communicated the value of rest throughout his Word, and rest is a core value with him.

INTRODUCTION

The snow blew through the tall pines as I stared through the windshield of my parked car. Scarcely anyone would visit this picnic area in the winter months, not even mosquitoes. I was breaking in a new outdoor sanctuary. For nearly twenty years I had established various private sanctuaries in states where I had served congregations: Iowa, Wisconsin, and Kansas. But this one would take on new significance. Not because of its magnificent trees, or vast acreage, nor because it was in my home state where I spent the first twenty-four years of my life. This outdoor sanctuary reigned because I had just given up my indoor sanctuary. After twenty-five consecutive years serving as a pastor of local churches, I no longer had a church. I was a preacher without a pulpit, a shepherd without a clearly defined flock, a leader without a following.

My wife, Lois, and I had just moved from Kansas to Minnesota in January—something only former Minnesotans would do. I had accepted a new position as a *pastor to pastors* with a district of one-hundred and forty churches. This was a newly formed position. While the opportunity to mold the position to fit my pastoral gifts excited me, there was a strange nakedness about it.

Women wear their homes, men wear their jobs, and pastors wear their churches. Few women enjoy living out of a suitcase. I had counseled several couples whose marriages were on the ropes simply because the husband couldn't settle down and the wife couldn't handle being uprooted like a homeless person any longer. Generally speaking women tend to settle in and nest, while men thrive on the thrill of a new challenge. Men will give up comfort for a new job as long as their wives are willing, and too often when they are not.

I have also sat with men who were jobless. The first month goes *okay* as long as there is some promise of finding new employment. By the third month these men are concerned. By the sixth month they are desperate. If a year has elapsed without landing a job, they feel devastated. Tears accompany doubts as they mutter, "What's wrong with me?"

It is every bit as dreadful for pastors who leave parish ministries and want to serve as pastor of a congregation again. The church is their extended family, identity, and cloth. I had watched fellow pastors be disrobed of their churches or voluntarily resign in distress with no place to go. I never wanted to go through what I had witnessed.

Taking this new position was like disrobing to help other pastors stay wrapped in their churches. I would examine what pastors needed in order to survive and thrive in pastoral ministry and equip them the best I could with God's help. But to do my new position justice I would have to resign from my congregation after being their pastor for thirteen years. I would relocate without a congregation waiting to receive me.

That day I gained a new appreciation for being a pastor. There is something precious about a shepherd's relationship with a flock and God's call to serve them. Presiding at child dedications, baptisms, weddings, birthdays, anniversaries, and funerals fuses pastors and parishioners together for years. I have lived long enough to have former parishioners walk up to me and remind me, "Pastor, you baptized me." "Pastor, you dedicated me." "Pastor, you married us." "Pastor, you did my husband's funeral." Opening the timeless Word of God for a congregation, sharing Christ in the community, discipling believers, and developing leaders shapes a pastor for eternity.

That first day in my new outdoor sanctuary I saw the significance of another day, the day I entered my first Sabbath-rest experience eighteen years earlier. It was a day when God reviewed my life with him. He revealed to me how I always looked for a pedestal to stand on because I felt so small. Early on it was art, then music, then ministry, then having a church. When things went well with the church, I felt tall. When things were troublesome, I felt like my pedestal was quaking beneath me and about to tumble with me on it. My identity was wrapped up in the church I served. That day was memorable because God brought me back to the basics.

He reminded me there was no greater calling than to be a Christian, a Christ follower. Doctor, professor, pastor, or any other label could not compare to the name of Christ. Jim Anderson, Christian, was the greatest position and finest title I could ever have. That identity could not be taken from me. With or without a job, I never needed to feel naked again, even if I didn't have a church. That was significant preparation for the day I would serve without a church wrapped around me. Resting in Christ's sufficiency was the best tool I could put in any pastor's survival kit, including my own.

For that matter identity in Christ is the finest gift one person can pass on to another regardless of career or other differences. Belonging to Jesus Christ puts us all in the same humble yet exalted position.

Sabbath-rest is not limited to prophet, priest, or king. Rest in Christ is offered to all who belong to him. May God use *For God's Sake, Rest! Discovering the Pleasure of His Rest* to deepen your rest in Christ as his pleasure resides in you.

Part I

REST, THE PLEASURE OF GOD

HOW CAN I PLEASE GOD BY RESTING?

That was not a legitimate question throughout much of my life. Pleasing God, man, or self was always linked to work, action, or accomplishment, but not rest! Rest was for infants, the sick, the elderly, and those who had earned it by working.

You might be surprised to learn that we were made to please God by resting. Many of the same elements that bring rest into our lives bring pleasure to God when we participate in them.

God is pleased when we reflect his image through rest as well as work. God is pleased when we rest by trusting his Word. God is pleased when we enter his Sabbath as a sanctuary of time. God is pleased when we adopt his perspective through rest. God is definitely pleased when we make His rest our pleasure. These topics of Scripture are essential to resting *for God's sake.*

May you be blessed and God pleased as you discover the pleasure of his rest.

CHAPTER ONE

REST, THE PLEASURE
OF HIS IMAGE

I PLEASE GOD BY REFLECTING HIS IMAGE

Thus the heavens and the earth were completed in all their vast array. By the seventh day God had finished the work he had been doing; so on the seventh day he rested from all his work. And God blessed the seventh day and made it holy, because on it he rested from all the work of creating that he had done.

(Genesis 2:1-3)

Made in the image and likeness of God, I am likely to rest.

(Jim Anderson)

For years my wife, Lois, and I had heard others talk about their trips to Lake Louise in Banff National Park. "It is so beautiful, you have to go there and see it for yourself." Nestled in the Canadian Rockies, in the province of Alberta, Lake Louise has captured the hearts of admirers for centuries.

Not until Lois and I were given an all-expense paid vacation for our thirtieth wedding anniversary did we schedule a trip to Lake Louise. I had no idea the trip would teach me so much about God and about myself. I didn't know that Lake Louise was going to give me a deeper understanding of spiritual rest.

For years we had vacationed in Colorado and experienced the grandeur of the American Rockies, but this sight stimulated our senses like none other. Towering snow-capped mountains stand vertically on both sides of the lake. As we looked down the long narrow waterway, our eyes fixated on the huge, sparkling glaciered mountain known as Mount Victoria.

Tom Wilson was the first white man to discover the lake in 1882 and named it Emerald Lake. No wonder—its water resembles the turquoise color of the precious stone. Two years later the name was changed to Lake Louise in honor of Princess Louise Caroline Alberta, wife of the Governor General of Canada from 1878 to 1883 and the fourth daughter of Queen Victoria. No matter what it is called, the total visual experience is a heart stopper.

I marveled, *what a work of art!* But before the day was over the scene would teach me more about God's rest than God's handiwork; this panoramic view increased my pulse rate and put me at ease simultaneously.

The moment Lois and I thought we had seen the lake in all her glory, the sun came out, and Lake Louise reflected the image of Mount Victoria. The lake augmented her beauty by absorbing the image of the mountain.

Just as water contains the intrinsic ability to bear the image of objects far more impressive than itself, I realized *so do I!* A reflection on water serves as a reminder of the uniqueness of man. Like water, I was created with the ability to bear an image. I bear nothing less than the image of God, the Creator of all. Distinct from all other created things, man was created *in the image and likeness of God*: "Then God said, 'Let us make man in our image, in our likeness, and let them rule over the fish of the sea and the birds of the air, over the livestock, over all the earth, and over all the creatures that move along the ground'. So God created man in his own image, in the image of God he created him; male and female he created them" (Genesis 1:26-27).

As I read these verses my soul begged for an answer to the question, *how is the image and likeness of God reflected in man?* Knowing we would ask, the Author answers such questions within the context of the text. As God is the ultimate ruler, so he lets man rule in the caring image of God: "...and let them rule over the fish of the sea and the birds of the air, over the livestock, over all the earth, and over all the creatures that move along the ground." The image of God is evident in man as man rules the creatures of God's creation. Since God empowered man to rule, seeing man rule must give God pleasure.

When our two sons were still boys living at home, the three of us often went fishing together. For years it was toilsome work, untangling and tying line, baiting hooks and taking fish off. Eventually these lads became good fishermen. What was once as painful as a hook in the finger became a pleasure to watch because they were doing something in my likeness. To this day I will phone and ask our grown sons, Scott and Nate, "Have you been fishing lately?" Likewise they are prone to call me with the news, "Dad, I caught a big one!"

If we are made in the image and likeness of God, we are also apt to work. Much of our work may pertain to our privileged role as rulers of God's provision. However, work embraces much more than ruling as we expand our creative energies in the likeness of our creator. It is not that we become gods or even become more like God by ruling or creating; rather we reflect what God has already instilled within us. The acts of creating and making in Genesis chapter one are referred to as work in Genesis chapter two: "Thus the heavens and the earth were completed in all their vast array. By the seventh day God had finished the work he had been doing; so on the seventh day he rested from all his work. And God blessed the seventh day and made it holy, because on it he rested from all the work of creating that he had done" (Genesis 2:1-3).

Holy God worked the works of creation and continues to work as master of all. Work and all its related tasks of creating, making, ruling, planting, gathering, and managing preceded the fall of man. Bearing the image and likeness of God, man worked apart from any penalty or consequence of sin. It is safe to say that since God empowered man to work, God takes pleasure in seeing mankind at work. The person who refuses to work within his or her God-given capacity or realm of responsibility lives in contempt of the image and likeness of God within him or her. However, we are not to *overwork* as if it were the only way in which the image of God is evident in our lives. Many of us live as if work were the only way by which we can please God. We are constantly on the go and feel guilty when we are not.

REST AND THE IMAGE OF GOD

I will never forget the day I visited a counselor. A few months after leaving one congregation for another I began to experience severe anxiety. I felt like I was being squeezed in a vice between the expectations of all the new faces that stared at me every Sunday and my self-imposed ideals. After telling the therapist my story, I left myself wide open with the question, "Well, what do you think?"

She simply said, "The person in front of me is one of the most restless, driven people I have ever met." How humbling! I wanted to please God so much that I was neglecting one of the primary means of doing so—rest!

Contrary to my driven lifestyle, I realized that rest is actually a means of God showcasing his image in me. Made in the image and likeness of God, I am likely to rest as he shows me by example how to rest.

> *If my life is going to clearly reflect the image of God,*
> *I am going to have to learn how to rest.*

In contrast to the first six days of creation, on the seventh day God does not speak or work. Twice it is stated that God *rested*. Old Testament scholar John Sailhamer cites an important link between the rest theme and the unique creation of man:

> It is likely, as well, that the author intended the reader to understand the account of the seventh day in light of the "Image of God" theme of the sixth day. If the purpose of pointing to the "likeness" between man and his Creator was to call upon the reader to be more like God (e.g. Leviticus 11:45), then it is significant that the account of the seventh day stresses that very thing which the writer elsewhere so ardently calls upon the reader to do: "rest" on the seventh day (Exodus 20:8-11).[1]

> I am the LORD who brought you up out of Egypt to be your God; therefore be holy, because I am holy.
>
> (Leviticus 11:45)

> Remember the Sabbath day by keeping it holy. Six days you shall labor and do all your work, but the seventh day is a Sabbath to the LORD your God. On it you shall not do any work, neither you, nor your son or daughter, nor your manservant or maidservant, nor your animals, nor the alien within your gates. For in six days the LORD made the heavens and the earth, the sea, and all that is in them, but he rested on the seventh day. Therefore the LORD blessed the Sabbath day and made it holy."
>
> (Exodus 20:9-11)

If my life is going to clearly reflect the image of God, I am going to have to learn how to rest. Rest is of value to both God and man. The author of the Pentateuch, the first five books of the Bible, points out that the life of God and man intersect during periods of rest. Rest is so important to the God-man relationship that God called one day of the week—the Sabbath—a day of rest! The Hebrew word for rest is *Shabbat*, from which comes the word Sabbath. However, God's definition of rest may differ somewhat from our contemporary understanding of rest. From God's perspective rest is more than sleep or leisure. After all, God doesn't get tired: "Do you not know? Have you not heard? The LORD is the everlasting God, the Creator of the ends of the earth. He will not grow tired or weary, and his understanding no one can fathom" (Isaiah 40:28).

When I read that God rested on the seventh day from all His work which He had done, I wondered, "What is it that God did that was rest? He must have done something other than sleep."

DIVINE REST IS CLOSURE

Divine rest is closure. Before there can be closure, some activity or segment of time must begin. Genesis 1:1 tells us that God had indeed begun an era of creative activity, and that creative activity had been brought to a close. An act of closure is significant according to the value of that which precedes it. Genesis 2:1-3 tells us that something had been finished and this act of completion is the basis of divine rest, as commentator James G. Murphy explains, "The resting of God arises not from weariness, but from the completion of His task. He is refreshed, not by the recruiting of His strength, but by the satisfaction of having before Him a finished good."[2]

The first book about the Sabbath that impacted me was *Ordering Your Private World* by Gordon MacDonald. His insights remain helpful to me as I seek to understand and apply the Sabbath concept to my own life:

High-tech systems planners like to use the phrase "closing the loop" to describe the completion of a phase in an electrical circuit. They also use the phrase when they want to say that a task has been completed or that every person in a project has been informed or consulted.

So you could say that on the seventh day, God closed the loop on His primary creation activity. He closed it by resting and looking back upon it to survey what had been accomplished.

A Sabbath rest is, first of all, a time of looking backward, of loop-closing. We gaze upon our work and ask questions like: "What does my work mean?" "For whom did I do this work?" "How well was the work done?" "Why did I do this?" and "What results did I expect, and what did I receive?"

To put it another way, the rest God instituted was meant first and foremost to cause us to interpret our work, to press meaning into it, to make sure we know to whom it is properly dedicated.[3]

Closure requires that we have the power to stop working. Genesis 2:2 declares twice that God rested, and three times it states that he ceased making. C.F. Keil states, "God completed the creation of the world with all its inhabitants by ceasing to produce anything new...."[4] It is conceivable that God could have continued to create yet another universe or simply added another strain of insects to the present existing earth, but did not before resting. He had the power to cease his work. He controlled his work; his work did not control him.

It therefore can be said that in light of the likeness of God in man I demonstrate God's likeness by bringing closure to my work. This ability makes me unique compared to the rest of the created order, which does not voluntarily cease its endless cycle of activity. Closure has powerful implications for workaholics, those of us who are obsessed with work and even work at our play. The Sabbath becomes a test to determine if a person is in control of his work or his work is in control of him.

As a means of curtailing my own workaholic tendencies, I have found it helpful to set aside a time each week to record what I did during the past six days. I simply finish the sentence: *This week I* _____. I then list the tasks completed over the past seven days. The list embraces all aspects of life: doctor appointments, household chores, key conversations with family members, and of course loads of work-related endeavors. Nothing that comes to mind is too small for the list. Recording seemingly insignificant tasks or conversations has a role in registering a sense of closure and accomplishment. This means of charting progress contributes to a lighthearted mood, putting a smile on an otherwise stress-filled face. Perhaps it was more than a smile on my face. Perhaps it is the image of God within me and the pleasure of God inducing the smile.

I believe God modeled daily closure for us as well as weekly closure in Genesis one and two. He brought closure to his work each day with the words, "It is good," even though the total project of creation remained unfinished. Then at the end of the sixth day he said, "It is very good."

DIVINE REST IS BLESSING

Divine rest is blessing: "And God blessed the seventh day...." (Genesis 2:3). Blessing is the act of bestowing some good on an object or person. God had *seen* that all he had made was good (Genesis 1:4, 10, 12, 18, 21, 25, and 31). Now he includes the seventh day in that goodness. However, this declaration regarding the seventh day is distinct compared to statements following the days of creation for three reasons. First, before the seventh day it was the contents of creation that were seen as good and not specifically the days themselves. The seventh day is the first day that is recognized as good or *blessed*. Second, God does not simply see that it is good but specifically gives it his blessing. Third, the word *blessed* is distinguished from good because it is associated with life. The notion of blessing does not appear until the creation of living creatures of the sea and sky (Genesis 1:22). An identical blessing is given to man with the addition of *dominion*. Once again John Sailhamer's commentary clarifies the point: "As soon as 'living beings' are created, the notion of 'blessing' is appropriated because the blessing relates to the giving of life."[5]

In his work, *The Sabbath Belongs to Israel*, W. Zimmerli goes as far as to say, "God takes this day and impresses upon it some special importance. He puts into this day the powers of life...."[6] This statement about the Sabbath is supported by Exodus 31:17: "It is a sign between Me and the sons of Israel forever; for in six days the Lord made heaven and earth, but on the seventh day He ceased from labor, and was refreshed" (Exodus 31:17, NASB).

The root meaning of the Hebrew word translated *refresh* in Exodus 31:17 is life or soul (nefesh). The form of the Hebrew verb is reflexive, meaning the subject *refreshes himself*. While it may be difficult to understand why God would need to refresh himself, each person has experienced the self-refreshing powers of the human body. When a person ceases to do and starts to rest, the body begins to refresh, restore, and repair itself.

The craving for rest is instinctive; fatigue draws a weary athlete to the bench, bed rest is the remedy for the common cold, and a business executive under stress seeks retreat. The concept of Sabbath-rest orders what human experience verifies—namely that the refreshing powers of life are received through declared periods of rest. This is the blessing of the Sabbath. It was given to refresh our lives.

The Jewish writer Abraham Joshua Heschel likewise understands the Sabbath to be a day full of life:

Every seventh day a miracle comes to pass, the resurrection of the soul, of the soul of man and of the soul of things. A medieval sage declares: The world which was created in six days was a world without a soul. It was on the seventh day that the world was given a soul. This is why it is said: "and on the seventh day He rested *vayinnafash*" (Exodus 31:17); *nefesh* means a soul.[7]

Unfortunately the act of blessing a day of rest grinds against many western practices. Our work ethic continues to make people who need rest feel guilty. Voices of the past challenge us to work harder and longer days. Voices of the present whisper, *"Supermarkets and shopping centers are now open seven days a week. One day is just like all the rest."* A competitive spirit nags, *"You must use down time to get ahead."* A day of rest is scoffed at; the concept of rest is cursed. In contrast God blesses rest, relieving troubled consciences of unnecessary guilt.

Men and women demonstrate their likeness to God by following God's example and personally blessing their labor. Verbal blessing is a rare gift belonging only to God, angels, and man. Sabbath-rest gives man an opportunity to practice the art of blessing. As God blessed the day, so should man. As God looked upon his week's work and declared it good, so should man. This is rest and refreshment to both man and his surroundings.

The image and likeness of God is reflected in each of us as we see that our work is good and we bless rest, specifically our own rest. *Am I distinguishing myself from plant and animal life by exercising my ability to bless? Do I have a day or at least a weekly block of time to practice the divine knack of blessing as God intended? Is rest at the top of my list of recipients of my blessing?* As a person made in the image and likeness of God, I am moved to please him right now by pausing to bless this moment of rest. I find it essential and delightful to set aside a day or block of time each week to pump life (nefesh) into my surroundings by saying: *It is good! I bless you!*

DIVINE REST IS HOLY

And God blessed the seventh day and made it holy

(Genesis 2:3)

You are to be holy to me because I, the LORD, am holy

(Leviticus 20:26)

For it is written: "Be holy, because I am holy"

(I Peter 1:16)

On occasion I ask people, "Is rest a four-letter word?" Literal minds immediately go to work counting letters asserting "Of course it is!" In contrast more figurative thinkers immediately connote four letter words with coarse speech unfit for polite use. They react with a resounding "No way!"

Regardless of thought patterns, busy people treat rest like it is an unmentionable. It is perpetually on our minds but suppressed among our passions. We dream of it but dare not yield to it. We avoid the urge to rest for fear of looking lazy, being unproductive, losing out to the competition, or failing to meet self-imposed goals. In contrast God calls rest *holy*.

The word "holy" appears in Scripture approximately six hundred times. By far the most common declaration is *God is holy!* Closely connected to the declaration that God is holy is the command that we are to *be holy*. As an aid to the process of becoming holy, God has given us holy things or places. What surprised me was the fact that the first thing God called holy was neither a thing nor a place.

God's work week, as described in Genesis one, was spent creating many *things*; yet none of those things was specifically called *holy*. The word *holy* does not come into play until the seventh day. It was not a *thing* that was first called holy but *time*—specifically a time of *rest* (Shabbat). Rest is the word from which comes the word *Sabbath*. Jewish theologian Abraham Heschel points out the significance of God calling the Sabbath *holy*:

> How extremely significant is the fact that it is applied to time: "And God blessed the seventh day and made it holy." There is no reference in the record of creation to any object in space that would be endowed with the quality of holiness. This is a radical departure from accustomed religious thinking. The mythical mind would expect that, after heaven and earth have been established, God would create a holy place—a holy mountain or a holy spring—whereupon a sanctuary is to be established. Yet it seems as if to the Bible it is holiness of time, the Sabbath, which comes first.[8]

To my astonishment I saw that it was a segment of time that was first called holy resembling the character of God. The root idea of holiness is one of separateness or the act of setting apart. Thus when the text says that God sanctified the seventh day, it is to be distinguished from the other days. It is special, not ordinary! God's ability to rest was a demonstration

29

of his own holiness. I am beginning to understand that my passion to meet him in periods of rest is an indication of my desire to be holy. James Montgomery Boice explains the connection between rest and holiness: "God sets the Sabbath day apart to teach that we are to enter not only into His rest but also into His holiness. The two go together, because holiness is the opposite of sin, and sin is what makes us restless."[9]

Unlike any object that has to be purchased, made, or carried, time is with each person and possessed by all. Heschel has profoundly identified the significance of the Sabbath in Jewish history: "The Sabbaths are our great cathedrals; and our Holy of Holies is a shrine that neither the Romans nor the Germans were able to burn."[10]

I had to think about that: *Do I have a cathedral of time that no one else can burn or destroy? What sacrifices will I have to make to meet God weekly? Have I identified a time and place for my weekly meeting with God?* I know that I need to identify a cathedral of time that I can enter and where I can meet God.

> *As parents and grandparents take pleasure in their sleeping children, so God takes pleasure in our rest.*

When our children were small, Lois and I would often lie down with our sons to get them to nap in the afternoon or to go to sleep at night. There were plenty of times when we would have loved to take naps ourselves, but our agenda was to help them settle down and go to sleep for their own good. We would lie down, read books, tell stories, and pray until they finally closed their eyes and went to sleep. As Lois and I now cherish the privilege of doing the same with our grandchildren, we now realize that such times are some of the most precious in a parent-child relationship. This intimacy provided the foundation for our lifelong relationships with our sons.

Throughout Scripture God is referred to as Father. Jesus consistently urged his followers to think of God as their Father. For example The Lord's Prayer begins, "Our Father in Heaven" (Matthew 6:9). I find it helpful to think of God as a parent who lies down beside his child to quiet him and help him go to sleep. God uses rest to merge my temporal life into his eternal being. Through rest, I find closure, blessing, and holiness.

As grandparents Lois and I not only enjoy playing with our grandchildren, we like to peek in their rooms while they are asleep. Those active little bodies and inquisitive minds have momentarily ceased running, climbing, and asking questions. A child at rest is a precious picture of health, satisfaction, and peace. As parents and grandparents take pleasure in their sleeping children, so God takes pleasure in our rest.

It can be said that man demonstrates his likeness to God during periods of rest. It is my privilege to demonstrate the likeness of God within me by following the pattern of the first Sabbath. God takes pleasure in seeing us rest, since rest that is set apart for meeting with our Holy God is itself holy. Is rest a four letter word? Yes, it is a *holy* one.

Some time ago I saw a photo of a beautiful autumn scene. The trees in the picture had turned into flaming shades of yellow, orange, and red. The picture had obviously been taken on a calm day since the lake beneath the forest was casting a perfect reflection of the trees. I studied the photo for some time before noticing something peculiar. The photo hanging on the wall was actually upside down. The reflection on the water was so good that I assumed it was the real thing and not a reflection at all.

I have often thought about that picture and asked myself, *How well do I reflect the likeness of God in whose image I was created?* I have to honestly say my reflection has been a broken image at best. Hardly did I fool anyone about my reflection of God during the years I produced whitewater with my anxious thoughts and hasty lifestyle. Today I can say that I have at last come to the realization that the reflection of God's image in my life is impossible without rest.

Prayer

Lord God, your majesty is expressed in all that you have made and done both great and small. I am honored to be made in your image and privileged to have the opportunity to reflect your image and likeness during my time on earth. Forgive me for clouding your image with selfishness and fear. I long to reflect your image in all I do and say at work, play, or rest. In Jesus' name and for his sake I pray, Amen.

Questions to Ponder

1. How does my work reflect God's character?
2. How do I bring closure to periods of work?
3. When do I pause to bless my work?
4. When do I rest without guilt?

CHAPTER TWO

REST, THE PLEASURE

OF HIS TRUST

I PLEASE GOD BY TRUSTING HIM

Bear in mind that the LORD has given you the Sabbath; that is why on the sixth day he gives you bread for two days.

(Exodus 16:29)

How are we going to get the life that has no lust, no self interest, no sensitiveness to pokes, the love that is not provoked, that thinketh no evil that is always kind? The only way is by allowing not a bit of the old life to be left; but only simple perfect trust in God, such trust that we no longer want God's blessings, but only want Himself.[11]

(Oswald Chambers)

A St. Cloud businessman known for his integrity, energy, and generosity has died."[12]

So read the headlines the day after Dad died. He spent fifty years building a business and developing an honorable name in the community. He did it largely with trust. He trusted people and enhanced their trust in one another. Family, friends, employees, even competitors came to show their respect at his memorial visitation and funeral. Many who once worked for him came to honor him, including some whom he had fired.

I frequently meet people who knew Dad and share fond memories of times with him. I hear them say, "Your Dad gave me my start in business. Without him I don't know where I would be today." His trust won him many friends.

Trust also has its heartaches. Dad trusted to a fault at times. There were those who proved themselves untrustworthy by taking advantage of his trust for their own personal gains. I saw the pain in his eyes more than once after a trusted business partner had selfishly siphoned off money and walked away from a partnership. He often hired people who were hard-up for work; some of them became long-term loyal employees. Others had to be released because of dishonesty or theft. All things considered I don't think Dad would have changed a thing. His trust gave people opportunities to grow and reach their potential.

Dad received great pleasure when people made good on his trust and developed into trustworthy people in life and business. He also received many blows from those who abused it, but he never quit trusting.

I have come to realize that God takes great pleasure when I make good on his trust. All I have is entrusted to me by God, even the ability to earn a living is a gift from God (Deuteronomy 8:18). Trust is the big idea behind many Bible texts. Exodus sixteen is a prime example. The fledging nation of Israel is forced to trust God for their daily provision of food, which came in the form of bread known as manna:

> Each morning everyone gathered as much as he needed, and when the sun grew hot, it melted away. 22 On the sixth day, they gathered twice as much—two omers for each person—and the leaders of the community came and reported this to Moses. 23 He said to them, "This is what the LORD commanded: 'Tomorrow is to be a day of rest, a holy Sabbath to the LORD. So bake what you want to bake and boil what you want to boil. Save whatever is left and keep it until morning.'" 24 So they saved it until morning, as Moses commanded, and it did not stink or get maggots in it. 25 "Eat it today," Moses said, "because today is a Sabbath to the LORD. You will not find any of it on the ground today. 26 Six days you are to gather it, but on the seventh day, the Sabbath there will not be any." 27 Nevertheless, some of the people went out on the seventh day to gather it, but they found none. 28 Then the LORD said to Moses, "How long will you refuse to keep my commands and my instructions? 29 Bear in mind that the LORD has given you the Sabbath; that is why on the sixth day he gives you bread for two days. Everyone is to stay where he is on the seventh day; no one is to go out." 30 So the people rested on the seventh day.

> (Exodus 16:21-30)

The whole wilderness excursion was an exercise in trust. Thus far in the journey they had made pretty good on the Lord's trust. They had walked right out of Egypt at his command. They had marched through the Red Sea at his command with walls of water on each side and Egyptian chariots in revengeful pursuit behind them. This nation of slaves was now free and homeward bound. They could enjoy parading to the Promised Land, unless they failed to trust God for routine provisions such as food.

Whenever I travel I don't get very far before I begin to think about food: *Where am I going to eat? What's next on the menu? I hope it's not more gas station food.* I find it easy to compare one meal to the next and allow food to occupy my thoughts and conversations. I also have plenty of company when it comes to such conversations. In fact I would have fit right in with the Israelites in the wilderness. In the desert the whole community grumbled against Moses and Aaron. The Israelites said to them, "If only we had died by the LORD's hand in Egypt! There we sat around pots of meat and ate all the food we wanted, but you have brought us out into this desert to starve this entire assembly to death" (Exodus 16:2-3).

Food is not the first thing I think about when it comes to trusting God. Prayer at meals is such an easy ritual, hardly requiring any thought. So I say to myself, *I will save my trust for bigger things.* But when I don't get what I have in mind I find myself groaning inside. When the disappointment occurs for a series of meals, I easily voice my opinion. So it was with the Israelites who had trusted God when their backs were against the pyramids or rushing chariots; they showed their lack of trust by complaining about food. They would soon learn that the one who had freed them would also feed them as their provider: "I will rain down bread from heaven for you. The people are to go out each day and gather enough for that day. In this way I will test them and see whether they will follow my instructions."

From their response I don't think manna was the Israelites' first choice. I know it wouldn't have been mine. The lesson is the same for me as it was for the Israelites. I am to trust God not only for the provision of food, but the kind of food he provides. He purposely gave them manna to teach them that life is not about food, but trusting what God says. "He humbled you, causing you to hunger and then feeding you with manna, which neither you nor your fathers had known, to teach you that man does not live on bread alone but on every word that comes from the mouth of the LORD" (Deuteronomy 8:3).

Making good on God's trust also pertains to following instructions. Like the Israelites I find it so natural to listen selectively to instructions and see how far I get without the details I left behind. The result is usually the same; I have to go back and follow the instructions step by step before I get the desired results.

For many years I heard it said, *experience is the best teacher,* and figured that experience must be the preferred method of learning. Then one day I heard someone add the phrase, *unless you can learn any other way.* If I don't follow instructions, I am destined to learn by experience, which is often painful and costly.

The Israelites were prone to figure out their own way of putting life together rather than trust the instruction manual God had provided. Each day they were to gather enough for that day and no more, because what they did not eat would spoil by the following day. They were literally to trust God for their daily bread; not too hard an assignment being that their God was God Almighty who defeated the undefeated Egyptians. The former slaves knew God was powerful, but was he really good? Will he really lead us through the wilderness? Or will he be like the father who forgot to pick up his child at school after a special event? As trustworthy as God was some did not trust him for the next day's bread and hoarded it for themselves to ensure they would not go hungry the following day. "Then Moses said to them, 'No one is to keep any of it until morning.' However, some of them paid no attention to Moses; they kept part of it until morning, but it was full of maggots and began to smell. So Moses was angry with them" (Exodus 16:19-20).

By the next day maggots had spoiled the picnic, and the leftovers reeked. No doubt the smell seeped from tent to tent, identifying those who chose to hoard and not trust. Food was not the only thing that spoiled; their relationship with Moses was spoiled and their relationship with the Lord was in jeopardy. Learning by experience was costly.

Another issue of trust had to do with the Sabbath. Whatever religious routines were engrained in the descendents of the patriarchs, Abraham, Isaac, and Jacob, they were pretty well washed out during the four hundred year imposition of pagan Egyptian culture. As slaves it was unlikely that they had any regular day off, especially in the years of the recent pharaohs. Could they handle a break in their monotonous routine of gathering for themselves?

The Sabbath would come with a miracle of its own. On the sixth day the people could gather all they needed for the seventh day, and it would not spoil. The *Shabbat* was more than a day off; it was separate or holy. Literally the Shabbat was a day to *cease* their gathering and labor in general.

Could they handle a day of rest? Would they devote themselves to the pleasure of their deliverer and provider? After all, the entire Sabbath was to be a holy Sabbath to the LORD. This loaded phrase communicated ownership and pleasure. The Sabbath was first and foremost an offering of trust to the Lord designed for his pleasure. Finally, could those who get weary accept a gift of rest from the one who does not get weary? That which pleased God was to be a relief and pressure release to all who trusted him. "Bear in mind that the LORD has *given* you the Sabbath; that is why on the sixth day he gives you bread for two days. Everyone is to stay where he is on the seventh day; no one is to go out. So the people rested on the seventh day" (Exodus 16:29-30).

Yes, the Lord was pleased with those who were able to break with the patterns of their previous existence and trust God to provide according to his word. But not every one trusted God's provision; not everyone accepted the gift of rest; not everyone gave God pleasure one day a week. "Nevertheless, some of the people went out on the seventh day to gather it, but they found none. Then the LORD said to Moses, 'How long will you refuse to keep my commands and my instructions?'" (Exodus 16:27-28).

Obviously God was not pleased with their compulsive gathering as they failed to cease doing on the Sabbath what they were told to do every other day.

GATHERING

Gathering or making a living, as it is called today, is rewarded by free progressive societies. Traditionally, America is a privileged society which champions the resourcefulness of hard workers who apply themselves wholeheartedly to their endeavors. Their ingenuity and energy create opportunities, including employment for others. Such individuals are rewarded by communities for gathering much. God is not opposed to gathering; he is the one who told the Israelites to do so in the first place. God rewards gathering as long as it is accompanied by the will power to cease, demonstrating trust in God as the ultimate provider.

I have wondered at times, *where does gathering go wrong?* The drive to gather more than I need is typically driven by one of two dynamics. The most obvious is greed, a resolve to possess more than I need simply out of selfishness. Being the *best* gatherer can become an obsession fueled by egoistical motives. Greed may lead to egotism if egotism isn't already the root cause of greed.

The other dynamic for gathering more than I need is driven by fear—fear that I may not have enough someday. Those who suffered through the Great Depression will never forget what it was like to *go without*. The plague of going to bed hungry etched itself into minds that were determined to never lack again. No matter what their earnings were throughout adulthood, they worked like they were dirt poor, because that *gut* feeling never left them. The 1930s they spoke of produced a large percentage of workaholics, people who were compulsive workers and put their work before health and loving relationships. Love was expressed as the gathering of a masterful provider. Children of the Great Depression generally became good providers but mediocre parents; many were materially rich and relationally poor.

> *It is interesting to listen to the comments that outsiders, particularly those from Third World countries, make on the religion they observe in North America. What they notice mostly is the greed, the silliness, the narcissism.*
>
> (Eugene Peterson)

Once again it must be emphasized that gathering is good and ambition admirable. But I must ask myself, *when is enough, enough? Where rests my power to cease gathering?* In a day of rocket fuel and turbo engines I need to be as interested in stopping power as starting power. What is around the wheels should grip my attention as much as what is under the hood. I am personally thankful that brake technology has improved along with engine technology. At least once every winter I find myself praising God for antilock brakes. A generation that values *high impact* must bear in mind that *impact* is not a positive word without brakes.

The Sabbath was a day to test brakes. Every seventh day was a test to see if gathering was in control mode or on *run away*. It was a day to evaluate whether greed had taken root in the past week. Likewise every seventh day was set aside to read the fear gauge. It was time to ask a familiar question, *"Do I rely solely on my abilities to gather, or do I solemnly trust the God who gave me the ability to gather?"* (Deuteronomy. 8:18). Trust is the ingredient that is commonly lacking when I cannot stop gathering. The Sabbath is about trust. Those who have a hard time ceasing their work and resting sufficiently for even one day a week lack trust. Trust is what working brakes are made of.

Hebrews chapter eleven has been called God's Hall of Faith. The chapter opens with a definition of faith and goes on to list individuals who lived by it. All these people had one thing in common—faith. Nothing was more essential to their connection with God Almighty. Hebrews 11:6 states why faith is so valuable: "And without faith it is impossible to please God...." There is simply no substitute for pleasing God. Trust is simply another word for faith. Like faith, trust gives God pleasure.

THE SABBATH PRINCIPLE

The Sabbath principle asserts: *If I set aside (make holy) one day out of seven for God's pleasure, He will make six days of work as good as seven.* In fact I will be better off, healthier, stronger, and smarter having ceased my work and rested that one day. It is a win/win offer. The Sabbath principle awards God the pleasure he deserves while drenching me in his goodness. There is only one condition—trust.

Some may argue, "The Sabbath has little or nothing to do with pleasing God today. It was for the Hebrew sojourners and Jews today who choose to obey its complicated rules." On the contrary both the Sabbath principle and the journeys of those who crossed the desert thirty-five hundred years ago have powerful implications for people today, especially Christians.

The Apostle Paul bridged the divide between the Old and New Testaments by urging the Corinthian church to learn from the errors of the very people spoken of in Exodus 16: "These things happened to them as examples and were written down as warnings for us, on whom the fulfillment of the ages has come" (I Corinthians 10:11). Furthermore Paul quoted Exodus 16:18 in II Corinthians 8:15, "As it is written: 'He who gathered much did not have too much, and he who gathered little did not have too little.'" In both texts the recipients of the inspired Word of God were urged to trust God to provide and not hoard, as if God could not be trusted to provide as he had promised. The issue of trust is central to the Sermon on the Mount. Our Lord Jesus challenges us to trust our Heavenly Father like the simple creatures of his creation:

> Look at the birds of the air; they do not sow or reap or store away in barns, and yet your heavenly Father feeds them. Are you not much more valuable than they? [27] Who of you by worrying can add a single hour to

his life? [28] And why do you worry about clothes? See how the lilies of the field grow. They do not labor or spin. [29] Yet I tell you that not even Solomon in all his splendor was dressed like one of these. [30] If that is how God clothes the grass of the field, which is here today and tomorrow is thrown into the fire, will he not much more clothe you, O you of little faith? [31] So do not worry, saying, 'What shall we eat?' or 'What shall we drink?' or 'What shall we wear?' [32] For the pagans run after all these things, and your heavenly Father knows that you need them. [33] But seek first his kingdom and his righteousness, and all these things will be given to you as well. [34] Therefore do not worry about tomorrow, for tomorrow will worry about itself. Each day has enough trouble of its own.

(Matthew 6:26-34)

If the Sabbath principle is truly a principle and not a temporary solution to desert wanderers, it should be transferable to other peoples, times, and cultures. I have often asked myself, *Does the Sabbath principle have any relevance for other times and places? Is the trust required of the Israelites who ate unspoiled manna on the seventh day to be emulated by other generations?* Marva Dawn in *Keeping the Sabbath Wholly* emphasizes the life-related truth of the Sabbath principle with this true story:

> The story is told of a wagon train on its way from St. Louis to Oregon. Its members were devout Christians, so the whole group observed the habit of stopping for the Sabbath day. Winter was approaching quickly, however, and some among the group began to panic in fear that they wouldn't reach their destination before the heavy snows. Consequently, several members proposed to the rest of the group that they should quit their practice of stopping for the Sabbath and continue driving onward seven days a week.

> This proposal triggered a lot of contention in the community, so finally it was suggested that the wagon train should split into two groups—those who wanted to observe the Sabbath and those who preferred to travel on that day. The proposal was accepted, and both groups set out and traveled together until the next Sabbath day, when one group continued while the other remained at rest.

> Guess which group got to Oregon first. You're right. The one who kept the Sabbath reached their destination first. Both the people and the horses were so rested by their Sabbath observance that they could travel much more vigorously and effectively the other six days of the week. God honors those who honor his commands.[13]

Kirk owns a marina in northern Minnesota, where summer comes late and winter comes early. It is alleged there are only two seasons where he lives—*winter and rough sledding*. His business is open April through November and that is stretching it. Weekend business trickles in between April and June as well as September through November. June through August sales soar as customers buy everything from boats to minnow buckets. If there is a business that cannot afford to close one day during the summer, it is Kirk's Land O Lakes Marine. Ill-advised as it may seem, Kirk closes his store on Sundays, even during those busy summer months. His store is closed on one of the two busiest days of the week because Kirk believes in the Sabbath principle: *Set aside one day out of seven for God's pleasure, and He will make six days of work as good as seven*. His trust pays off year after year as Kirk has a solid business and many loyal customers.

Howard Dayton in *Money Matters* makes the point that rest is largely a trust issue that is as applicable to our lives as it was to the first recipients of the fourth commandment:

> I believe this Old Testament principle of resting one day out of seven has application for us today. This has been difficult for me, particularly in times of "plowing or harvesting" when a project deadline is approaching or I am under financial pressure.
>
> Why? Rest is often an issue of faith. Is the Lord able to make our six days of work more productive than seven days? Yes! The Lord instituted this weekly rest for our physical, mental, and spiritual health.
>
> Our example in this is Christ. Even through the time appointed for his public ministry was only a few years, He still took time to be alone with the Father. He made his relationship with the Father a priority, and so should we.[14]

GOD'S MATH

Ceasing to gather is a struggle I face every week. To stop working when there is so much to do appears to be foolish and the lazy way. Only after failing to trust God on numerous occasions have I learned God's math: when it comes to work, six is more than seven.

After years of resistance I came to trust God's math. At first it was out of fatigue that I learned to rest. Then I discovered that I actually got more done after times of rest. Rest became a productive thing. Time was actually saved when I ceased to work and rested.

On one occasion I was leading a group of church leaders through a Sabbath-rest experience, which I will introduce later in this book. After several hours of divorcing ourselves from our work, we came together for a debriefing. One very busy associate pastor, whose senior was on sabbatical, raised his voice in astonishment, "We just saved ourselves a lot of time." He was referring to the clarity of thought and direction received as he rested from work and trusted in God. Not only renewed energy, but new insights for solving problems are granted to those who rest from their labors.

Trust in God expressed as rest allows me to ponder what is really important. A long-range, even eternal, perspective is a by-product of rest. Like climbing to the top of a tower, I get my bearings and redirect my erroneous energies. I am often reminded during times of restful solitude that relationships are more important than completing mundane tasks or arranging agendas for *the right outcome*. On occasion after a time of rest, I have walked away with an outline for a whole sermon series. It was like a reward for trusting and not worrying or working.

There is something mysterious about the Sabbath; something supernatural beyond the physical, mental, and emotional impact of rest. Does God show up when his people rest? Various attempts have been made to explain away the manna as a natural phenomenon—like "honeydew excretion of two types of insects or aphids that live on the numerous tamarisk trees in the region" or "lichen."[15] Besides being less than appetizing, these explanations are rather porous. Walter Kaiser identifies the numerous problems with explanations that rule out the supernatural occurrence of the manna and agrees that something miraculous has taken place:

> Both of the above suggestions run into trouble: Bodenheimer could not account for the stinking decay or the melting (he promptly relegated these textual features to a misinterpretation or an interpolation in the text). Furthermore, the manna continued to provide food for the Israelites for almost forty years, not just for the three to six weeks in July and August as Bodenheimer's suggestion would necessitate. It was also produced in quantities far exceeding what either of these methods could possibly deliver. Thus we agree with Rawlinson (2:40): Manna "must be regarded as a peculiar substance, miraculously created for a special purpose, but similar in certain respects to certain known substances which are still produced in the Sinai region."[16]

No explanation that rules out supernatural involvement satisfies reader curiosity. Furthermore there is no natural explanation for manna not rotting on the Sabbath, when it rotted every other day of the week that it was held over. The Sabbath was a divine gift saturated with the supernatural. *Yes, God shows up when I rest in honor on him!* Therefore, there should be no embarrassment concerning a supernatural boost for practicing the Sabbath principle today. We should not be surprised when God honors and empowers those who willingly express Sabbath principle trust in him today. A timeless principle is at work. As the Scripture says, "Anyone who trusts in him will never be put to shame" (Romans 10:11, Isaiah 28:16).

HOW FAR DO I HAVE TO GO TO PLEASE GOD?

We are surrounded by opportunities to please God like never before. For instance, the familiar Bible verse, "Therefore go and make disciples of all nations..." (Matthew 28:19) once required becoming a trained missionary and living in a distant land. Today thousands engage in short term cross cultural missions throughout the world that lead to hundreds of thousands coming to Christ each year. I have had the privilege of visiting Russia twelve times. I never dreamed of speaking in Russian churches, leading Russians to Christ, teaching Russian pastors, and leading short term teams to help plant Russian churches. Serving God cross culturally has been one of the biggest thrills of my life. But you don't have to board a jet destined for a far away land to serve God in far away places. You can stay at home and share Christ around the world by email; whereas letters took months emails take moments before there is a reply.

A world of disciple-making has also come to our doorsteps because most every community is now international. The church I most recently served opened a preschool. To our amazement over half of the children enrolled were from India. Word got out among their immigrant parents that this was a caring preschool and would accommodate their children. The fact that we already had a doctor from India serving as an elder made it easier for some of these families to visit church services and hear the gospel.

Obviously we please God by serving as we walk through doors of opportunity available to us today. However, there is another means of pleasing God that has always been far more accessible than the new easy-access, high-profile ways of serving available today. Every person regardless of ability can participate in this means of pleasing God. It is called trust. Are you *making good* on God's trust by trusting him to provide through lean times, through illness and tragedy, or through waves of work that threaten to tow you under? Is that trust expressed through an ability to cease gathering for yourself and others? Is your trust demonstrated in acts of rest on a weekly basis? It is time to *make good* on God's trust by experiencing the Sabbath principle for his sake and pleasure. God takes pleasure in our rest, for Sabbath-rest is the pleasure of his trust.

Prayer

Dear Lord, all of your words are trustworthy and all of your deeds are done in righteousness. Please forgive me for not trusting you to care and provide for me. I have worked through times of rest because I did not trust you. I have allowed both anxiety and greed to rule my life. I long to please you by trusting you and offering significant times of rest to you. In Jesus' name and for his sake I pray, Amen.

Questions to Ponder

1. Am I driven by anxiety because I have not trusted God's provisions and promises?
2. Am I driven by greed to get ahead of others for my ego's sake?
3. Am I consistently working through times of rest because I do not trust the Lord?
4. What progress have I made placing my trust in God's provision and promises?
5. How will I please God with rest in the future?

CHAPTER THREE

Rest, the Pleasure
of His Sabbath

I Please God by Entering His Sabbath-Rest

It is a Sabbath unto the Lord.

(Exodus 20:10)

The sin of working constantly, excluding time for God, deserved a place in the Ten Commandments. We argue against the Sabbath commandment more than all the rest.[17]

(David Hansen)

FREE TO REST

Freedom was the last word uttered by a tortured William Wallace in Mel Gibson's movie *Braveheart*. "Give me liberty or give me death" expressed the passion of Patrick Henry and numerous early American patriots. The late Martin Luther King is best remembered for his vibrant freedom speech delivered on the steps at the Lincoln Memorial in Washington D.C. on August 28, 1963:

Let freedom ring from the heightening Alleghenies of Pennsylvania! Let freedom ring from the snowcapped Rockies of Colorado! Let freedom ring from the curvaceous peaks of California! But not only that; let freedom ring from Stone Mountain of Georgia! Let freedom ring from Lookout Mountain of Tennessee! Let freedom ring from every hill and every mole-hill of Mississippi. From every mountainside, let freedom ring.

When we let it ring from every village and every hamlet, from every state and every city, we will be able to speed up that day when all of God's

44

children, black men and white men, Jews and Gentiles, Protestants and Catholics, will be able to join hands and sing in the words of the old Negro spiritual, "Free at last! Free at last! Thank God Almighty, we are free at last.[18]

Freedom is an American byword. Attempts to free people in South Korea, South Vietnam, Kuwait, Afghanistan, and Iraq have motivated Americans to go to war. We fight to keep it for ourselves and achieve it for others. The issue in question for me does not debate our achievement of freedom, but our use of freedom.

America's forefathers fought for freedom of speech. Today twenty-first century Americans fear censorship for being politically incorrect. While there is religious freedom, fewer Americans are practicing their religion this century compared to the last century. Americans continue to travel freely throughout the country but fear walking anywhere alone at night. While no one in America is legally a slave, millions now live in bondage to one addiction or another. While more time and money are spent on leisure activities, millions of Americans are restless and don't know how to rest. Rest is one of the many privileges of any free nation. Freedom, however, does not guarantee that people know how to rest. Tilden Edwards describes the acute nature of this twenty-first century restlessness dilemma in his book, *Sabbath Time*:

> The rhythm of life for countless people, set up by the culturally pressured way, thus emerges as one that oscillates between driven achievement (both on and off the job) and some form of mind numbing private escape. This crazed rhythm, based on a distorted view of human reality, increasingly poisons our institutions, relationships and quality of life.[19]

As essential as rest is to human happiness, symptoms indicate that free people have to be re-parented regarding rest. Parents mandate periods of rest for their young children but deny themselves the rest needed to be good parents. The restless pattern becomes more and more ingrained as attempts to provide more or play more continue. Ironically, many free people have to be reminded of the benefits of rest. I am one of them.

THINGS GO BETTER WITH REST!

Rest provides many practical benefits. Most obvious is recovery from fatigue. Without rest bodies break down and attention spans diminish.

Without rest God's creatures do not feel or function well. We are simply more useful and productive when rested.

Safety is another. Driving home late one evening, I realized that I was too tired to continue. I decided to stop for the night and stay in a motel that was in view. In my weariness I entered a one way street going the wrong way. A police officer stopped me. I explained to him that I was very tired and was about to drive to the motel in front of the one way street. The officer said, "I won't give you a ticket providing you go directly to that motel and get some rest." I was not in a position to argue with him. Accidents happen to tired people.

Productivity is yet another. As unproductive as rest may appear to the person who is constantly preoccupied with thoughts of work, rest greatly improves productivity. Counselor and author Alan Loy McGinnis notes that perpetual work can be deceptive and actually counterproductive:

> The person who is addicted to work often is not nearly so effective as he or she would like to think. Many of the studies show that such persons do more but accomplish less. They give the appearance of turning out a blizzard of work, but in the long run they often do not accomplish as much as the less-driven person. High achievers are committed to results, whereas the driven person is simply committed to activity.

> Driven workers have a way of flattening out in their careers. Dr. Charles Garfield says one can almost predict the professional trajectory of workaholics. They rise quickly on the basis of their initial contribution, and then they level off and end up managing the details of their careers instead of delegating those details to people they trust.[20]

Things go better with rest! Rested people are healthier, happier, safer, work harder, get along better, and make better decisions. If there is a universal recommendation for improving people and performance, it is rest! After all, rest is a gift from God.

REST, GOD'S GIFT TO MAN

Rest is a gift from God to man. A night of sleep, Sabbath, and rest from war all have one thing in common within Scripture: they are gifts from a loving God who understands man's need for rest.

It is in vain that you rise up early and go late to rest, eating the bread of anxious toil; for he *gives* to his beloved sleep.

(Psalm 127:2 ESV, italics mine)

Bear in mind that the LORD has *given* you the Sabbath; that is why on the sixth day he *gives* you bread for two days. Everyone is to stay where he is on the seventh day; no one is to go out.

(Exodus 16:29 italics mine)

The LORD replied, "My Presence will go with you, and I will give you rest."

(Exodus 33:14)

Praise be to the LORD, who has given rest to his people Israel just as he promised. Not one word has failed of all the good promises he gave through his servant Moses.

(I Kings 8:56)

And the kingdom of Jehoshaphat was at peace, for his God had given him rest on every side.

(II Chronicles 20:30)

Like cattle that go down to the plain, they were given rest by the Spirit of the LORD. This is how you guided your people to make for yourself a glorious name.

(Isaiah 63:14)

Like any other gift rest is easily consumed without gratitude. I have to admit that I can exercise my freedoms of speech, travel, ownership, and religion for days without thinking about the many young men and women who died in wars to grant and prolong these precious gifts of freedom. I fear that many adults are much like small children who tear open Christmas gifts on Christmas day but cannot recall who gave them a single gift. The best they can do is say, "Santa Claus."

The Scriptures guide me to view rest as a gift of God. Instead of stewing about being tired, I must learn to give thanks for every breath of rest, remembering that throughout history many have craved the rest that is free to me.

> *The Sabbath-keeping commandment is a gift of mercy from the heart of a loving God who knows the burden, the entrapment, the bitter bondage of work.*
>
> (Karen Mains)

Slaves are not free to rest as they want or need. They are given rest only because their masters realize that without it their usefulness will be short term. This is the backdrop of the fourth commandment found in Exodus chapter twenty and Deuteronomy chapter five. It was given firsthand to slaves who had experienced precious little rest.

> Then a new king, who did not know about Joseph, came to power in Egypt. [9] "Look," he said to his people, "the Israelites have become much too numerous for us. [10] Come, we must deal shrewdly with them or they will become even more numerous and, if war breaks out, will join our enemies, fight against us and leave the country." [11] So they put slave masters over them to oppress them with forced labor, and they built Pithom and Rameses as store cities for Pharaoh. But the more they were oppressed, the more they multiplied and spread; so the Egyptians came to dread the Israelites [13] So they ruthlessly made the people of Israel work as slaves [14] and made their lives bitter with hard service, in mortar and brick, and in all kinds of work in the field. In all their work they ruthlessly made them work as slaves.
>
> (Exodus 1:8-14)

God's gifts of rest are reasons to gratefully worship God. The freedom to rest was founded in the mercies of God. Israel was shackled by Egypt, a nation far superior to any on earth at the time. There was no human strength that could possibly separate the iron jaws that contained this nation of slaves. If God Almighty heard their cries, only then would the Israelites ever experience the freedom Abraham, Isaac, and Jacob cherished. The hope of freedom from slavery and rest from unceasing labor, dwelt in the Lord God who values rest.

> So God looked on the Israelites and was concerned about them.
>
> (Exodus 2:25)

The LORD said, "I have indeed seen the misery of my people in Egypt. I have heard them crying out because of their slave drivers, and I am concerned about their suffering."

(Exodus 3:7)

Remember that you were slaves in Egypt and that the LORD your God brought you out of there with a mighty hand and an outstretched arm. Therefore the LORD your God has commanded you to observe the Sabbath day.

(Deuteronomy 5:12-15)

Once freed from Egypt, Israel was not to forget that God set them free and gave them rest by his mercy. In this sense the Sabbath was a weekly memorial to remind them of days past when rest was not free. As the Israelites enjoyed their Sabbaths for generations to come, they were to remember that God in his mercy freed their ancestors from their agony under a ruthless empire. Likewise, they were never to take rest for granted but cherish it as a gift from God.

REST, MAN'S GIFT TO GOD

I find it convenient to interpret Scripture solely from my self-absorbed perspective. After all, I am part of a culture which perpetually asks, *what's in it for me?* But I cannot blame it all on culture. I am quite comfortable being self-centered. When I read the narrative about God freeing slaves, I assume that God did it solely for the sake of the captives. Out of context it appears the Lord God freed the nation of slaves from the iron furnace of Egypt purely out of compassion.

However, my self-centered interpretation falls short of God's point of view. While God is compassionate there is more to the historical narrative.

The Lord through Moses made it plain to Pharaoh that his interest in the slave nation of Israel was less about freedom and more about worship, less about Israel and more about God. "Let my son go, so he may worship me" (Exodus 4:23).

God declared his intent boldly without reservation to Pharaoh and the world beyond. He called for the release of slaves for a higher reason than human freedom. God was setting them free for himself. He would set them free so he could better enjoy them in their times of work and rest. As I read about rest I must come to a turning point where I say, *it's not about me.*

God's gifts of rest urge us to thank him and supply us with opportunities to worship him.

Must I Obey the Sabbath if I Am Not Tired?

I find it most tempting to slight the Sabbath principle when I am well rested, at ease, and not particularly desperate for God. During these self-sufficient moments I am prone to ask myself, *why take a Sabbath-rest when I don't need one?* I tend to interpret the fourth commandment exclusively on the basis of my need and enjoyment of rest. I ask myself, *what if I don't need to rest? What if am not tired? If I am not tired, does that mean I don't need to observe the Sabbath concept?*

Contrary to my self-focused interests, the fourth commandment does not say: *Take a Sabbath when you think you need it.* It supersedes my need for rest. The heart of the fourth commandment pulsates within a short phrase—one that my self-centered flesh wants to ignore. It is a phrase about which few commentators say anything. It is a phrase which is more fundamental than my desire or need for rest. The fourth commandment was not given just because I need rest as a self-centered being. It was given that I might please God as a rested being: "It is a Sabbath unto the Lord" (Exodus 20:10). "But the seventh day is a Sabbath to the LORD your God" (Deuteronomy 5:14).

That which is unto the Lord is dedicated to him and designed to give the Lord pleasure. I am commanded to rest for God's enjoyment. Even the land was to take a rest unto the Lord every seventh year, which was a major gift of rest to the entire nation. "But in the seventh year the land is to have a Sabbath of rest, a Sabbath to the LORD. Do not sow your fields or prune your vineyards" (Leviticus 25:4).

I ask myself, *how am I to make Sabbath-rest a Sabbath unto the Lord? How can I make the Sabbath a pleasure to the Almighty?*

First, a Sabbath unto the Lord is made to reflect his character. It is to be holy, for the Lord is holy. Treating something as holy means it is to be set apart from the common *stuff* of life.

A culture that has no time for rest has no time for holiness and no time for God. That is the culture that flows in me. For God's sake, that culture must be drained from my veins each week. As I get rightly configured by entering a Sabbath-rest, time itself becomes insignificant.

When I enter a Sabbath-rest I enter into a different time zone—God's zone. It could be called a timeless zone. As I check out of this spinning globe to be with the one who is beyond time itself, there is a sensation of timelessness which God enjoys and I need. I enter into a different place—God's place. I succumb to someone else's agenda—God's agenda. To do so I must resist the temptations that whisper, *this is a waste of time*. I make an effort to step out of my routine. It is like taking a scenic route on a trip when I am driven by an apparent need to get somewhere in a hurry. I must dismiss the discomfort of being out of control. It is like leading a meeting and purposely turning the meeting over to another person who may change the agenda and take it in a different direction. Over the years I have become more trusting of God to lead my meeting with him. His is a holy agenda.

Second, a Sabbath unto the Lord puts his work ahead of mine. That means I cease my work long enough to recognize and appreciate his unfathomable works. I pause to look at God's creative work just as he did on the first Sabbath. This is the emphasis of the Exodus version of the fourth commandment. Like a flashback to the account of creation, Exodus returns to Genesis chapter two: "For in six days the LORD made the heavens and the earth, the sea, and all that is in them, but he rested on the seventh day. Therefore the LORD blessed the Sabbath day and made it holy" (Exodus 20:11).

If God paused to say his creative work was indeed good (Genesis 1:31), it ought to grab our attention at least once a week. A Sabbath-rest experience begs to be spent outdoors. I have often said, "The best of life is spent outdoors." Cities tend to reflect the achievements of man. Creation reflects our Creator God. In the words of David, "The heavens declare the glory of God; the skies proclaim the work of his hands" (Psalm 19:1).

When I pause to ponder his workmanship, I take myself less seriously and become more self-abandoned. As I have opportunity to view the Bridger Mountains of Montana or the Canadian Rockies in Banff National Park, I am reminded of my place by the expanse of his creation. The same thing happens when I observe the intricacy of small creations: I don't have to go far to find them.

Kansas is not a particularly popular vacation state. It is best known as the long east-west state that vacationers yawn through on their way to and from the Rockies. Nonetheless, Kansas is full of God's spectacular designs. I know because I lived there for thirteen years.

One warm summer day I was sitting under a park pavilion during my weekly Sabbath-rest when a spider web caught my eye. Had I been in my normal work mode at church or home I would have reached for a broom and swatted it to pieces, adding some expressions of repugnance that such creatures had encroached upon the dwelling place of man. Instead, I began to examine it carefully. With the thread-like substance glittering in the sunlight, I noticed the threads were spaced evenly apart. *"How did it do that?"* I muttered to myself. I imagined how it may have been constructed. Several long tiny tight ropes would have to be strung and fastened to fixed objects in all directions. The spider must then find a center point and go around and around evenly. *What a marvelous design,* I thought to myself. Then I began to question: *What blueprints did the spider review as it spun the web? What measuring devices did it have to space the threads so evenly? Like Michelangelo painting the Sistine Chapel, did it have to step back several feet from its masterpiece to get an overall perspective? What architecture or engineering school did it attend in order to construct this structure which serves as both its home and restaurant? By the way, what's the recipe for that substance that is nearly invisible yet remarkably strong?*

I began to think about the spider's brain. *What brain?* I thought to myself. *It can't be bigger than the head of a pin. What intelligence does this spider have?* All questions led to a maker who programmed the spider to do what I cannot do. What a marvelous Creator he is! No wonder the Apostle Paul declared: "For since the creation of the world God's invisible qualities—his eternal power and divine nature—have been clearly seen, being understood from what has been made, so that men are without excuse" (Romans 1:20).

I thought to myself, *where have I been that I have not noticed such marvels? All my life spiders have been spinning webs. I have been spinning my own webs, at times with less intent than a spider. I have expended much energy with perpetual motion driven by anxiety.*

Third, a Sabbath unto the Lord celebrates deliverance. In addition to the emphasis on creation in Exodus, the Deuteronomy account of the fourth commandment includes an emphasis on deliverance:

> Observe the Sabbath day by keeping it holy, as the LORD your God has commanded you. [13] Six days you shall labor and do all your work, [14] but the seventh day is a Sabbath to the LORD your God. On it you shall not do any work, neither you, nor your son or daughter, nor your manservant or maidservant, nor your ox, your donkey or any of your animals, nor the alien within your gates, so that your manservant and maidservant may rest, as you do. [15] *Remember that you were slaves in Egypt and*

that the LORD your God brought you out of there with a mighty hand and an outstretched arm. Therefore the LORD your God has commanded you to observe the Sabbath day.

(Deuteronomy 5:12–15, italics mine)

The Sabbath was a time to remember days spent in bondage. Like the children of Israel born in Egypt, I was born in bondage, the bondage of Adam's original sin and mine as well.

While my timeframe postdates the era of Moses' Israelites by three thousand years, the same God who delivered them delivered me. In fact I have much more to celebrate since I know God's redemptive deliverance through the Messiah, Jesus Christ. Sabbath-rest becomes holy to the Lord God as I assess the many times God has rescued my life. I think of the close-call accidents that could have taken my life, illnesses that could have been fatal, and the many roadblocks in church work that were impasses until the Lord passed my way like a Mighty Deliverer. Most of all I celebrate salvation through Jesus Christ, the only substitute for the punishment due my sin. He delivered me from the eternal death of my sin and the eternal hell I deserved as a sinner.

FOR GOD'S SAKE

Divine pleasure, not human need, is the greatest reason for observing the Sabbath principle. The key question is not: how rested am I after a Sabbath-rest experience? Nor how productive am I after a Sabbath-rest? The key question I must ask myself is: *Did I enter my chambers of rest for the pleasure of God?* After all, he set me free for his pleasure.

After years of embracing a Sabbath-rest practice for my own perceived need for rest and the desire to become more productive, I now tell myself, *for God's sake, rest!* Variations of the phrase *for God's sake* appear throughout Scripture:

He restores my soul. He guides me in paths of righteousness for his name's sake.

(Psalm 23:3)

Help us, O God our Savior, for the glory of your name; deliver us and forgive our sins for your name's sake.

(Psalm 79:9)

For the sake of the house of the LORD our God, I will seek your prosperity.

(Psalm 122:9)

Now, our God, hear the prayers and petitions of your servant. For your sake, O Lord, look with favor on your desolate sanctuary.

(Daniel 9:17)

O Lord, listen! O Lord, forgive! O Lord, hear and act! For your sake, O my God, do not delay, because your city and your people bear your Name.

(Daniel 9:19)

For we do not preach ourselves, but Jesus Christ as Lord, and ourselves as your servants for Jesus' sake.

(II Corinthians 4:5)

What is more, I consider everything a loss compared to the surpassing greatness of knowing Christ Jesus my Lord, for whose sake I have lost all things. I consider them rubbish that I may gain Christ.

(Philippians 3:8)

Daniel 9:17, "For your sake, O Lord..." expresses a desire that the Lord's reputation and character be esteemed above all others, including that of the worshiper. What pleases the Almighty motivates the spokesman. When I pray or say *for God's sake* or *for Jesus' sake,* I desire to align my behavior to what gives God pleasure. I curb my appetites and actions so as to be an asset and not a liability to his interests on earth. While God can take care of himself, I am protective of his name and character in the face of scoffers. I am rightfully defensive, not about me but about him.

When it comes to pleasing my Master, I could take lessons from my Springer Spaniels who seemingly live to please me. This is most true of Abby, our five-year-old Springer. She is the most affectionate dog I have ever met. She follows me wherever I go. When I return home from a trip, she whines until I greet her. When I take her in the boat fishing, she wants to lick my face the whole time; she's the only fishing buddy who can get away with that kind of behavior. She loves to fetch for me, and her master-pleasing bent is most pronounced when we are pheasant hunting with our hunting buddies. No matter who drops the bird she is faithful to deliver all birds to her master's hand.

When it comes to pleasing my Master I have a ways to go before ranking with the best of Springer Spaniels. My master, the Lord Jesus Christ, deserves my complete desire to please him whatever the cost to me.

Am I a Human Doing or a Human Being?

Living for God's sake requires service and silence. My Christian experience as a young person emphasized service. My home church hummed with performance as accomplishments for God were rewarded. The words of well meaning people still ring in my mind: *"Use your talents for God," "Please God by serving,"* and, *"If at all possible, become a minister."* Good advice had it been balanced with an understanding of being and the theology of rest.

The Bible is full of acts of service and good works that require effort and energy on our part. We were created to do good works: "For we are God's workmanship, created in Christ Jesus to do good works, which God prepared in advance for us to do" (Ephesians 2:10). But good works have their limits. The verses that precede verse ten emphatically state that we are not saved by our good works: "For it is by grace you have been saved, through faith—and this not from yourselves, it is the gift of God—not by works, so that no one can boast" (Ephesians 2:8-9).

The Apostle Paul's teaching regarding salvation was clear; salvation was by grace through faith, not works. However, when it came to sanctification, works were extremely important. By every inference sanctification was by works, not grace. There was little understanding of the role that rest played in holiness.

A constant stream of deeds reduces us to human doings—a frame of mind that says, *I am only as good as what I do. I have worth as long as I am able to produce.* This familiar belief system reflects slavery in ancient Egypt and the notions of the many industrialized nations; it devalues who we are.

In contrast we are human beings with worth beyond our ability to produce and serve. Peter Scazzero, Pastor of New Life Fellowship in Queens, New York, describes how the shift from functioning as human doings to human beings transformed first his life and then the church: "For the first time, I understood what it meant to minister out of who you are, not what you do. My discovery was contagious. We went from being *human doings* to *human beings*. The result has been a rippling effect, very slowly, through the entire church."[21]

We more closely resemble human beings when we cease *doing* long enough to know God as the Supreme Being. A Sabbath unto the Lord takes us from doing to being, which is the thrust of Psalm 46: "Be still, and know that I am God; I will be exalted among the nations, I will be exalted in the earth" (verse 10). This verse conveys the essence of the fourth commandment. The fourth and fifth commandments are the only commandments of the ten that are stated as positives: *Remember the Sabbath* and *Honor your father and mother.* The other eight are stated as *You shall not.* Psalm 46:10 conveys the essence of the fourth commandment in a somewhat negative form—be still. In other words *cease doing.* Cease is a common definition for Sabbath. *Be still* as opposed to doing the many seemingly urgent duties and performing personal agendas. *Be still* emphasizes being over doing.

In my stillness I note God's sovereignty and the fact that he will be exalted among nations and in the entire earth. Knowing God will be exalted gives me hope beyond my frustrating attempts to bring my little world under control. Instead of perpetually working my agenda as a control freak, I cease and take note of God's supreme control. Knowing God will be exalted shifts my trust from man's attempts to conquer evil to God's almighty greatness and goodness (Psalm 62:11-12).

As I write this paragraph, the date is July 7, 2005. This morning four bombs exploded in London—three on the subway and one on a bus. The death count is thirty-nine and rising. I believe that the war on terror is just that—a war. Governments, military, and law enforcement must work together in an attempt to eliminate terrorism. I also believe the real object of my faith must be God, not man. No matter what happens, God will be exalted among nations and on the earth. So I take a moment to ponder who is really in control. It is not about me or my efforts. It is about God. Therefore I am still before him.

Psalm 46 calls us to pause and take note of the God over all. There is a strange little word that mandates that we be still and know who is God. It is not translated, only transliterated so it can be pronounced. Sooner or later every Bible student is apt to ask, "What does *Selah* mean?"

PSALM 46

For the director of music. Of the Sons of Korah.
According to alamoth. A song.

God is our refuge and strength,
an ever-present help in trouble.
[2] Therefore we will not fear, though the earth give way
and the mountains fall into the heart of the sea,
[3] though its waters roar and foam
and the mountains quake with their surging.

                                                          Selah

[4] There is a river whose streams make glad the city of God,
the holy place where the Most High dwells.
[5] God is within her, she will not fall;
God will help her at break of day.
[6] Nations are in uproar, kingdoms fall;
he lifts his voice, the earth melts.

[7] The LORD Almighty is with us;
the God of Jacob is our fortress.

                                                          Selah

[8] Come and see the works of the LORD,
the desolations he has brought on the earth.
[9] He makes wars cease to the ends of the earth;
he breaks the bow and shatters the spear,
he burns the shields with fire.
[10] "Be still, and know that I am God;
I will be exalted among the nations,
I will be exalted in the earth."

[11] The LORD Almighty is with us;
the God of Jacob is our fortress.

                                                          Selah
                                              (Psalm 46:1-11)

Selah means rest. The word occurs three times in Psalm 46, a total of
seventy-one times in the Psalms, and three times in Habakkuk. As these
texts were set to music, Selah instructed the singers to rest and allow all
an opportunity to ponder what they were singing. In his melodic way with
words Charles Spurgeon provides commentary on the meaning of Selah:

"Selah." In the midst of such a hurly-burly the music may well come to a
pause, both to give the singers breath, and ourselves time for meditation.
We are in no hurry, but can sit us down and wait while earth dissolves,

and mountains rock, and oceans roar. Ours is not headlong rashness which passes for courage; we can calmly confront the danger, and meditate upon terror, dwelling on its separate items and united forces. The pause is not an exclamation of dismay, but merely a rest in music: we do not suspend our song in alarm, but retune our harps with deliberation amidst the tumult of the storm. It were well if all of us could say, "Selah," under tempestuous trials, but alas! Too often we speak in our haste, lay our trembling hands bewildered among the strings, strike the lyre with a rude crash, and mar the melody of our life-song."[22]

Selah means "stop the music!" Think about what you are singing. Recognize the one you are singing about or singing to. Selah complements the command to be still and know that I am God.

THE REST MAKES THE MUSIC

Years ago I played violin in a community orchestra. My musical reflexes have since diminished considerably. Performance is now limited to the closet. Nevertheless, music left a profound impact on my life. At some point in my musical training I grasped the value of the rest in music. Rests make music more dynamic. Silence strengthens the sound that remains and adds suspense, causing listeners to anticipate what is next. Great composers know how to use rests to enhance their creations.

One of the differences between amateur and professional musicians is a matter of respect for the rests. Rests do not require instrumental technique, fine tone quality, or the ability to carry a tune. Rests should be the easiest to play or sing, since they require no sound. However, for the undisciplined musician they are often most difficult.

Proud musicians occasionally play or sing slightly into the rests, seizing the opportunity to show off their fine tone at the expense of musicianship. Others jump in before rests are over for fear of falling behind. In the work world greed and fear are root causes for skipping periods of rest. Unfortunately, western ways reward such behavior calling it diligent, industrious, studious, and resourceful.

Music is primarily about the composer. Only as the musician honors the composer will the music be worthy of the one who wrote it. So it is with our lives.

Life is not about us. It is about the Creator who gives us life. Each of us can have a part in making beautiful music if we surrender being the center of attention. Perhaps that is the reason we debate about the Sabbath and sidestep any attempt to make it applicable to our lives. Sabbath-rest, for God's sake, requires a revolution!

COPERNICAN REVOLUTION

A Sabbath unto the Lord requires more than discipline and self-denial. It requires a revolution. Years ago I picked up a copy of Pastor Erwin Lutzer's insightful book, *Failure, the Back Door to Success*. Lutzer candidly shares an illustration that helped him turn his self-focused trend into a God-centered lifestyle:

> Remember Copernicus? He was the astronomer who rejected the theory that the planets rotated around the earth. He found it difficult to explain planetary motion according to this scheme. So he proposed a new theory, namely, that the sun is the center of the universe. With this theory, he found that the motion of heavenly bodies could be more easily explained.
>
> I knew I needed my own "Copernican Revolution." Until now, my world was at the core of my life. God was worked in only when needed. Now I decided that He would be on center stage, and my world—schedules, sermons, and exams—would rotate around Him. This, of course, necessitated adjustments.[23]

Without a personal revolution the thought of celebrating a Sabbath unto the Lord is apt to be boring if not repulsive. Without such a revolution a Sabbath unto the Lord flies in the face of my agenda, even my prayer requests. Without a revolution I pray constantly for God to prosper me, make my life easy, and full of problem-free fun—or I don't pray at all.

After a revolution I ask, *what would you like to do with my life?* I even rest beyond my personal need for rest because it pleases him. After a revolution I see that God does not exist simply to bless me. I exist to bless him. So I pray that God would bless me so I can bless him. After all, without him I am nothing and have nothing with which to bless him.

Sabbath-rest is also a weekly realignment. After being knocked out of alignment by the ruts of a world that totally resists such a revolution, Sabbath-rest realigns my life with the revolution I have experienced. Sabbath-rest reverses any *have it your way* trends that have wormed their way into my thinking.

Has the time come for your Copernican Revolution? Are you ready to rest for God's sake? Are you ready to live for his sake? Request a revolution today!

Prayer

Dear Heavenly Father, I realize that I am not the center of the universe. I am not the center of anything. I lay down all of my self-centered desires and invite you to not only be my Savior but my center as well. I don't know how to live in this new way, so I ask you to direct my paths to you every day in every way. In Jesus' name and for his sake I pray, Amen.

Questions to Ponder

1. Do I oscillate between driven achievement and some form of mind numbing private escape?
2. Do I claim that God set me free *for me* or *for himself*?
3. If my life were a concert, would my audience say that I am playing through the rests?
4. Have I had my Copernican Revolution?

CHAPTER FOUR

REST, THE PLEASURE
OF HIS PERSPECTIVE

I PLEASE GOD BY EMBRACING
HIS PERSPECTIVE

The LORD said, "Go out and stand on the mountain in the presence of the LORD, for the LORD is about to pass by." Then a great and powerful wind tore the mountains apart and shattered the rocks before the LORD, but the LORD was not in the wind. After the wind there was an earthquake, but the LORD was not in the earthquake. [12] After the earthquake came a fire, but the LORD was not in the fire. And after the fire came a gentle whisper.

(I Kings 19:11-12)

C. S. Lewis observed, "As long as you are proud, you cannot know God. A proud man is always looking down on things and people: and of course, as long as you are looking down, you cannot see something that is above you."[24]

"Our lives can become messy, a fog can roll in so thick that we can't see even one step ahead. Special guidance may be called for. There are times when it's good to ask a wise person to turn his or her chair toward us, to look deeply into our hearts, to help us gain perspective, to see what we're too blind to see, and to uncover what in our self-deceiving ways we hide from ourselves."[25]

THE LOSS OF PERSPECTIVE

When Lois and I planted a church, it taxed my reserves more than any other life experience. We made the commitment to do so during my last quarter of seminary. We were able to commute to and from our future home nearly every weekend. Seven families and two single men had committed monthly financial support to the potential church. That was enough to secure our meager salary. Only six families were planning to make the fledgling group their church home, and one of them was transferred to another state before we moved to the community. Lois and I soon felt like pioneers in our own country.

The first year I discovered that most of the people who had once expressed an interest in planting a church had shifted their attention to their teenagers. The advantages of established churches with youth pastors and well-run youth ministries overruled the adventures of church planting. Naturally they declined the offer to be part of the church plant and settled into their familiar churches.

The second year erupted like a volcano as conflicting agendas surfaced like hot lava rushing down a mountainside. After two years I admitted that it was only by God's grace that Grace Evangelical Free Church had survived.

We rebounded the third year recovering from some attendance loss due to the previous year of conflict. I personally recovered from a physical breakdown caused in part from the year of conflict. I discovered I could potentially work and worry myself to death, and I learned to value rest by experiencing what happens when I go without it for an extended period of time.

The fourth and fifth years of the church provided steady numerical growth. The spiritual development of young families was remarkable. Most of the congregation had not been raised in Christian homes. Many had become believers during their college years and were clueless as to how to establish a Christian home. Being raised in Christian homes was a huge advantage for Lois and me. Despite the narrow differences in age, we were like spiritual parents to them. These families became especially dear to us.

Year six challenged Grace Evangelical Free Church to once again live within its name. Stepping out in faith, the congregation broke ground and began building a church building that would fit its purposes. Building projects are notorious for making or breaking churches. Had the congregation known what would transpire shortly after signing the building contract, they may not have broken ground. The building was not the problem; it was leadership.

Just as the congregation took the giant step, young professionals who had been successful in their first jobs were promoted. That word usually meant transfer.

Many of the promotions came without an option to stay in the area, since entire departments were being transferred to other cities. The unemployment rate in the area would soon exceed twenty percent. These were the bright, young Christians that had developed into church leaders, deacons, potential elders and lots of faithful workers. Most tragic was the moral failure of our church chairman, which took place as the building was being constructed. The ranks of leadership were greatly reduced.

Six weeks after moving into the new facility our building committee chairman (not the same person who was in moral failure) pulled me aside after an evening service. He proceeded to ask me an all-too-familiar question, "Do you have a moment?" I had become gun-shy of the all-too-familiar conversation that followed, but for some reason I was ambushed this time. Brian and I had communicated nearly every day during the design and construction phases. With a solid Christian background, engineering, finance, and communication skills, he was the one leader I couldn't do without. Besides, Brian was my hunting buddy and we had just been out pheasant hunting the day before. *Not Brian! Yes Brian!* His company was moving him two hours away; not far, but too far to commute. He was to begin work at his new location in six weeks and he and his family were to move within three months.

Monday morning I got up and wandered to the basement. I fell to my knees and began to sob from my gut. It was like the cornerstone had just been pulled from everything I had invested in for the past six years. It was about more than a building or a career. It was about a ministry friendship.

Year seven was bittersweet. It was sweet because of all the new people that filed into the new building for worship services. Each month we broke all previous Sunday morning attendance records. Many of the new people were like the hungry young Christians who came when we first started the church. Normally I would have thrived on the situation, but the bitter had eroded the sweet.

I missed so many people. I had not only weathered the storms of their development but had come to depend on their skills. Without them we were now at our attendance high and leadership low. There were so many gaps in leadership and open positions, and I was still the only pastor on staff. The workload was great and the emotional load was greater.

There were so many victories to ponder and moments of grace to share. I could have been recharged with drive and purpose as I was seven years earlier, but I had lost something and didn't know what. Figuratively speaking, I was blind and couldn't find my way out of the bitter side of things. Like a blind man I needed someone to lead me out of the darkness, my blindness.

About the time so many were moving out of the area, Tom moved into a neighboring community. Tom was on staff with the Navigators, a parachurch organization well known for its ministries in the military and on college campuses. His new assignment reflected the Navigators strategic expansion into communities. Tom, a seasoned veteran, had about fifteen years of life and ministry experience on me. As a simple, unpolished farm boy at heart, Tom knew God and understood people. While I was long on explanation, Tom was long on application, and that's what I needed!

Tom would listen to me for hours regardless of the topic. Hesitant to interrupt, he waited until I took a long pause before inserting a few well-chosen words that helped order my thoughts. Then he would probe with honest questions, smiling patiently as I searched for a safe answer. Sometimes Tom would burst into laughter. My response varied from agitation to relaxation. By the end of each meeting I was taking myself and my situation less seriously. More than once I heard Tom say, "You lose perspective."

Technically speaking, "Perspective is the art of picturing objects on a flat surface so as to give the appearance of distance or depth."[26] Applying this definition to my thinking, I would have to say that I was viewing events as one-dimensional, magnifying all that seemed hopeless while screening out anything representing hope.

Figuratively speaking, perspective is "The effect of the distance of events upon the mind. Perspective makes happenings of last year seem less important."[27] An example of a loss of perspective is recorded by Robert Louis Stevenson, "Sleeping or waking, I beheld the same black perspective of approaching ruin.[28]

Throughout history many of God's most remarkable servants have suffered from a loss of perspective.

While I was not in any life-threatening situation, I was definitely losing hope because of my loss of perspective. I could not think big picture.

Unpleasant as it was, I would eventually thank God for sending Tom my way to point out my loss of perspective. I would also discover that I was not alone in my loss.

Throughout history some of God's most remarkable servants have suffered from a loss of perspective. No one made a more emphatic declaration that Jesus was the Christ than John the Baptist. While others inquired and investigated, John pointed to Jesus:

> The next day John saw Jesus coming toward him and said, "Look, the Lamb of God, who takes away the sin of the world! [30] This is the one I meant when I said, 'A man who comes after me has surpassed me because he was before me.' [31] I myself did not know him, but the reason I came baptizing with water was that he might be revealed to Israel." [32] Then John gave this testimony: "I saw the Spirit come down from heaven as a dove and remain on him. I would not have known him, except that the one who sent me to baptize with water told me, 'The man on whom you see the Spirit come down and remain is he who will baptize with the Holy Spirit.' [34] I have seen and I testify that this is the Son of God." [35] The next day John was there again with two of his disciples. [36] When he saw Jesus passing by, he said, "Look, the Lamb of God!" [37] When the two disciples heard him say this, they followed Jesus.
>
> (John 1:29-37)

Convinced of who Jesus was, John was convincing—so much so that his disciples began to follow Jesus. John knew his own identity as the voice preparing the way for the Christ (John 1:23), and he knew who Jesus was—the Christ. I would have never guessed that John would lose perspective based on his clear pronouncement of Jesus as the Christ.

However, there came a day when even John lost perspective. Blinded by his own circumstances, John lost perspective: "After Jesus had finished instructing his twelve disciples, he went on from there to teach and preach in the towns of Galilee. [2] When John heard in prison what Christ was doing, he sent his disciples [3] to ask him, 'Are you the one who was to come, or should we expect someone else?'" (Matthew 11:1-3).

John's question has baffled many Bible students over the centuries. I find his question contradictory to what John had so confidently stated at the baptism of Jesus. I ask myself, *had John forgotten the first day he spotted Jesus in the crowd and those words about Jesus that flowed out of his mouth? What about Jesus' baptism, the dove descending, and the thunderous words from* heaven, "This is my Son, whom I love; with him I am well pleased" (Matthew 3:17)? Was it now all a myth to John?

Years ago I visited Israel. Numerous attractions stuck in my mind for weeks after returning home. But no location fused itself to my emotions more than a hole in the ground. Hewed straight down into solid stone was a cistern, originally designed to store water. These cisterns not only held water; they held prisoners, as the Prophet Jeremiah experienced: "So they took Jeremiah and put him into the cistern of Malkijah, the king's son, which was in the courtyard of the guard. They lowered Jeremiah by ropes into the cistern; it had no water in it, only mud, and Jeremiah sank down into the mud" (Jeremiah 38:6).

For centuries these old cisterns served as caverns for detaining prisoners. Too deep for any prisoner to climb out of without help, cisterns hardly required guards.

I stared at the opening from ground level. It was about the size of a manhole cover. I imagined myself looking up through the hole from the bottom of the stone pit and seeing only a circle of light. Our guide described the conditions at the bottom of the hole as damp, dirty, muddy, and sometimes full of water. Peering into the hole I realized there was no way out, not even to *relieve* myself. Prisoners were at the mercy of their captors. If they were to receive any food or fresh water, it would have to be dropped into the hole at the top of the cistern.

Our guide in Israel was a Bible scholar who fit the land and Scripture together like a giant jigsaw puzzle. As we stood over the open hole of the cistern, he indicated that John the Baptist had likely spent time in a prison like this. I cringed at the thought. *Could I question John the Baptist for losing perspective in such a hole as this? No wonder John lost perspective and needed a word of assurance from Jesus:*

Jesus replied, "Go back and report to John what you hear and see: [5] The blind receive sight, the lame walk, those who have leprosy are cured, the deaf hear, the dead are raised, and the good news is preached to the poor. [6] Blessed is the man who does not fall away on account of me." [7] As John's disciples were leaving, Jesus began to speak to the crowd about John: "What did you go out into the desert to see? A reed swayed by the wind? [8] If not, what did you go out to see? A man dressed in fine clothes? No, those who wear fine clothes are in kings' palaces. [9] Then what did you go out to see? A prophet? Yes, I tell you, and more than a prophet. [10] This is the one about whom it is written: "'I will send my messenger ahead of you, who will prepare your way before you.' [11] I tell you the truth: Among those born of women there has not risen anyone greater than John the Baptist; yet he who is least in the kingdom of heaven is greater than he."

(Matthew 11:4-11)

Jesus does not scorch John's ears with a scalding rebuke for his lack of faith. Instead, he speaks what must have been music to the prisoner's ears. Jesus knew that John had lost perspective while in a hole in the ground. So Jesus renewed John's perspective.

Years later I attended a Promise Keepers rally at the Washington Mall. Joining a million men in song, sermon, and prayer was unforgettable. But what I remember best was a question whispered in my heart: *Are you willing to be lowered in a hole for me?* Sitting on the ground I pondered the question for most of the afternoon. The question did not leave me until I was willing to be lowered into a dark pit where it would be so easy to lose perspective.

John the Baptist's ancient predecessor also lost perspective. It was said of John that he would, "Go on before the Lord, in the spirit and power of Elijah" (Luke 1:17). No one performed more magnificent miracles by the power of God than Elijah. Yet he would suffer as well from a loss of perspective on at least one occasion.

First Kings eighteen and nineteen provide a startling portrayal of lost perspective. Chapter eighteen contrasts the pitiful inability of idols to do anything for those who worship them, compared to the prevailing power of God demonstrated through the courageous Prophet Elijah. After a climactic victory over the prophets of Baal, chapter nineteen depicts him running for his life.

SYMPTOMS OF LOST PERSPECTIVE

Symptoms sabotage our best attempts to conceal our weaknesses. Hide, cover, suppress as we may, symptoms surface like frost on a fall pumpkin. As annoying and embarrassing as an *idiot light* on a dashboard of a car, symptoms force the issue. Symptoms indicate that something needs correction or adjustment.

Elijah would be remembered as the elite among prophets. His name is repeated twenty-nine times in the New Testament. Only Moses and Elijah appeared with Jesus on the Mount of Transfiguration. The very mention of Elijah was equated with the miraculous power of God Almighty. However, not even Elijah could escape the symptoms of lost perspective. In First Kings nineteen Elijah displays *the fear of man* as a symptom of lost perspective.

FEAR OF MAN

Now Ahab told Jezebel everything Elijah had done and how he had killed all the prophets with the sword. ² So Jezebel sent a messenger to Elijah to say, "May the gods deal with me, be it ever so severely, if by this time tomorrow I do not make your life like that of one of them." ³ Elijah was afraid and ran for his life.

(I Kings 19:1-3)

He who was once so fearless now fearfully runs for his life. Elijah had met King Ahab face-to-face and called him a troublemaker a few hours before this episode with Jezebel. Standing courageously before a mob of angry idolaters and four hundred cultic prophets, he boldly condemned their actions as Baal worshipers: "Elijah went before the people and said, 'How long will you waver between two opinions? If the LORD is God, follow him; but if Baal is God, follow him.' But the people said nothing'" (I Kings 18:21).

Elijah ran from the threat of one woman. True, she was not just any woman. She was Jezebel, queen of Israel, and arguably the most wicked woman to walk this earth. To this day her name is synonymous with the character of a wicked witch. The contrast in Elijah's demeanor is shocking. One day he rules in victory, the next he runs in defeat. His symptoms cause the faithful to shudder and ask, *"If Elijah the prophet can falter like this, what about the rest of us?"* His symptoms are real. Obviously he has lost something between chapters. His previous perspective is now out of focus.

DESPONDENCY

Fear is followed by a more dreadful symptom—despondency. Despite numerous miracles and victories, Elijah lost all hope of good overcoming evil. Prophet of prophets, miracle worker of miracle workers was Elijah; yet he was without hope that his renowned ministry had a chance against the evil of his day. At least, that's what he thought! Void of any request for help, the premier prophet of all time feels like a total failure. "While he himself went a day's journey into the desert. He came to a broom tree, sat down under it and prayed that he might die. 'I have had enough, LORD,' he said. 'Take my life; I am no better than my ancestors'" (I Kings 19:4).

Elijah's response reminds me that even the best of God's servants falter when losing perspective. It doesn't matter what God has accomplished through you or me previously, when we lose perspective it is over until perspective is regained.

Martyr Syndrome

Elijah's obsession with his own death may qualify as a martyr syndrome. He may have been using martyrdom to validate his sacrifice as heroic in order to take some of the sting out of defeat. Twice Elijah answers the Lord with the same statement: "I have been very zealous for the LORD God Almighty. The Israelites have rejected your covenant, broken down your altars, and put your prophets to death with the sword. I am the only one left, and now they are trying to kill me too" (verses 10, 14).

In his frame of mind there was only one thing left for Elijah to do—die. I do not question Elijah's sold-out readiness to become a martyr for the work of God. What baffles me is his desire to become a martyr, as if his death were a last ditch effort to salvage something out of defeat.

Oswald Chambers wisely warned: "Always guard against self-chosen service for God; self-sacrifice may be a disease. If God has made your cup sweet, drink it with grace; if He has made it bitter, drink it in communion with Him. If the providential order of God for you is a hard time or difficulty, go through with it, but never choose the scene of your martyrdom."[29]

Choosing the scene of his martyrdom is what I feel Elijah was doing. A martyr syndrome has at least a tinge of self-focus mingled with the cause. In his own eyes Elijah has done all he can do in his lifetime for the Lord's cause, and now he is about to die as the last faithful prophet. Given his perspective, dying is the only thing left for him to do. All of his faithful attempts to turn the tide have failed. With Jezebel's wrath in hot pursuit he is sure to die alone. That's what you think, Elijah!

In contrast martyrdom was the furthest thing from God's plan for Elijah. God saw to it that Elijah did not die. God transposed Elijah directly into his presence, a rare privilege enjoyed only by Enoch (Genesis 5:24). The degree to which Elijah's perspective was twisted is unveiled in I Kings 2:11, "As they were walking along and talking together, suddenly a chariot of fire and horses of fire appeared and separated the two of them, and Elijah went up to heaven in a whirlwind."

FROM SYMPTOMS TO CAUSES

Loss of perspective may be caused by physical needs and limitations. James points out that Elijah, who had prayed many miracles into reality, "was a man just like us. He prayed earnestly that it would not rain, and it did not rain on the land for three and a half years" (James 5:17).

Elijah's God-given ability to perform miracles did not exempt him from requiring sleep: "Then he lay down under the tree and fell asleep" (verse 6). Likewise he experienced hunger: "All at once an angel touched him and said, 'Get up and eat.' ⁶ He looked around, and there by his head was a cake of bread baked over hot coals, and a jar of water. He ate and drank and then lay down again" (II Kings 19:5, 6). The fact that Elijah's lack of rest, food, and water are mentioned in the narrative, leads me to believe that his physical condition played a role in his loss of perspective.

Physical conditions clearly impact psychological responses. Wartime interrogation of prisoners is often enhanced by denying them food, water, and sleep. Prisoners may eventually give in to the requests of their captors, having lost perspective as to what is more important—physical needs or top security information.

Every once in a while I meet people who insist on finding a spiritual answer for a physical problem. They apply more spiritual discipline when they need to go to the doctor and have a physical. Not all depression is spiritual or psychological. For some it is a matter of thyroid or chemical imbalance. I have inserted this paragraph as a suggestion to those who have not lost perspective; so much as they have lost physical wellbeing.

The text, however, unveils a greater cause for the disintegration of perspective. There has been a shift in focus between First Kings eighteen and First Kings nineteen. In chapter eighteen the subject is more often the Lord, and Elijah is the subject through which God performs miraculous deeds.

> At the time of sacrifice, the prophet Elijah stepped forward and prayed: "O LORD, God of Abraham, Isaac and Israel, let it be known today that you are God in Israel and that I am your servant and have done all these things at your command."
>
> (I Kings 18:36)

Elijah said, "As the LORD Almighty lives, whom I serve, I will surely present myself to Ahab today."

(I Kings 18:15)

In chapter nineteen, Elijah speaks primarily of himself, and the Lord is the object. God has all but dropped off his radar scanner. "I have had enough, LORD," he said. "Take my life; I am no better than my ancestors" (verse 4b). Verse ten states: "I have been very zealous for the LORD God Almighty. The Israelites have rejected your covenant, broken down your altars, and put your prophets to death with the sword. I am the only one left, and now they are trying to kill me too."

Perspective definitely shrinks when we become the subjects of our conversations and the solutions to our problems. We may step into the arena of high demand with high hopes as long as our physical, mental, and emotional resource gauges are on full. But once they are depleted, we sink like the Titanic at sea.

I find it noteworthy that Elijah sees himself as the last faithful prophet through which God can work in the previous chapter as well. "Then Elijah said to them, 'I am the only one of the LORD's prophets left, but Baal has four hundred and fifty prophets'" (I Kings 18:22).

Elijah's perspective was somewhat skewed even during his courageous showdown with the prophets of Baal. Misinformed as he was, Elijah still performed miraculous deeds in the face of great opposition. Yes, it is possible to do great works for God with a distorted view of ourselves. But distortion is sure to catch up with us, as it did with Elijah.

FROM CAUSES TO CURES

I am so thankful that in his wisdom God included First Kings nineteen in the Bible. Without it I would think that Elijah was superhuman and unlike the rest of us. I would dismiss him as either a freak or an angel. I might even go so far as to call him the fourth member of the Trinity. Elijah might do without this chapter, but I can't! It identifies his propensity to lose perspective as well as identifies the path to recovering a true perspective.

Sandwiched in-between repeated claims by Elijah that he alone remains faithful is a short narrative which reveals a key to restoring perspective:

The LORD said, "Go out and stand on the mountain in the presence of the LORD, for the LORD is about to pass by." Then a great and powerful wind tore the mountains apart and shattered the rocks before the LORD, but the LORD was not in the wind. After the wind there was an earthquake, but the LORD was not in the earthquake. [12] After the earthquake came a fire, but the LORD was not in the fire. And after the fire came a gentle whisper. [13] When Elijah heard it, he pulled his cloak over his face and went out and stood at the mouth of the cave. Then a voice said to him, "What are you doing here, Elijah?"

(I Kings 19:11-13)

A WORD FROM GOD

A Word that Comforts

Compared to the fierce conflict of chapter eighteen, chapter nineteen unfolds quietly. Instead of tense dialogue, solitude permeates the scene. Elijah flees to a place of solitude in the wilderness. He falls asleep by himself. None other than the voice of God arouses him. His conversation is with God and God alone. Intimacy with God dominates the text. John Eldredge describes well the value of solitude: "To recover his heart's desire a man needs to get away from the noise and distraction of his daily life with his own soul. He needs to head into the wilderness, to silence and solitude. Alone with himself he allows whatever is there to come to the surface."[30]

The narrative redirects our attention from the sensational to the serene. Like Elijah we anticipate God will show up in the spectacular: wind, earthquake, and fire. Each time we are informed that the Lord was not in any of these attention grabbers: "But the LORD was not in the wind." "But the LORD was not in the earthquake." "But the LORD was not in the fire."

Instead, Elijah is directed to a quiet, personal setting to receive the word he needs. Elijah does not need more fanfare, conflict, or strife. He needs solitude and quiet assurance that God was there, is there, and will be there for him whatever happens and wherever he goes. He needs a gentle whisper from God, "And after the fire came a gentle whisper...What are you doing here, Elijah?" (I Kings 19:11-13). It is in solitude that God's voice is heard, a whisper within. The comfort is not so much in what God says but in the fact that God has spoken. The silence has been broken by the voice of God. Therein lies the comfort, even if his voice asks a question for which we have no good answer.

A Word that Sends

The next verses describe Elijah's completion of his journey. He was not to stew in self-pity any longer, for God had a clear plan for continuing what he had begun through Elijah. Elijah had to accept that it was no longer about him. It was time to pass the mantle on to others who will continue what he has been doing.

There comes a day for each of us when the question shifts from, *what is God going to do through me* to *what is God going to do through the next generation?* Restoring perspective is contingent on our willingness to accept that others will play a major role in the next chapter of God's kingdom plan. Elijah's next move was to anoint others to continue what God had begun through him—the most significant being the young Prophet Elisha:

> The LORD said to him, "Go back the way you came, and go to the Desert of Damascus. When you get there, anoint Hazael king over Aram. [16] Also, anoint Jehu son of Nimshi king over Israel, and anoint Elisha son of Shaphat from Abel Meholah to succeed you as prophet. [17] Jehu will put to death any who escape the sword of Hazael, and Elisha will put to death any who escape the sword of Jehu.
>
> (I Kings 19:15-17)

A Word that Corrects

Any view that distorts reality must be corrected in order for God's perspective to be restored. Elijah had believed that he was the last faithful follower of the Lord. While he had witnessed repeated apostasy on the part of the people he loved, Elijah was not alone. God corrected him, informing him there were as many as seven thousand in Israel who had not given in to Baal worship: "Yet I reserve seven thousand in Israel—all whose knees have not bowed down to Baal and all whose mouths have not kissed him" (verses 15-18).

Like Elijah we need a word from God which comforts, sends, and corrects. These ingredients are essential to the restoration of a true perspective.

Chapter nineteen is about restoring perspective in a restful setting. There are times when a dramatic encounter with God grabs our attention, like Moses experienced with the burning bush (Exodus 3) or Saul's blinding-light encounter with Christ (Acts 9). However, when it comes to restoring perspective, rest works best! As I once told a dear pastor who was hooked on his own adrenaline, "You can't change the oil while the engine is running." He was the engine that needed to be shut down for repairs and maintenance.

It has taken me a long time to resist the urge to speed up in order to catch up with God. I have always had a tendency to press more into a day than twenty-four hours would hold. I have run from one activity to the next, multi-tasking all the way. While I am tempted to speed up in an attempt to catch up with God, it is more often slowing down, shutting down, and shutting off that is necessary; even though it feels so wrong.

PERSPECTIVE EASILY LOST

Even as I write this chapter, I find it easy to lose perspective. Seldom is it one event that distorts perspective. An accumulation of events has been eroding an accurate perspective for months.

In August my mother had emergency surgery at age eighty-five. She was given a twenty-five percent chance of survival. Three days later Mom's vitals were dropping, and I began to think about writing her obituary. On the fourth day after surgery Mom amazed all of us, including doctors and nurses, as she showed strong signs of recovery. We didn't think she would make it through August, but she did. September brought new complications causing us to doubt she would make it through the month, but she did. After two months of being in the hospital and nursing home, Mom finally came home. It is now Christmas and Mom is still living at home with assistance. I am relieved along with my siblings. However, all three of us admit that numerous hospital and home visits, discussions, and decisions with medical teams have taken their toll on us.

My perspective was losing altitude faster than a B-52 full of bombs and out of fuel.

During this same period of time, I encountered a number of deaths at my part-time job as a trucking company chaplain. Two weeks before Christmas I attended a funeral of a truck driver who died of cancer. The week before Christmas I talked at length with three widows of drivers whose husbands had died suddenly during the fall months. One of the accidents happened just three days before Christmas. Being the bearer of bad news several times did not seem to bother me until the day after Christmas, Sunday.

Just before church I went downstairs to let our two dogs out. When I opened the door I was stunned by a very unpleasant odor. Cricket, our fifteen-year old English Springer Spaniel, had lost control of her bowels. In the midst of cleaning up the mess, I began to have thoughts about putting her down. *She is blind, but sees better than she hears. She has a heart murmur and is very arthritic. What's next?* We had talked about putting her down more than once but always delayed it since she was such a fighter and still had spring in her desire if not in her legs. The thought of taking her out of her discomfort suddenly gave me discomfort. Today I cringed as I thought; *this is going to be more difficult than I thought.*

Cricket had been a stabilizing factor for our boys during a move across three states, fifteen years earlier. As our boys grew up, they would snuggle up to her and allow her to comfort them whenever they had bad days. She had been a great family pet for so many years; it was hard to imagine our home without Cricket. Besides, she was a hunting buddy to me and our boys. She had flushed and fetched so many birds with such enthusiasm. She never quit on us. Then there were the puppies. Cricket had given us a litter of five and hovered over her daughter while she gave birth to a litter of eight. With her puppy and hunting days behind her, she still yearned for affection. *This isn't going to be easy*, I thought to myself. I felt ill as *putting her down* crossed my mind.

Once the mess was cleaned up, I got ready for church where I would take another blow. When I arrived a dear friend, who had agreed to do a very specific favor, told me that he would not be available to help out. It was a very legitimate excuse; I just wasn't in the mood for excuses that morning. I was experiencing self-pity, the most sincere kind. *I've given so much to so many people the last few months. Why can't someone come through for me when I need them? I don't want to see or talk to anyone this morning. I can't wait to get out of here and go home.* My perspective was losing altitude faster than a B-52 full of bombs and out of fuel.

As with Elijah, Jeremiah, and John the Baptist, the loss of perspective may appear to be sudden and drastic. However, the build up to the loss may be weeks or months in process. Loss of perspective may follow victories over immense opposition which leaves a person physically, emotionally, or spiritually depleted.

PERSPECTIVE, A GOD'S EYE VIEW

God never needs to consult a committee for a new or renewed perspective. He is the committee on true perspective—Father, Son, and Holy Spirit. God never needs to gather more information. He is omniscient, knowing all things. God never needs to step back to get a different view. He sees all things from all angles at once for he is omnipresent. God doesn't need time to think about what he will do or how he will respond. He is eternal and knows how all events turn out—past, present, and future. God doesn't lose perspective because of fatigue. He doesn't get tired. God is true perspective!

We are none of the above, yet God desires that we view heaven and earth as he views them. That's a unique privilege and if it requires settling down into a restful state of solitude, it is worth it and God is worthy of it.

I still lose perspective even after citing all these examples and having my perspective restored many times. The difference is that I recognize it more readily for what it is and back off from activity by inserting rest into my life. I have learned to say, *It's OK to rest for a few hours or a day until I can think clearly again.*

I am not necessarily talking about sleep. As the undisciplined college student said to himself the night before finals, *When in doubt, sack out!* Sleep has its restoration power when it comes to tired bodies and sleepy minds. However, as I emphasized in chapter one, *rest divine* is something more than sleep. More will be said on the nature of rest in future chapters.

What must be emphasized is this: the cost of going forward is too great when you don't know where you are. All too often busy people continue to do what they have done in the past, year after year without a clear perspective. They resemble a boxer who is out on his feet; he has been hit solidly in the head and has a concussion. He remains on his feet, only partially aware of what is going on. He continues to flail away at his opponent, ridiculously ineffective, until the referee stops the fight or his opponent floors him. Many people who were once effective workers have marginalized themselves by just working harder and longer after losing perspective. Others may slip into a mental funk so deep they minimize whatever abilities they once applied to their work and lose all enthusiasm for life itself.

WISDOM LITERATURE

A true perspective pleases God. I say this because so much of Scripture is given that God's people might gain and regain a true perspective. There is a section of the Old Testament known as Wisdom Literature: Job, Psalms, Proverbs, Ecclesiastes, and Song of Solomon. These books and passages of Scripture claim they are able to make the reader wise as in the case of Psalm 19:7-14:

> The law of the LORD is perfect, reviving the soul. The statutes of the LORD are trustworthy, making wise the simple. [8] The precepts of the LORD are right, giving joy to the heart. The commands of the LORD are radiant, giving light to the eyes. [9] The fear of the LORD is pure, enduring forever. The ordinances of the LORD are sure and altogether righteous. [10] They are more precious than gold, than much pure gold; they are sweeter than honey, than honey from the comb. [11] By them is your servant warned; in keeping them there is great reward. [12] Who can discern his errors? Forgive my hidden faults. [13] Keep your servant also from willful sins; may they not rule over me. Then will I be blameless, innocent of great transgression. [14] May the words of my mouth and the meditation of my heart be pleasing in your sight, O LORD, my Rock and my Redeemer.

I find it interesting that the Psalmist's purpose in internalizing the wisdom of the Scriptures is to please the Lord: "May the words of my mouth and the meditation of my heart be pleasing in your sight, O LORD, my Rock and my Redeemer" (verse 14).

I find it even more interesting to observe that so much of the wisdom literature is written not by writers who *have* God's perspective chapter after chapter but writers who are *searching for* his perspective. They are people whose whole lives were pilgrimages in search of God's perspective. Through a painful process of elimination these sojourners found it by resting on simple truths that were readily available to them throughout life. Such was Solomon's recommendation to centuries of readers at the end of Ecclesiastes: "Remember your Creator in the days of your youth, before the days of trouble come and the years approach when you will say, 'I find no pleasure in them'" (Ecclesiastes 12:1).

Psalm seventy-three is one of my favorite psalms. It was written by Asaph, who headed the service of music during the reigns of David and Solomon. I love the way he admits his struggle with envy and unveils the process of restoration from a faulty, envious perspective to a true, godly perspective.

> Surely God is good to Israel, to those who are pure in heart. [2] But as for me, my feet had almost slipped; I had nearly lost my foothold. [3] For I envied the arrogant when I saw the prosperity of the wicked. [4] They have no struggles; their bodies are healthy and strong. [5] They are free from the

burdens common to man; they are not plagued by human ills. [6] Therefore pride is their necklace; they clothe themselves with violence. [7] From their callous hearts comes iniquity; the evil conceits of their minds know no limits. [8] They scoff, and speak with malice; in their arrogance they threaten oppression. [9] Their mouths lay claim to heaven, and their tongues take possession of the earth. [10] Therefore their people turn to them and drink up waters in abundance. [11] They say, "How can God know? Does the Most High have knowledge?" [12] This is what the wicked are like—always carefree, they increase in wealth. [13] Surely in vain have I kept my heart pure; in vain have I washed my hands in innocence. [14] All day long I have been plagued; I have been punished every morning. [15] If I had said, "I will speak thus," I would have betrayed your children. [16] When I tried to understand all this, it was oppressive to me [17] till I entered the sanctuary of God; then I understood their final destiny. [18] Surely you place them on slippery ground; you cast them down to ruin. [19] How suddenly are they destroyed, completely swept away by terrors! [20] As a dream when one awakes, so when you arise, O Lord, you will despise them as fantasies.

(Psalm 73:1-20).

Asaph admits his former envy as well as his need for a change in perspective. Verses twenty-one and twenty-two represent a huge breakthrough in the Psalmist's attitude. Asaph looks back and sees how blinded he was by his loss of perspective: "When my heart was grieved and my spirit embittered, [22] I was senseless and ignorant; I was a brute beast before you."

I cannot count the number of times I have looked back with embarrassment at my short-sighted, despondent attitude and murmured, *How could I have been so blind, so faithless, so foolish, after all the ways God has shown his love to me?*

Asaph now sees clearly and experiences genuine prosperity as he reviews the immeasurable privilege of knowing God. In contrast, the present pleasure of the ungodly is short-lived as their fate is destruction.

Yet I am always with you; you hold me by my right hand. [24] You guide me with your counsel, and afterward you will take me into glory. [25] Whom have I in heaven but you? And earth has nothing I desire besides you. [26] My flesh and my heart may fail, but God is the strength of my heart and my portion forever. [27] Those who are far from you will perish; you destroy all who are unfaithful to you. [28] But as for me, it is good to be near God. I have made the Sovereign LORD my refuge; I will tell of all your deeds.

(Psalm 73:23-28)

When it comes to regaining perspective, there is nothing new under the sun. Some who have gone before us figured it out long ago. As D. Martyn Lloyd-Jones said of Augustine, "The great St. Augustine knew it; for quite a period he had this restlessness of soul and at last he cried out, 'Thou hast made us for Thyself, and our souls are restless until they find their rest in Thee.'"[31]

All of Scripture is God breathed (II Timothy 3:16-17) and therefore readily available to give us a perspective adjustment as we prayerfully desire God's view of things. A *bird's eye view* is an old cliché used to describe the advantage a bird has as it hovers overhead and sees what is not visible from the ground. The bird sees the big picture while ground creatures, including man, see only parcels of ground and objects that block distant landscapes. Better than a bird's eye view is a God's eye view. God sees all—past, present, and future—all the time. The Scriptures are written from a God's eye view to help us gain his perspective.

Several years ago I was teaching through the Book of Ephesians when a parishioner challenged the point I was making about our privileged position in Christ. The text in discussion was Ephesians 2:4-7:

> But because of his great love for us, God, who is rich in mercy, [5] made us alive with Christ even when we were dead in transgressions—it is by grace you have been saved. [6] And God raised us up with Christ and seated us with him in the heavenly realms in Christ Jesus, [7] in order that in the coming ages he might show the incomparable riches of his grace, expressed in his kindness to us in Christ Jesus.
>
> (Ephesians 2:4-7)

After I read aloud verses four through seven, he blurted out, "But that's God's perspective!"

"You are absolutely right," I responded, "and that's the perspective God wants us to have as we live our lives on earth."

As I seek to please God during my few and fragile days on earth, I now realize that maintaining God's perspective in a short-sighted world has no substitute. I can serve God in many ways, but God is pleased when I diligently devote myself to maintaining his perspective. Like it or not, I must admit that rest is always a part of the maintenance agenda. So I pray with the Psalmist: "May the words of my mouth and the meditation of my heart be pleasing in your sight, O LORD, my Rock and my Redeemer" (Psalm 19:14).

Prayer

Lord God, blessed be your name now and forever, for your perspective has always been clear and true. Neither sin nor sorrow has ever clouded your view or understanding. You alone see and know all things with precise clarity. You alone are true and the measure of truth throughout all eternity.

Forgive me for the many times I have entertained sinful and self-centered thoughts that have clouded my perspective and sent me into a mental funk. Thank you for providing a true and renewed perspective that pleases you. In Jesus' name and for his sake I pray, Amen.

Questions to Ponder

1. Can I recall a time when I lost perspective? If so, describe it.
2. Assuming I have lost perspective at some time, how did I regain a true perspective?
3. If I were in a condition of lost perspective today, what would I do to get out of it?
4. What practice(s) would help me maintain a proper and true perspective?

CHAPTER FIVE

REST, THE PLEASURE
OF HIS PEOPLE

I PLEASE GOD BY MAKING
HIS REST MY PLEASURE

If you keep your feet from breaking the Sabbath and from doing as you please on my holy day, if you call the Sabbath a delight and the LORD's holy day honorable, and if you honor it by not going your own way and not doing as you please or speaking idle words, then you will find your joy in the LORD, and I will cause you to ride on the heights of the land and to feast on the inheritance of your father Jacob." The mouth of the LORD has spoken.

(Isaiah 58:13-14)

One of the largest obstacles to true Sabbath-keeping is leisure.... Leisure is what Sabbath becomes when we no longer know how to sanctify time. Leisure is Sabbath bereft of the sacred. It is a vacation—literally, a vacating, an evacuation.[32]

(Mark Buchanan)

Sabbath-rest is a time to set aside lesser pleasures and be filled with eternal joy in a temporal setting.

(Jim Anderson)

In every age people manage to worship the works of their hands at the expense of God's pleasure. The original recipients of Isaiah's message blatantly worshiped images formed by their own hands: "The craftsman encourages the goldsmith, and he who smoothes with the hammer spurs on him who strikes the anvil. He says of the welding, 'It is good.' He nails down the idol so it will not topple" (Isaiah 41:7).

Shades of idolatry advance as twenty-first century man becomes more and more amused with his technological discoveries. Computers, cell phones, digital cameras, and satellites are great tools and toys, but terrible treasures. While I enjoy the use of all such devices, I am amused at what happens when a storm takes out the satellite signal to my television. I am also amazed when an entire company is immobilized whenever its computer system goes down. I chuckle every time I hear the most familiar question asked by cell phone users, "Can you hear me now?" Too often I am that cell phone user. Such disruptions remind us that our devices are worthy of our use, but never our worship.

I have also been tempted to worship the work I do with people as opposed to my work with things. There is a tendency to worship seemingly higher ranking jobs that require higher education and social skills compared to worshipping manual labor. If we do not worship how we rank in the work force, we may settle for worshipping the material goods and services our jobs make affordable to us.

Gordon Dahl made a profound statement in his book, *Work, Play, and Worship in a Leisure Oriented Society*:

> "We worship our work, work at our play,
> and play at our worship."[33]

The temptation to worship our work gives birth to another temptation—the temptation to work at our play. Good employment pays bills and makes luxuries and leisure activities possible. Once golf clubs, country club memberships, fishing rods and boats are purchased, they beg to be used. As they are used there is a desire on the part of their owners to be proficient at their use in order to justify their purchase. Gradually leisure becomes serious business. Before we know it play has become work.

We work at our play when we take leisure activities more seriously than our jobs or families. Preoccupation with sports teams and hobbies while on the job can be dangerous. It also produces mediocre work. As the saying goes, "Never buy a car that was made on Monday or Friday." The implications being that on Mondays workers are still decompressing from their weekend leisure activities, and on Fridays they are thinking about what they are going to do when the buzzer rings and the weekend begins.

LEISURE ACTIVITIES

A search on the web for the word "leisure" brought up 303,000,000 hits, compared to 7,700,000 a few years ago. To say that we live in a leisure-minded world is an understatement. One of the more interesting websites out there is *Men of Leisure Limited*.

Men of Leisure Limited is dedicated to the spread of leisure in all forms. It is our duty to educate all peoples about the transforming power of the leisure philosophy, to guide them in their quest for leisure, and in due time to declare each of them an official man of leisure! We shall provide quality products, sound advice, links to the leisure world, and leisure reviews to all men no matter what their stature in life.[34]

LEISURE ACTIVITIES CANNOT REPLACE GOD

Leisure activities have their place. It is no secret that I like to hunt and fish. Such activities helped keep our family close, especially during the years Lois and I were raising teenage boys. Compared to girls, boys tend to be less communicative, keeping their parents guessing as to what they are thinking. On the way home from hunting or fishing trips both of our sons chattered about numerous subjects. Every family needs to have at least one leisure activity. They are a means of parenting and keeping family members together.

They have also been a significant means of friendship and interaction with men. When it comes to teaching men, nothing compares with getting in a boat together. After all, that's what Jesus did (Matthew 8:23). Once they are in the boat you have a captive audience; they can either listen or swim to shore.

Leisure activities serve as good introductions to rest. They help us wind down and relax after intense periods of work. Leisure activities also serve as effective bridges after extended periods of rest. They help us transition back into our work zones.

I would be a full-fledged hypocrite if I frowned on people having fun and experiencing pleasure as God intended. The Apostle Paul warned against deceptive teachers who forbid the enjoyment of God's creation:

Such teachings come through hypocritical liars, whose consciences have been seared as with a hot iron. They forbid people to marry and order them to abstain from certain foods, which God created to be received with thanksgiving by those who believe and who know the truth. For everything God created is good, and nothing is to be rejected if it is received with thanksgiving.

(I Timothy 4:2-4)

THE LIMITS OF LEISURE

Leisure activities have their place. They also have their limits. First of all, leisure activities cannot replace God any more than work can replace God as a focal point of worship. Solomon went to extremes stimulating his senses with every delight known to man. He pursued pleasure hoping it would unlock the meaning to life. He discovered pleasures could not complete him. They couldn't even quench his thirst for pleasure.

I thought in my heart, "Come now, I will test you with pleasure to find out what is good." But that also proved to be meaningless. ² "Laughter," I said, "is foolish. And what does pleasure accomplish?" ³ I tried cheering myself with wine, and embracing folly—my mind still guiding me with wisdom. I wanted to see what was worthwhile for men to do under heaven during the few days of their lives.

(Ecclesiastes 2:1-3)

I denied myself nothing my eyes desired; I refused my heart no pleasure. My heart took delight in all my work, and this was the reward for all my labor. ¹¹ Yet when I surveyed all that my hands had done and what I had toiled to achieve, everything was meaningless, a chasing after the wind; nothing was gained under the sun.

(Ecclesiastes 2:10-11)

By seeking happiness through pleasure, Solomon pressed against pleasure's limits. The pursuit of pleasures failed him. Pleasure loses its luster when pleasure becomes the purpose of life. The pursuit of pleasure cannot replace the pursuit of God as a purpose for life. Solomon went on to say, "He has made everything beautiful in its time. He has also set eternity in the hearts of men; yet they cannot fathom what God has done from beginning to end" (Ecclesiastes 3:11). Since God set eternity in the heart of man, only the pursuit of the Eternal One can satisfy man's enormous craving for purpose. As the theologian Augustine said, "Thou hast made us for Thyself, O God, and the heart of man is restless until it finds its rest in Thee."

Another downside to working at our play is financial. Leisure activities are not affordable to all. Yet many who cannot afford them are consumed by them. Those who work extra hours so they can obtain leisure toys are often exhausted before they can enjoy them. In order to work at our play, we have to first work for our play.

The pursuit of pleasures often drives a desire for more money. Leisure activities compel people to seek more demanding jobs to feed their hobby horses. Better-paying jobs typically require more education, extended workdays, and longer commutes. Ironically the efforts that make leisure activities affordable consume remaining energy and time for enjoying them. The demand for more money to support leisure activities usually leads to less leisure enjoyment. When it is all said and done, one has a big house with a garage full of toys that rust out before they wear out. Randy Alcorn makes this very point in his book *Money, Possessions and Eternity*. "What I am pointing out is simply a law of life—the tyranny of things. And the central issue is not the things themselves, but the depletion of the resources of time, energy, enthusiasm, and money that could have been invested in the kingdom of God."[35]

The pursuit of affluence for any reason may produce the same vacuums as poverty. David Mckenna has coined the word *affluenza* in describing the ill effects of wealth:

Affluenza is a strange malady that affects the children of well-to-do parents. Though having everything money can buy, the children show all the symptoms of abject poverty—depression, anxiety, loss of meaning, and despair for the future. Affluenza accounts for an escape into alcohol, drugs, shoplifting, and suicide among children of the wealthy. It is most often found where parents are absent from the home and try to buy their children's love.[36]

Others manage to find time for leisure activities at the expense of worship. For them the day to pray has been exchanged for a day to play. Thus they play at their worship. Hope in the pleasures money can buy subtly replaces hope in God. Paul warned those who are rich in this world not to make such a shift in their focus and passion: "Command those who are rich in this present world not to be arrogant nor to put their hope in wealth, which is so uncertain, but to put their hope in God, who richly provides us with everything for our enjoyment" (I Timothy 6:17).

Since God richly provides everything for our enjoyment, leisure has its place. Ironically that proper place is not found by pursuing leisure. Like money, leisure activities make good servants, but terrible masters. Decades ago A.W. Tozer identified the perpetual conflict within mankind that takes place when God is replaced as the king of human hearts.

Our woes began when God was forced out of His central shrine and things were allowed to enter. Within the human heart things have taken over. Men have now by nature no peace within their hearts, for God is crowned there no longer, but there in the moral dusk stubborn and aggressive usurpers fight among themselves for first place on the throne.[37]

Leisure activities find their rightful place as people invite God to take his rightful place as their hope. When hope in leisure replaces hope in God, hopelessness prevails.

> *I have found a pleasure beyond leisure. I believe it is God's pleasure.*

While leisure activities have limited value for those who can afford them, God offers lasting satisfaction to all who come to him. God's full and free offer is recited in both the Old and New Testaments for all who are tired and weary of pursuits that fail to satisfy.

Come, all you who are thirsty, come to the waters; and you who have no money, come, buy and eat! Come, buy wine and milk without money and without cost.

[2] Why spend money on what is not bread, and your labor on what does not satisfy? Listen, listen to me, and eat what is good, and your soul will delight in the richest of fare. [3] Give ear and come to me; hear me, that your soul may live. I will make an everlasting covenant with you, my faithful love promised to David.

(Isaiah 55:1-3)

The Spirit and the bride say, "Come!" And let him who hears say, "Come!" Whoever is thirsty, let him come; and whoever wishes, let him take the free gift of the water of life.

(Revelation 22:17)

What an offer to all regardless of social status or income! No one has to moonlight or take a second job to obtain this offer.

I have lived enough years craving more time, money, and freedom to enjoy leisure activities. I have also had moments when I could have been rightly accused of working at my play. I still take pheasant hunting pretty seriously. No matter how aching tired I may be after chasing roosters through the tall grass, I never want to quit. As one hunter's son quizzed his Dad, "What does Jim have against those birds? What did they ever do to him?"

Today I could fill my life with more leisure and less work. I have never had more access to the things I once lived to do. I could be a leisure lord, traveling the world, taking cruises, hunting other species of birds, enjoying more than one Canadian fishing trip a year, and buying leisure toys. However, if I became a lord of leisure, leisure would become a lord of me.

Truthfully an increase in leisure activities does not appeal to me. It's not that I experience guilt when engaged in them nor sigh with self-pity as one who sacrifices leisure to serve God and others. I honestly have the life I want. I have found a pleasure beyond leisure. I believe it is God's pleasure.

Recently I met a man whose experience in this mode of pleasure far exceeds mine. After fifty-one years of enjoyable marriage he has been a widower for the past six years. At the age of seventy-eight, Max is a retired minister living on Social Security. If anyone is worthy of a life of full-time leisure, it is Max. He has earned his keep, serving churches for over a half century. However, stooping to a life of leisure has no appeal to him. His hobby is helping people. He serves as interim pastor where needed, encourages pastors to hang in there, and gently counsels unwed couples living together to break it off or get married.

I sense no driven workaholic tendencies in the man. Max portrays pure pleasure in God and a passion to see God loom large in the lives of others. Max has the contentment many crave but few find. He is living the pleasure of God.

PLEASURES CANNOT REPLACE RIGHT

Second, leisure activities cannot replace what is right. Isaiah chapter fifty-eight addresses worshipers who think God should bless them for fasting and keeping a Sabbath ritual while they freely exploit the needy and poor. They act as *a nation that does what is right* while enjoying pleasure at the expense of others:

> "Shout it aloud, do not hold back. Raise your voice like a trumpet. Declare to my people their rebellion and to the house of Jacob their sins. ² For day after day they seek me out; they seem eager to know my ways, as if they were a nation that does what is right and has not forsaken the commands of its God. They ask me for just decisions and seem eager for God to come near them. ³ 'Why have we fasted,' they say, 'and you have not seen it? Why have we humbled ourselves, and you have not noticed?' Yet on the day of your fasting, you do as you please and exploit all your workers. ⁴ Your fasting ends in quarreling and strife, and in striking each other with wicked fists. You cannot fast as you do today and expect your voice to be heard on high."
>
> (Isaiah 58:1-4)

As an act of denial they suppress their exploitation by doing as they please (verse 3). In every age among people of all ages wrongs are buried under pleasures. When guilt pangs pierce we tend to anesthetize them with sensations of pleasure. While hearing a cry for help we turn up the volume on the music we enjoy. When witnessing suffering on the evening news we channel surf to our favorite pleasure programs. Pleasure blinds us to wrong and avoids what is right.

In contrast God says forsake your pleasure and do what is right. Get right with your fellow man. Pleasure is not an antidote for wrong. Pleasure, even when innocent, distracts from doing what is right. In doing what is right we uncover and correct wrong.

PLEASURES CANNOT REPLACE REPENTANCE

Third, pleasures cannot replace repentance. Sin dulls the pleasure sensors. It jams the circuits that communicate pleasure to the brain and every other part of a being. What once brought pleasure now brings boredom. One must now go to extremes to stimulate the body's pleasure sensors. Some turn to drug use. Having given up on pleasure, some choose to arouse fear sensors through daredevil stunts. After normal pleasure sensors have been singed, I know of only one way to restore them. Repentance restores pleasure.

Isaiah's message calls for repentance for all the sinful ills of ancient Israel. The opening chapter of Isaiah is an invitation to reason with the

Lord regarding sins committed. Throughout the book *repent* is cited along with its near equivalent *return*.

> "Come now, let us reason together," says the LORD. "Though your sins are like scarlet, they shall be as white as snow; though they are red as crimson, they shall be like wool. [19] If you are willing and obedient, you will eat the best from the land; [20] but if you resist and rebel, you will be devoured by the sword." For the mouth of the LORD has spoken.
>
> (Isaiah 1:18-20)

> Like birds hovering overhead, the LORD Almighty will shield Jerusalem; he will shield it and deliver it, he will "pass over" it and will rescue it. [6] Return to him you have so greatly revolted against, O Israelites.
>
> (Isaiah 31:5-6)

> Seek the LORD while he may be found; call on him while he is near. Let the wicked forsake his way and the evil man his thoughts. Let him turn to the LORD, and he will have mercy on him, and to our God, for he will freely pardon.
>
> (Isaiah 55:6-7)

> "The Redeemer will come to Zion, to those in Jacob who repent of their sins" declares the LORD.
>
> (Isaiah 59:20)

While visiting friends in Atlanta, Lois and I heard a sermon from the most unpretentious senior pastor I have ever met—Pastor Buddy Hoffman of Grace Fellowship Church in Snellville, Georgia. The church Buddy serves is by no measure small. Yet when I met him before the service he impressed me as being one step up from a street person. His head was completely shaven. His clothes were extremely plain and his shoes looked like something designed for gardening. Without facade this man communicated grace and truth. Buddy spoke slowly, even for a person in the south. I was so impressed by his un-impressiveness that I got the message: this is a pastor and church that lives up to the name, Grace Fellowship Church. This was also the experience of our friends who came to the church in need of grace and truth.

Buddy spoke of repentance as a progression. Repentance moves from awareness to awakening and on to alteration. In order to truly repent one must have an awareness of personal sin before God. As a person becomes aware of personal sin, he or she begins to own up to the fact that he or she is indeed a sinner who has committed sins against God and man. This leads to awakening.

Awakening occurs when someone is disturbed by the devastating consequence of sin. Sin has made him an enemy of God. God is therefore just in sending him to hell. As he is awakened to the reality that God is good and just in contrast to his sinfulness, the sinner calls out to God in readiness to accept God's solution to the dilemma. A desire to do something about sin has been awakened. It is at this point that a person becomes receptive to God's free gift of salvation through Jesus Christ.

Having received, Christ a person has the power to alter his or her desires and behavior. It may be a total turnabout where a person leaves his or her former lifestyle. It may be a process of change that includes peaks and valleys before the person rids himself of the sinful habits that once ruled.

Buddy's sermon was not out of a textbook. He spoke as one who had experienced and observed again and again the transforming power of God activated by repentance in all of its stages: awareness, awakening, and alteration. People are hungry for grace and truth, and Buddy gives it to them.

Repentance in Old Testament Hebrew means to bring back or return. In New Testament Greek the word repentance is the descriptive compound word *metanoia*. Meta communicates change as in the word metamorphosis. Noia pertains to the mind. Repentance is a change of mind so as to change behavior.

God invited the Israelites to change more than their outward demeanor and posture. He wanted more than the apparent humility of an external ritual. God called them to repentance, an inward change of mind and heart.

Unfortunately change does not come easy for human beings, especially where sin is involved. We will deny, rationalize, and project our sin on others before claiming ownership of our sins. Most often we need to be confronted. Gentle confrontations are not always effective. *In your face* confrontations are often mandatory. We do not posture ourselves for change until we take ownership of our sin. Isaiah was sent to get in the face of the Israelites for their pretentious behavior toward the Sabbath. They pretended to keep the Sabbath while exploiting the poor.

Is this the kind of fast I have chosen, only a day for a man to humble himself? Is it only for bowing one's head like a reed and for lying on sackcloth and ashes? Is that what you call a fast, a day acceptable to the

90

LORD? [6] "Is not this the kind of fasting I have chosen: to loose the chains of injustice and untie the cords of the yoke, to set the oppressed free and break every yoke? [7] Is it not to share your food with the hungry and to provide the poor wanderer with shelter—when you see the naked, to clothe him, and not to turn away from your own flesh and blood? [8] Then your light will break forth like the dawn, and your healing will quickly appear; then your righteousness will go before you, and the glory of the LORD will be your rear guard.

(Isaiah 58:5-8)

God promises to change his demeanor toward sinners once repentance works its change in the minds and hearts of transgressors. He is quick to reply and repay with kindness towards the repentant:

Then you will call, and the LORD will answer; you will cry for help, and he will say: "Here am I." If you do away with the yoke of oppression, with the pointing finger and malicious talk, [10] and if you spend yourselves in behalf of the hungry and satisfy the needs of the oppressed, then your light will rise in the darkness, and your night will become like the noonday. [11] The LORD will guide you always; he will satisfy your needs in a sun-scorched land and will strengthen your frame. You will be like a well-watered garden, like a spring whose waters never fail. [12] Your people will rebuild the ancient ruins and will raise up the age-old foundations; you will be called Repairer of Broken Walls, Restorer of Streets with Dwellings.

(Isaiah 58:9-12)

The Lord rewards repentance by satisfying desires in unlikely places, giving strength where there was once weakness, and prospering his people according to his good pleasure. Through repentance God provides what the pursuit of pleasure could not. Repentance produces joy that is no match for leisure activities.

Genuine repentance is followed by joy. I find this connection between repentance and joy extremely interesting. This connection is obvious in Isaiah chapter fifty-five. The call to repentance in verses six and seven is followed by a promise of intense joy.

Seek the LORD while he may be found; call on him while he is near. Let the wicked forsake his way and the evil man his thoughts. Let him turn to the LORD, and he will have mercy on him, and to our God, for he will freely pardon.

(Isaiah 55:6-7)

You will go out in joy and be led forth in peace; the mountains and hills will burst into song before you, and all the trees of the field will clap their hands. [13] Instead of the thornbush will grow the pine tree, and instead of briers the myrtle will grow. This will be for the LORD's renown, for an everlasting sign, which will not be destroyed.

(Isaiah. 55:12-13)

JOY IS THE EMOTION OF HEAVEN

It is also noteworthy that repentance produces a shared experience of joy in heaven and earth at the same time. When repentance happens, both heaven and earth rejoice. Luke chapter fifteen has been labeled the lost-and-found department of the Bible. The chapter contains three parables about three lost valuables: a sheep, a coin, and a son. There is rejoicing in heaven and on earth when each is found.

"And when he finds it, he joyfully puts it on his shoulders [6] and goes home. Then he calls his friends and neighbors together and says, 'Rejoice with me; I have found my lost sheep.' [7] I tell you that in the same way there will be more rejoicing in heaven over one sinner who repents than over ninety-nine righteous persons who do not need to repent."

(Luke 17:5-7)

REPENTANCE IS A PREREQUISITE TO JOY

Joy is the emotion of heaven. Joy is the true pleasure of God. Repentance transforms pleasure into joy. One cannot experience the joy of God without repentance, without turning around and facing God. There is no joy in running from God. Joy is reserved for those who run to him like the prodigal son returned to his father:

"When he came to his senses, he said, 'How many of my father's hired men have food to spare, and here I am starving to death! [18] I will set out and go back to my father and say to him: Father, I have sinned against heaven and against you. [19] I am no longer worthy to be called your son; make me like one of your hired men.' [20] So he got up and went to his father. "But while he was still a long way off, his father saw him and was filled with compassion for him; he ran to his son, threw his arms around him and kissed him. [21] "The son said to him, 'Father, I have sinned against heaven and against you. I am no longer worthy to be called your son.' [22] "But the father said to his servants, 'Quick! Bring the best robe and put it on him. Put a ring on his finger and sandals on his feet. [23] Bring the fattened calf and kill it. Let's have a feast and celebrate. [24] For this son of mine was dead and is alive again; he was lost and is found.'" So they began to celebrate.

(Luke 15:17-24)

True Christians repent. John the Baptist and Jesus began their ministries with the word *repent*. I have listened to many testimonies of believers in Russia and to the best of my memory they all began with the words, "I repented when...." In contrast *repent* has all but dropped out of the vocabulary of churches in the west.

In order to maintain the joy-filled Christian life, repentance must take residence as the official Christian response to sin. David tried to hide his sin of adultery with Bathsheba by covering it up with the murder of her husband, Uriah (II Samuel 11). Even though God had worked mighty victories and written volumes through him, David had no joy as long as he hid his sin. In Psalm thirty-two David expressed the grief he experienced during those unrepentant days:

> When I kept silent,
> my bones wasted away
> through my groaning all day long.
> [4]For day and night
> your hand was heavy upon me;
> my strength was sapped
> as in the heat of summer.
>
> Selah
>
> [5] Then I acknowledged my sin to you
> and did not cover up my iniquity.
> I said, "I will confess
> my transgressions to the LORD"—
> and you forgave
> the guilt of my sin.
>
> Selah
>
> [6] Therefore let everyone who is godly pray to you
> while you may be found;
> surely when the mighty waters rise,
> they will not reach him.
> [7] You are my hiding place;
> you will protect me from trouble
> and surround me with songs of deliverance.
>
> Selah
> (Psalm 32:3-7)

David's joy returned after he reinstated repentance as the programmed response toward sin in his heart. Once he confessed his sin and received forgiveness the songs of deliverance returned. David wrote Psalm fifty-one during the same era. Once again David expresses the dregs of unrepentance and craves for joy, the emotion of heaven:

> Have mercy on me, O God, according to your unfailing love; according to your great compassion blot out my transgressions. [2] Wash away all my iniquity and cleanse me from my sin.
>
> (Psalm 51:1, 2)

> Restore to me the joy of your salvation and grant me a willing spirit, to sustain me.
>
> (Psalm 51:12)

REPENTANCE IS A PREREQUISITE TO REST

Whenever I sin and fail to repent my joy evaporates. Sin drains joy. The removal of joy functions as a deterrent to sin. Once experiencing the heavenly emotion, one does not want to return to a meager life of pleasure. I simply don't want to go there again. No matter what momentary delight accompanies sin, it is no match for the joy God has in store for his people. The loss of joy drained out at the point of sin is too big a price to pay for the sensation of sin.

It may seem strange to devote so much space to repentance in a book about rest. However, repentance is a prerequisite to rest. Rest requires repentance as an admittance fee.

We may attempt to enter the rest of God while our innards churn with sin, but Sabbath-rest will remain a locked door. Sabbath-rest is a pleasure of God we cannot enter apart from repentance of sin and a change of heart.

Repentance seldom comes easy. We stonewall true repentance of the heart with all our defenses. David Hansen vividly depicts the resistance of the human heart toward investigation and change. David's depiction of the heart echoes God's word through Jeremiah: "The human heart is the most fiercely guarded piece of ground in the universe. The fortress is built up through years and years of self-justification and rationalization. The soul in sin feels alive, but it is dead".[38]

"The heart is deceitful above all things and beyond cure. Who can understand it? I the LORD search the heart and examine the mind, to reward a man according to his conduct, according to what his deeds deserve" (Jeremiah 17:9-10).

If any of us have any hope of experiencing the fruit of repentance that leads to Sabbath-rest, we must persistently ask God to crack open our hearts and investigate them until we have no other response than repentance. After all, repentance is the official Christian response to sin.

Before attempting to open the door to personal Sabbath-rest, we must each ask ourselves before God the following questions: *Have I ever truly repented of my sin before God? Have I become aware, awakened, and altered so as to turn fully away from my sin? Have I asked Christ to forgive me and my sin and invited him into my life? Do I desire his life-altering power, so I can turn about from my sin and face him the rest of the way? Am I a believer who has allowed sin to take root and grow in me, so that I need to confess my sin, turn from it, and resist it in the faith and power of Christ?*

Please take a moment, a day, a week, or whatever it takes to settle these issues before entering the door of Sabbath-rest.

REST BEYOND LEISURE

Fourth, pleasure or leisure activities cannot replace true Sabbath-rest. When activity replaces rest, fatigue diminishes joy, even if the activity is leisure. As self-indulgence takes precedence over Sabbath-rest, joy departs. This is not a new problem. Israel apparently experienced a depletion of joy while pretending to maintain a Sabbath practice and wondered why until God sent the Prophet Isaiah with the answer:

> "If you keep your feet from breaking the Sabbath and from doing as you please on my holy day, if you call the Sabbath a delight and the LORD's holy day honorable, and if you honor it by not going your own way and not doing as you please or speaking idle words, [14] then you will find your joy in the LORD, and I will cause you to ride on the heights of the land and to feast on the inheritance of your father Jacob." The mouth of the LORD has spoken.
>
> (Isaiah 58:13-14)

While the specific application of Isaiah fifty-eight rebukes anyone who thinks spiritual discipline can wash away human abuse, the deeper issue provides a more general application confronting the basic selfish nature of man. *Doing as you please* is confronted twice (verses three and thirteen) as the root cause of exploitation: You do as you please and exploit all your workers.

Sabbath-rest is a time to set aside what is less than the best for what is best. While you may not be exploiting anyone, you might allow your independence coupled with the leisure industry to exploit you. *Going your own way* is less than the best. *Doing as you please* is less than the best. *Speaking idle words* is less than the best. *Finding your joy in the LORD* is the best!

Once I refrain from practices that are less than the best, I am in a far better position to find my joy in the Lord. Once I taste the joy of the Lord, I will want to carry that taste of joy into the rest of my week. But it takes setting aside what I want to do to taste what God wants for me. He always knows what is best for me.

On occasion I am asked, "What's all this fuss about Sabbath-rest? Why not just take a day off once a week and do some lawn work or engage in some leisure activities? Why not just take a day off to do as you please?" While a day or weekend off for doing leisure as we please provides a divergence and relief from the pressures of work, it fails to produce the deep-cycle rest needed in a stressful, leisure-driven world.

In his article "Learning to Rest," J. Alex Kirk conveys his discovery that his leisure activity proved to be less than the best:

> Then one Sunday as I turned off the TV after the late afternoon game, I evaluated how I actually felt. In truth, after 15 hours of watching football over the previous two days, I was sluggish and my eyes were glazed over. All I really wanted to do after "resting" for the past two days was take a nice, long nap. I was trying to find rest in something that wasn't bad, but it didn't restore me. This realization was a bit startling at the time. I'm ashamed to say it took me several more years to shake my habit, but the realization that Sunday woke me to the bigger issue in my life: where does rest come from? For leaders, most of whom are enthusiastic and energetic, the discipline of resting is a foreign one. But to work this into your leadership journey is essential for a healthy and glad ending down the road.[39]

Leisure activities are overrated when it comes to providing deep rest. The relief they provide is short-lived. A steady diet of leisure leaves us empty inside. Leisure is simply not potent enough to bring rest into the dark restless recesses of the soul. While leisure may serve as a divergence from stress, it can also distract us from settings that help us identify the real stress producers. They will be identified in the next segment of the book.

Sabbath-Rest, When Divine and Human Pleasures Meet

It may appear that God's pleasure and my pleasure are opposites, never to be aligned with one another. That was my perspective in my teen years. I perceived that pleasing God would numb my pleasure sensors. Whatever God wanted for me was all work and no play. Later, I discovered that when I desire divine pleasure, God is pleased and so am I. Seeking God's pleasure is a win-win proposition.

After I encouraged a pastor to attend a Sabbath Retreat he replied, "God says a whole lot to me while I am cutting wood with a chainsaw." I thought to myself, *just think how much God would say if he turned the chainsaw off?*

A fellow workaholic like me can relate to his reply. He feels guilty as soon as he stops working. A running chainsaw that produces a pile of firewood pacifies guilt and disengages the mind enough for God to get a word in edgewise. I have a chainsaw. Using it is a good reprieve from sitting at a desk or computer all day. Though cutting wood produces sweat, it feels more like leisure than work.

Mundane work at which our minds are free from the strain of study or decision making is an opportunity for God to have a word with us. After all, God will take what we give him, and he is perfectly capable of speaking above the chatter of a chainsaw.

However, there is the issue of disrespect. If someone wanted to talk with me, I wouldn't keep the chainsaw running. It is disrespectful to keep on working when someone wants to talk to you. How much more when God speaks!

God can speak to us at any time, even with a chainsaw raging though a tree trunk; but God wants to speak to us while we are alert yet resting from work and leisure.

God wants us to enjoy him. When we find our pleasure in God, God is most pleased and glorified. In my estimation no one in recent decades has melded the pleasure of God and pleasure of man more passionately than Pastor John Piper. With reference to this pleasure Piper has coined the phrase *Christian Hedonism*:

Here is the rock-solid foundation of Christian Hedonism: God is most glorified in us when we are most satisfied in Him. This is the best news in the world. God's passion to be glorified and my passion to be satisfied are not at odds....

The aim of Christian Hedonism is to show why this is so. It aims to show that we glorify God by enjoying Him forever.[40]

> *The only way we will find the higher plateaus of joy is by weaning ourselves off the lower stuff, including leisure activities.*

Contrary to my early belief system, divine pleasure and human pleasure are not mutually exclusive. When I first experienced the pleasure of God as my joy, Psalm 34:8 and related verses became my reality: "Taste and see that the LORD is good; blessed is the man who takes refuge in him." "Delight yourself in the LORD and he will give you the desires of your heart" (Psalm 37:4). "Satisfy us in the morning with your unfailing love, that we may sing for joy and be glad all our days" (Psalm 90:14).

Sabbath-rest has become my focus time for setting aside both work and leisure, so that God's joy-filled rest may enter me without competition. I strongly believe that is how it is meant to be. The only way we will find the higher plateaus of joy is by weaning ourselves off the lower stuff, including leisure activities. Sabbath-rest is a time to set aside lesser pleasures to be filled with eternal joy in a temporal setting.

I enjoy the great outdoors. I like to hunt, fish, swim, work on the lawn, and cut wood for the fireplace, but not during my Sabbath-rests.

For the first time in my life I live on a lake. Skiing boats, fishing boats, and jet skis motor around the lake in the summer and snowmobiles in the winter. I have learned to not indulge in those enjoyable activities during my Sabbath-rest. By not indulging I allow a greater joy to seep into my life, the joy of the Lord. I cease doing as I please and make room for God to share with me what pleases him. I pray, "God, grant me the joy you experience. May your joy settle in my soul, joy that cannot be taken away by injury or age."

I have found the best use of a lake during a Sabbath-rest is to not use it. Sabbath-rest is the enjoyment of being. God doesn't ask that we do anything during a Sabbath-rest so we might know that he enjoys us as human beings apart from what we can do. I don't ask the lake to provide a ride, a swim, or a fish. I don't ask it to do anything for me. I let it be because it has worth and gives joy for just being, apart from what it can produce. It is best to let it be. Having bonded my pleasure with God's pleasure, both work and leisure are carried out with greater joy.

Sabbath-rest is the sanctuary of lovers. Throughout the Bible, God uses a number of caricatures to portray our relationship to him: a potter and his clay, a shepherd and his sheep, a lord and his servants, a teacher to his students, a father to his children, a friend to his friends. But God saved the best until last—a bridegroom and his bride. Christ is the Bridegroom and the Church, made up of his people, the Bride (Ephesians 5:22-33, Revelation 19:7-9). True lovers need neither the accomplishment of work nor the entertainment of leisure to be in love. They just need each other.

Steve McVey brings this concept home emphatically in his book, *Grace Walk*: "How foolish I was when I thought that God's main interest was in what I did for Him. I lived as if He wanted a maid to serve Him, when what He really wants is a bride who loves Him so much that she is consumed with knowing Him intimately!"[41]

Sabbath-rest is not only the pleasure of God; it is the pleasure of his people. It is the joy, the emotion of heaven that loss of health or home cannot remove. Unlike so many leisure activities, you don't need to get a second job to pay for it. You need a sanctuary of time that neither work nor play can destroy.

Here is an old hymn with a new melody. Make it your prayer, your theme song.

JESUS I AM RESTING

Jesus I Am Resting Resting
David Hampton / Jean Sophia Pigott

Chorus 1
Jesus I am resting resting
In the joy of what Thou art
I am finding out the greatness
Of Thy loving heart

Verse 1
Thou hast bid me gaze upon Thee
And Thy beauty fills my soul
For by Thy transforming power
Thou hast made me whole

Verse 2
Oh how great Thy loving kindness
Vaster broader than the sea
Oh how marvelous Thy goodness
Lavished all on me
Yes I rest in Thee Beloved
Know what wealth of grace is Thine
Know Thy certainty of promise
And have made it mine

Verse 3
Simply trusting Thee Lord Jesus
I behold Thee as Thou art
And Thy love so pure so changeless
Satisfies my heart
Satisfies its deepest longings
Meets supplies its ev'ry need
Compasseth me round with blessings
Thine is love indeed

Verse 4
Ever lift Thy face upon me
As I work and wait for Thee
Resting 'neath Thy smile Lord Jesus
Earth's dark shadows flee
Brightness of my Father's glory
Sunshine of my Father's face
Keep me ever trusting resting
Fill me with Thy grace [42]

Prayer

Dear Lord God, grant me that joy that can only be found in you. May
your joy settle in my soul—joy that cannot be taken away by injury or age.
I long to feast in the pleasure that you enjoy, for you are my pleasure. You
are my leisure activity. In Jesus' name and for his sake I pray, Amen.

Questions to Ponder

1. Does the quote from Gordon Dahl represent my life in any way(s)?
   "We worship our work, work at our play, and play at our worship."
2. Do I expect more from my leisure activities than God intends for me to receive from them?
3. Have I truly repented of my sin?
4. Am I experiencing joy, the emotion of heaven? Am I expressing it through work, through leisure activities, through Sabbath-rest?

Part II

PLEASING GOD, AT REST FROM WORK

HOW CAN I REST FROM WORK?

By now you have gotten the picture that pleasing God exceeds working for God in some capacity. Pleasing God includes rest, even if you like your work. God wants you to enjoy him above and beyond the work you enjoy. God wants you to relax and enjoy him apart from work on the job, work at home, even work you regard as hobbies.

The next five chapters are designed to guide you into a weekly Sabbath experience. Chapter six describes my own reluctance to begin such a practice and the treasures I discovered once I finally yielded to the Holy Spirit's prompting. Chapter seven depicts the Sabbath as a day to *release* your concerns and release yourself from the rigors of labor. Chapter eight urges you to *review* your life before God as a means of *cleaning house* through repentance. Chapter nine encourages you to *remember* your God, given that the Sabbath was intended to be a day to recall God and his works of creation and salvation. Appendix A provides a practical Sabbath-rest exercise designed to guide you through *release, review,* and *remember*. Chapter ten emphasizes the futuristic aspect of the Sabbath as a weekly occasion to focus on eternity and the believer's final home in heaven. Appendix B will assist you in becoming more heavenly minded during your earthly existence.

As you keep reading you will experience the relief God has prepared for you as you learn how to please him through rest.

CHAPTER SIX

SABBATH-REST,

A TIME TO DISCOVER

Find rest, O my soul, in God alone; my hope comes from him.

(Psalm 62:5)

Helicopters require almost constant attention, and it would appear that God has designed human beings to run best with a weekly spiritual re-calibration. His Sabbath principle is one that can't be repeatedly ignored without doing damage to your soul. God seems to have made us to function best when one day each week is designated for resouling, or restoring, or attending to our spiritual needs.

(David R. Mains)

The minister who fails to practice what he preaches places himself in a precarious position. Unfortunately, it is a position few preachers avoid. Just ask their families.

I remember vividly the Sunday I preached on the fourth commandment, "Remember the Sabbath day, to keep it holy." It was November 4, 1984. This sermon represented many hours of diligent preparation, studying numerous texts which were related to the Sabbath. I was confident that I had captured the main themes of the Sabbath. Main points were well-thought-out and supported by sub-points. Illustrations connected the congregation to the texts. The introduction reflected my recent trip to Israel, where I witnessed Sabbath-keeping as it has been practiced for thousands of years. The sermon was to end with a stunning quote from the atheist Voltaire, "I can never hope to destroy Christianity until I first destroy the Christian Sabbath."[43]

On paper it was a winner. When it came to delivery, I was stumped. The sermon seemed to go on forever. I used many words to describe simple points, forcing the service into overtime. I kept fumbling the conclusion until finally I admitted that I had not implemented any kind of a Sabbath practice in my own life. *I'm no example of Sabbath-rest,* I thought to myself. I didn't need to say it out loud; it was obvious. I seldom felt or looked rested. Sure, as a man of many hobbies, I knew how to take a day off for leisure. Nonetheless, the practice of holy rest was a mystery to me. *Just when was a minister to do this anyway? Saturday is like the day before finals and Sunday is obviously no day of rest for pastors.* This sermon was an intellectual exercise which my conscience could not bear. The minister who preaches about rest without taking rest sabotages his own ministry.

As time elapsed it appeared that I had once again eluded the mysterious practice of the Sabbath. Yes, I had previously wrestled with the concept. A tour of the Middle East had enabled me to witness Orthodox Jews observing the Sabbath with great precision earlier that fall. I witnessed a total mercenary shut down in honor of the living God. While it was little more than an idle ritual for some, others reaped the benefits of spiritual rest and reflection.

In flight between Egypt and Switzerland, Dr. Lareau Lindquist, then president of the Institute of Holy Land Studies, suggested that I take a week to fast and pray in search of God's direction for my weary life. I had been halfway around the world and was still not refreshed. Little did I know that spiritual rest was more than sightseeing. I shrugged off the good advice thinking, *how could I take a week off for spiritual direction after being gone from my ministry for two weeks?*

Upon returning to the States, I quickly shifted into gear hoping to make up for time away from work. I was also determined to make the most of the trip by organizing my slides and recording my impressions—still no implementation of precious Sabbath-rest.

It was time to heed the advice of many voices and search for significant spiritual rest.

One month later Tom Bussard, whom I wrote about in chapter three, suggested that I spend one day a week away from the office renewing perspective on my life and work. His perception was right, but I did not do it. My dilemma was similar to that of Peter Scazzero, who fought for years the fear of becoming morbidly introspective:

> Our great dilemma, and mine for years, is that I was too busy building a bigger church and looking for ways to have a greater impact. Who had time for this kind of morbid introspection? Wouldn't reflection time slow down the work of God? What good for God and others could come out of tapping into my unconscious or unidentified wishes, fears and hopes?[44]

I had read *Ordering Your Private World* and figured that Gordon Mac-Donald just couldn't relate to anyone serving as the solo pastor of a middle-sized church. The pastor of the middle-sized church has limited staff and is asked to be all things to all people. Author and church consultant Lyle Schaller's comments are notable: "As a group the pastors with the highest level of frustration, fatigue, and guilt may be those serving congregations averaging between 160 and 240 at Sunday morning worship."[45]

Ordering Your Private World was both intriguing and convicting. I found the chapter *Rest beyond Leisure* most troublesome. MacDonald views nineteenth century English Parliamentarian William Wilberforce as a busy man who modeled Sabbath-rest:

> Wilberforce's check and balance to a busy life was Sabbath; he had come to understand genuine rest. Wilberforce had discovered that the person who establishes a block of time for Sabbath-Rest on a regular basis is most likely to keep all of life in proper perspective and remain free of burnout and breakdown.... From the beginning of all history, it has been an axiom at the base of healthy living; unfortunately, it is a principle badly misunderstood by those whose lives are driven to achievement and acquisition.[46]

I had survived November only to be greeted with the news that our closest friends in the church would be moving from the area. Craig was a faithful deacon and adult Sunday school teacher, seminary quality. Seven years earlier Craig had come to the church as a new believer. We had enjoyed nearly two years of one-to-one weekly disciple-making sessions. It was my privilege to watch him grow and mature. His wife, Cindy, was my wife's closest friend. One by one we had watched several core church families move from the area. Each time a co-laborer left, my workload and heartache increased. Waving goodbye to Craig and Cindy was more than I could bear. I was physically tired, emotionally bruised, and above all spiritually drained. It was time to heed the advice of many voices and search for significant spiritual rest.

With the temperature below zero on a frigid December morning, I left the church office and drove to a wilderness park a dozen miles from the church. Equipped with wool socks, army combat boots, long underwear, stocking hat and overcoat, I entered the park, bearing only a jug of juice for physical nourishment. The church phone would have to answer itself. Considering my fatigue, I would not have been able to comfort the afflicted or afflict the comfortable any longer. Like Moses climbing Mount Sinai, I risked letting God's sheep tend for themselves.

Desperate for direction, I headed out. Seated in my compact Dodge Colt, I began to relax. It felt so good. It is amazing how relaxed a restless person can become once they are removed from the circumstances of their anxiety. Like peeling the skin off an onion, I began to shed layers of concerns that had plagued me for years. Quietly, I began to release my work, recalling that it was God's church in the first place. I began to review my entire life, recognizing that I had often sought significance from something less than the Savior who died for me and his church.

It is remarkable how warm you can stay on a cold day with just sun rays penetrating the windshield of your car. Only occasionally is it necessary to turn on the car to circulate warm air. One can concentrate on a cold day!

After nearly five hours of sitting in the car, I took a walk through the wooded ravines. It was far more than a casual stroll. This was an opportunity for the Holy Spirit to restore the splendor of God in my life. At one point I stopped in the middle of a maple grove and sat on the ground, leaning all my weight against a tree. I remained perfectly still for some time, thoroughly enjoying the contrasts of sunlight and shadow. Then something broke the silence. A whitetail doe and her fawn came into view. Unalarmed, they grazed in front of me for several moments. I heard another sound from the direction where the deer had appeared. Sure enough, it was an impressive ten-point buck with a broad well-balanced set of antlers. He immediately caught sight of me. I stayed as stiff as the tree that supported me. He did not know what to think of me. Without breaking his gaze, he moved his massive neck and head up and down. I did not move. The buck proceeded to step behind a tree, which hid most of his body from my sight. It was a showdown to see who would move first. I did not flinch. Suddenly the buck jumped from behind the tree heading in the direction from which he had come. Shortly after, the doe caught scent of me, circled, and eventually disappeared with her fawn. As I continued to rest beneath the tree, one thought occupied my being: *the one who cares for these, watches over me.*

That night I went to bed relaxed and refreshed having experienced at least a fraction of what God enjoyed on the seventh day and intended for man. I had released my concerns to the Lord and reviewed my life for flaws in my relationship with God that resulted in a warped perspective on life. That leisurely walk through the woods was one of the most memorable of my life.

This first Sabbath experience would set the stage for many to follow. The pattern that developed over a period of years will be disclosed in the next four chapters.

Prayer

I thank you Lord, for bringing many people into my life who encouraged me to walk the path of Sabbath-rest. Forgive me for resisting your servants and grieving your Spirit with my stubborn ways. I praise you as Lord of the Sabbath for considering my need for rest from the beginning of time and being patient with me until I considered my need. In Jesus' name and for his sake I pray, Amen.

Questions to Ponder

1. Am I guilty of telling others about rest and not taking it myself?
2. On a scale from one to ten, ten being the most tired, how tired am I?
3. Do I have a weekly block of time for Sabbath-rest that will help me keep all of life in proper perspective and help me avoid burnout and breakdown?

CHAPTER SEVEN

SABBATH-REST,
A TIME TO RELEASE

Six days do your work, but on the seventh day do not work, so that your ox and your donkey may rest and the slave born in your household, and the alien as well, may be refreshed.

(Exodus 23:12)

Sometimes our difficulties and fears become like precious antiques. We love to talk about them, but we would not give them up for anything.[47]

(Henry Blackaby)

FROM RICHES TO RAGS

Long ago in a country far away lived a nobleman named Nils. Nils and his wife had a son named Victor. Nobility gave Victor access to private land, hired servants, and a lifetime of opportunity. A nobleman's son did not have to work. Work was for the people noblemen hired to keep their prestigious standard of living enviable. The potential advantages of nobility expanded as Victor entered adulthood.

Nobility, however, comes with expectations. This was no exception. It was difficult to lose the privileged position of nobility and next to impossible to rise to nobility. But there was one great equalizer that could lift one to that privileged status or reduce one to a begging peasant—marriage. Nils sternly warned Victor that he was to "have no social ties with the landless commoners." Victor had a good life ahead of him; he had it made as long as he did not fall in love and marry a peasant girl.

Victor spent much of his leisure time hunting, which often brought him to the perimeters of his father's land. It was there at the edge of his family's property that Victor met a poor widow's daughter named Mathilda. Walks outside Victor's home became less about hunting and more about Mathilda. As love stories go, one thing led to another until Victor fell in love with her. Whatever it was about Mathilda that attracted him, it was more powerful than land or nobility. Victor would marry Mathilda.

Victor had done the one thing that negated his nobility. He had married a peasant girl without a cottage. He would be disinherited and banished from his parents' land. He was forced to leave his home, and since Mathilda had no home the newlyweds voyaged across the Atlantic Ocean to a new world where land was plentiful. Once landing in New York's harbor, they journeyed west through forest and farm until they found a climate worse than the one they left in Sweden. They settled in Minnesota.

Victor was twenty-seven and Mathilda just seventeen. For Mathilda it was simply the exchange of one hard life for another. Victor, however, endured strenuous physical labor foreign to his life of leisure and nobility in Sweden. He worked with timber harvesting the virgin white pine forests of northern Minnesota. Later he and Mathilda bought farmland in central Minnesota. Together they tilled the rocky soil and raised eight children on the farm.

One of those children was named Elmer. Elmer experienced nothing of his father's childhood nobility. What little Elmer learned about nobility came as Victor reminisced about the old country. In contrast, hard work molded Elmer's childhood. He watched his father work himself out of a hole and into some degree of prominence only to see him lose it all. Once the farm and the large farmhouse were paid for, Victor cosigned a business loan for two of his sons. The timing couldn't have been worse as the Great Depression swept through the land and the farm was taken as collateral. Elmer watched his father die suddenly from a kidney infection shortly after the tragic loss. From Elmer's perspective, one could not work hard enough in the hope of establishing some security!

Elmer left farming and began logging in the northern part of the state, hauling logs first with horses and later with trucks. He also applied his ingenuity toward loading and hauling huge stones from granite quarries. Heavy work became his trademark. He eventually became a road construction contractor. While Elmer submitted bids for new jobs, he also worked a bulldozer until cancer took his life at age sixty eight. Work was intensely physical for Elmer. The drive to survive never left his veins. Elmer never knew retirement. Scarcely did he know how to spend a day in leisure.

Elmer left behind a wife, a daughter, and a son named Harold. That same drive to survive lodged itself in Harold. At a young age he assisted his father during the Great Depression as a measure of survival. World War II brought an even more literal meaning to the word as Harold survived thirty missions over Germany as a B-24 pilot. Following the war he drove a truck for his father until the day he was too ill to drive another mile. At age thirty-four Harold was pulled from his truck and sent to the Veterans Hospital in Minneapolis where he would spend fifteen weeks in recovery from rheumatic fever. That would be the end of his truck-driving career. Doctors told him that he could no longer do physical work. Those words would create a rift between Harold and his father who viewed work as physical. Hiring and managing people along with accounting and strategic planning did not qualify as work.

While rheumatic fever would put an end to Harold's truck driving, it would not end his trucking. The blessing of his physical limitations would send him into management, which was his greater asset. Harold did not just survive work; he loved it. He thrived on solving the challenges of an ever-changing trucking industry. He worked through his thirties, forties, fifties, sixties, seventies and well into his eighties. He lived to say, "My seventies were my best years." Retirement was never a consideration and occupied no place in his vocabulary.

In his eighties he was diagnosed with pulmonary fibrosis. Oxygen tanks and tubes were not very compatible with his manner of running a business: "If I am on oxygen I have to stay home, and if I have to stay home, I won't be on oxygen." While Harold did submit to the oxygen tank, he was not a very good oxygen patient. At age eighty five he was seen walking slowly between the office door and his car on a Wednesday evening. The next day he celebrated Thanksgiving with his family. That evening he contracted a fever and made a final trip to the hospital. Within a week he was gone.

Harold left behind his wife, two sons, and a daughter. The second son and middle child inherited the worst of his workaholic tendencies. Like Dad I became an entrepreneur, but not as a businessman. Far from the smell of diesel fuel, I attended seminary and became a church-planting pastor. The risks of planting a church nearly bankrupted my physical, mental, and emotional reserves. At age thirty I experienced an incapacitating illness initiated by fatigue. A case of atypical mononucleosis led to hepatitis and put me in bed for six weeks. It took nearly a year to fully recover.

I share all this personal history because of the pattern it presents. Each generation had to discover on his own that life has an edge, a place of no return. Like my father I had to learn the hard way—I can work myself to death. I can worry myself to death.

Prior to the six weeks spent in bed, I had worked hard and worried much in an all-out-effort to hold a fledgling church plant together. Willing to die trying I had not yet learned that everyone could not be pleased, at least not by me. Night after night I struggled to go to sleep. When I finally dozed off, our ten-month-old son would wake up screaming in pain because of a chronic ear infection. I attempted in vain to go back to sleep, usually tossing and turning until dawn. I would go to work tired day after day.

As hard as I tried and as much as I worried, I could not stop three families from leaving the church, a small percentage that left big scars. Two months after the dust had cleared and the losses were counted, the impact of my sleeplessness erupted, like a long fuse between the time of stress and its incapacitating effects.

One Saturday morning I could barely get out of bed. I did not preach the next day. I preached the following Sunday after giving this mysterious illness a week to leave. The next week I attempted to work as usual. By Friday I was back to where I began nearly two weeks earlier. I remember sitting in the surgery waiting room with Lois, while our ten-month-old had tubes put in his ears to reduce ear infections. That morning sitting on a chair was as strenuous as lifting barbells to my maximum capacity. I wanted to collapse on the floor.

That afternoon we drove home from the hospital together. I can't remember if I drove or held our youngster. What I do remember is that going a few miles seemed to take forever. Our son was on the mend and I was not. It was a beautiful spring day, so I decided to lie out in the sun for a few moments hoping to feel better. I could hear Lois on the phone describing my symptoms to the doctor and stating emphatically, "Jim is not getting better."

The next morning I went into the clinic for more extensive blood work. The results told the truth of my condition. Only after a prolonged period of rest would I feel better. What surgery could quickly do for our son, only long bed rest could do for me. I did not preach and did practically no church work the next four weeks.

The doctor instructed Lois to guard me from any potentially stressful phone calls. Most encouraging were the daily calls from my Dad who understood because he had once been in the same prone position for several weeks. Lois was also to guard me from working. I would sneak books between the blankets and read them when she assumed I was sleeping. She would come in and confiscate them, only to have to do it again. Later she learned that I had outlined the entire book of Joshua in anticipation of preaching a series from the book.

Most of the time was spent trembling under the covers, begging God to make me well again. Grandiose dreams of serving big churches melted down to hopes of being able to be a pastor and preach to a handful of people. I loved my work and wanted to return to it. But it was not to happen until I learned some lessons. I needed to be released from the constant preoccupation with work. There was a sense in which I was like a prisoner held in captivity.

SETTING THE CAPTIVES FREE

Jesus came to set the captives free—free from Satan, sin, and self. I am not surprised that captors despised his freedom ministry, like the owners who profited from a slave girl with a clairvoyant spirit (Acts 16:16-24). The reluctance of captives to seize the opportunity to be free does puzzle me. Not even those in his hometown of Nazareth recognized freedom or the one who frees when it was offered to them.

One day Jesus walked into his hometown synagogue and read publicly from the Scriptures: "The Spirit of the Lord is on me, because he has anointed me to preach good news to the poor. He has sent me to proclaim freedom for the prisoners and recovery of sight for the blind, to release the oppressed..." (Isaiah 61:1, Luke 4:18).

Some were obviously angered by his reference to these words from the Prophet Isaiah being fulfilled in him at that moment. Perhaps others were agitated by his inference that they needed good news, freedom as prisoners, recovery of sight, and release from oppression: *Who does he think he is anyway, the Messiah? We remember him running around these streets as a small boy. How dare he think that he knows what we need?*

Praise God he slipped away from the attempt on his life that day (Luke 4:28-30). He lived to die another day and set us free from our sins, long before we knew we were captives. That explains why most people don't plead with Jesus to free them and why others despise any reference to captivity; they don't know they are captive to do Satan's will (II Timothy 2:26). I must include myself as one who was not desperate enough to recognize my captivity. Praise God for those who recognize their bondage and allow Jesus to set them free.

SABBATH, A TIME TO RELEASE CRIPPLES

Jesus went down to Capernaum where he proceeded to teach in the synagogue on the Sabbath. Not only did he teach, he also freed a man held captive by an evil spirit. Before that Sabbath was over, he delivered many from their various afflictions and forms of captivity. Setting people free on the Sabbath was not only a trend with Jesus; he was quite intentional about it. In Luke six he healed a man with a withered hand on the Sabbath. In Luke chapter thirteen Jesus healed again on the Sabbath. This time it is a woman who was crippled.

> On a Sabbath Jesus was teaching in one of the synagogues, [11] and a woman was there who had been crippled by a spirit for eighteen years. She was bent over and could not straighten up at all. [12] When Jesus saw her, he called her forward and said to her, "Woman, you are set free from your infirmity." [13] Then he put his hands on her, and immediately she straightened up and praised God.
>
> (Luke 13:11-13)

These were more than healings from physical afflictions. They were acts releasing people form various forms of captivity, especially the grip of Satan.

It made no difference to the rulers of the synagogue. In their eyes freeing people from anything was work forbidden by Sabbath Law. Their lack of compassion for captives blinded them from seeing their gross hypocrisy.

> Indignant because Jesus had healed on the Sabbath, the synagogue ruler said to the people, "There are six days for work. So come and be healed on those days, not on the Sabbath." [15] The Lord answered him, "You hypocrites! Doesn't each of you on the Sabbath untie his ox or donkey from the stall and lead it out to give it water? [16] Then should not this woman, a daughter of Abraham, whom Satan has kept bound for eighteen long years, be set free on the Sabbath day from what bound her?" [17] When he said this, all his opponents were humiliated, but the people were delighted with all the wonderful things he was doing.
>
> (Luke 13:14-17)

SABBATH, A TIME TO RELEASE CRITTERS

Jesus pressed the issue of hypocrisy further with yet another healing on the Sabbath. The Pharisees experienced no disturbance of conscience as they walked by an invalid in the synagogue on the Sabbath. Yet they would think nothing of exerting themselves to free an animal caught in a well on the Sabbath.

> One Sabbath, when Jesus went to eat in the house of a prominent Phari-see, he was being carefully watched. [2] There in front of him was a man suffering from dropsy. [3] Jesus asked the Pharisees and experts in the law, "Is it lawful to heal on the Sabbath or not?" [4] But they remained silent. So taking hold of the man, he healed him and sent him away. [5] Then he asked them, "If one of you has a son or an ox that falls into a well on the Sabbath day, will you not immediately pull him out?" [6] And they could make no reply to this.
>
> (Luke 14:1-6)

The hypocrisy of the Scribes and Pharisees rested on their failure to acknowledge an essential element of the Sabbath. While straining themselves in an all-out-effort to prohibit work on this holy day, they violated the benevolent aspects. In truth there was nothing wrong with exerting energy to release a cripple or critter that was captive on the Sabbath. It was a day to set captives free. Any effort to set a cripple or critter free on the Sabbath was commendable. It was worshipping one's work efforts in place of worshipping God that was a true violation of the Sabbath. The fourth commandment establishes the profound purpose of the Sabbath.

> Observe the Sabbath day by keeping it holy, as the LORD your God has commanded you. [13] Six days you shall labor and do all your work, [14] but the seventh day is a Sabbath to the LORD your God. On it you shall not do any work, neither you, nor your son or daughter, nor your manservant or maidservant, nor your ox, your donkey or any of your animals, nor the alien within your gates, so that your manservant and maidservant may rest, as you do. [15] Remember that you were slaves in Egypt and that the LORD your God brought you out of there with a mighty hand and an outstretched arm. Therefore the LORD your God has commanded you to observe the Sabbath day.
>
> (Deuteronomy 5:12 -15)

> *The Sabbath serves as a circuit breaker to keep God's people from burning out.*

SABBATH SENSE

The Sabbath serves as a circuit breaker to keep God's people from burning out. Burnout is the result of being a captive to your work. One of the causes of burnout is a relentless effort to work until the job is done. What is commendable for short projects is dangerous for assignments that last for more than a week. I learned this the hard way. I could not continue to work as a church planter week after week without a weekly time of release, which was for me something more than a day off.

The Sabbath is comprehensive in scope. Everyone is to rest, from admirals to animals. In fact it is quite important that those in charge rest so those taking orders could get a rest from their domination. "Six days do your work, but on the seventh day do not work, so that your ox and your donkey may rest and the slave born in your household, and the alien as well, may be refreshed" (Exodus 23:12).

Several years ago I interviewed Eugene Peterson on the topic of the Sabbath. He spoke of an Exodus reason for the Sabbath and a Deuteronomy reason for the Sabbath:

> The Exodus reason is that this is what God did. We enter into the rhythm of creation and grace when we do this. The command functions to disengage us from our own work habits so that we can be prayerful people. Things become fulfilled in wholeness as we rest in God's action, not in our actions.

> The Deuteronomy reason is the social reason that we do this for the sake of those whom we're living with and working with. If we don't have a Sabbath, we turn people around us into slaves of our own ego, servants of our own ambition. It's socially oppressive not to keep a Sabbath. You were slaves four hundred years in Egypt, and I'm not going to let you do that anymore. I'm not going to let you do to anybody else what was done to you. This is really important for pastors because we need to give our wives, our children, our parishioners at least one day off from us. So we're not pushing our agenda for ministry or whatever else on them.[48]

The Sabbath is a commemoration of release from four hundred years of captivity. There was no freedom in Egypt for the Israelites, only captivity. Slaves were called to work any day of the week for any number of days in a row. The Israelites were not to go back into captivity even as their own masters.

The Sabbath is a celebration of freedom from every form of bondage. The Israelites were to celebrate freedom from their four hundred year captivity in Egypt. Sinners of every kind are to celebrate liberation from sin and Satan's death grip on their lives (Hebrews 2:14-15).

Work worshipers are to celebrate their freedom from the compulsion to work without ceasing. God in his mercy sets us free from the preoccupation of work to think of higher things. We are to think of him, for he is to be thanked. Jesus declared the Sabbath was not a curse to confine us but a gift to free us from harming ourselves: "Then he said to them, 'The Sabbath was made for man, not man for the Sabbath. So the Son of Man is Lord even of the Sabbath'" (Mark 2:27-28).

God's people are now free to serve God who released us by his powerful arm and gave us a day of rest as a proof of his compassion and the end of captivity. To a degree the Sabbath reverses the toilsome curse of original sin set forth at the fall of man (Genesis 3:17-19). The Sabbath gives us unlimited hope toward a full reversal of the curse in the age to come.

SABBATH, A TIME TO RELEASE CHRISTIANS

Jesus not only fulfilled the function of the Old Testament Sabbath by releasing the unfortunate from their bondage, He set a precedent for a day of release in the New Testament and the age to come. The Sabbath was a day of release. I would not expect Sunday and the age of grace to offer anything less. How fitting for church services to offer ministries of release, especially on Sundays.

Some Christian traditions still offer invitations during their worship services for attendees to receive Christ, healing, and deliverance from bondage, including satanic oppression. It is a means of offering release to people who are ready to be freed.

Jesus asked the man at the pool of Bethesda, "Do you want to get well?" (John 5:6). It remains an appropriate question as long as it is understood that human willingness is not the only prerequisite for wellness. God still teaches through infirmities (II Corinthians 12: 8, 9).

"Do you want to be released?" is just as appropriate in light of the gift of the Sabbath. What is the nature of your bondage? Is it physical, spiritual, emotional, or mental? What enslaves you? Is it an addiction or is it idolatry?

The longer I study the Sabbath and its pertinence to God's people today, the more I am persuaded that worship services offer a broad invitation to be released from all forms of bondage.

> *A weekly Sabbath-rest is often the difference between surviving and thriving in ministry.*

A SABBATH RELEASE

Looking back on my days as a local church pastor, I must confess that I did not regularly make use of worship services as a time of release from the bondages that ensnare people today. My Sabbath journey remained personal, not something I made compulsory for others. However, it was no secret that I practiced and promoted a weekly Sabbath for everyone. I cannot speak from experience regarding the relief a weekly Sabbath provides for business personnel, professionals, or factory workers. I can say with confidence, however, that a weekly Sabbath-rest is often the difference between surviving and thriving in ministry.

Ministers are as human as everyone else, perhaps more so. The call of God upon their lives does not exempt them from personal concerns. Pastors catch colds and flu bugs like everyone else. Their cars break down and roofs leak. Likewise ministers are vulnerable to financial difficulties. Even PKs, pastors' kids, may enter seasons of rebellion along with deacons' kids. There are ministry-related tensions as well.

A pastor's chief concern is often the complexity of work to which he or she has been called. The serious nature of pastoral work can easily become an emotional burden. While the medical doctor must make life-and-death decisions, the minister must give directions for eternal life. He or she is called upon to bring peace into many situations: the death of a child, a dispute among board members, dysfunctional families, sinners seeking repentance, and restless church shoppers, to name a few. Pastor John Lavender says the most difficult aspect of being a pastor is shifting gears:

For example, you have the tremendous demand of having to go from a funeral where you've had to help a young couple bury a child to a young couple preparing to get married and they're full of joy and excitement. You have to be real in both of those situations. It is very demanding, emotional, and wrenching, going from the requirements of being a leader to the demands of being a man alone with God.[49]

The pastors' visible positions make them vulnerable to criticism as well. During a church leader's retreat, the senior pastor's Sunday morning dress code became the topic of discussion. Like many of my colleagues, my platform apparel had changed considerably over the last twenty-five years. For years I wore suits and only on certain summer Sundays did I dress down to a sport coat. By the turn of the century I was wearing dress slacks with a well pressed shirt, with or without a tie, but no sport coat. One leader suggested I dress down even further, while the leader next to him barked out emphatically, "No way! He should always wear suits on Sunday mornings." I laughingly thought of how I might please them both by wearing a suit coat and tie over a t-shirt and a pair of shorts.

More serious issues may include: how much pastors should be paid, should his family live in the parsonage or buy their own home, how much time off should he or she be granted, should the pastor be an evangelist, shepherd, teacher, or administrator? Recently a pastor told me that one of his elders attacked him for using sports illustrations. While some parishioners identify with sports and sports figures, others disconnect their auditory nerve at the mere mention of them. While the church parking lot hums like a beehive with diverse opinions, a pastor and his wife may wonder, *Will all of this buzz eventually sting our children and steer them away from the church or even God?*

Add to this the immeasurable nature of pastoral work. Bottom lines such as bodies, bucks, and buildings are not necessarily trustworthy indicators of faithful service. While visible results are encouraging, they are not always an accurate barometer of a minister's character or worth. Jesus told the disciples: "Thus the saying 'One sows and another reaps' is true. [38] I sent you to reap what you have not worked for. Others have done the hard work, and you have reaped the benefits of their labor" (John 4:37-39).

Some pastors cultivate spiritually hard soil faithfully for years only to have others enjoy the harvest. If the pastor does not discover "the peace of God, which transcends all understanding" (Philippians 4:7) the weighty call of God may feel like an inescapable trap slamming down on him or her.

This is not God's intent. Burnout or breakdown is not necessary. Pastors can escape the apparent bondage of ministry without leaving the ministry.

RELEASE FROM MINISTRY BONDAGE

Ministers must recognize the obvious: even God rested from his work (Genesis 2:2). If the compassionate Creator rested, it follows that he would grant his creatures a break as well. The truth is he does not simply grant it, he commands it (Exodus 20:8-11). Seeing that God rested from his work and commands a weekly rest, the pastor should at least give himself the permission to rest.

Ministers must understand clearly that the people whom they serve are not their personal property. Peter reminds pastors to "Be shepherds of God's flock" (I Peter 5:2). A possessive attitude by the people in ministry eventually gives birth to an obsessive attitude toward the work of the ministry. Congregations belong to God. Unless ministers wrongfully add to the troubles of the flock, church problems are not a minister's personal problems. They must make the distinction between God as the owner of the flock and themselves as stewards. As stewards of the flock, pastors patiently bear the burdens of troubled people (Romans 15:1-3), without making them their own.

Pastors must also go through the act of releasing their personal and pastoral cares to the Lord. Before that is likely to happen, humility must replace the bondage of pride cultivated by *this is my church* notions. Humility is a prerequisite to releasing cares; therefore the imperative *humble yourselves* is the main phrase of I Peter 5:5-7:

> Young men, in the same way be submissive to those who are older. All of you, clothe yourselves with humility toward one another, because, "God opposes the proud but gives grace to the humble." Humble yourselves, therefore, under God's mighty hand, that he may lift you up in due time. Cast all your anxiety on him because he cares for you.

After addressing shepherds Peter instructs young men to humble themselves and cast their cares upon the one who cares for them. It is assumed the elders or shepherds had adopted the practice of surrendering concerns before being appointed to their shepherding tasks. Unfortunately most contemporary pastors have only an intellectual understanding of this practice. It took years of bearing unnecessary burdens of anxiety before I discovered the *transfer of crushing weight* the late J. Oswald Sanders described:

Anxiety implies "distraction of mind and heart in view of conflicting emotions." But the undershepherd need have no fear that the cares of his flock of God will be too heavy for him. By a definite act of mind and will, he can transfer the crushing weight of his spiritual burdens to the powerful shoulders of the God who cares.[50]

Cares will become sleep stealers if they are not released. Of greater concern, anxious pastors and parishioners alike become easy prey for the roaring lion to single out. In the context of releasing concerns, the Apostle Peter refers to the adversary: "Be self-controlled and alert. Your enemy the devil prowls around like a roaring lion looking for someone to devour" (I Peter 5:8).

As I see it Peter connects failure to release concerns with being vulnerable to Satan's schemes. If Satan cannot distract God's servants into careless attitudes about ministries, he will drive them out into the open with anxiety about performing ministries well. It is the anxious that succumb to the lion's dreadful roar. Driven by fear they spring into the open like panicky prey about to be pounced on by a devouring lion. Both parishioner and pastor are apt to become flushed prey for the evil one. The consequences of not releasing concerns can be disastrous.

THE SABBATH-CONCEPT IS FOR EVERYONE

During my twenty-five years of serving churches, I often heard from churched and unchurched people alike: "You're a pastor? Wow! You have a hard job." At the time I didn't think my job was harder than most. Looking back I am more aware of the joys of serving local churches. I am also acutely aware of the heartaches endured by those pastors I now shepherd. But there are many hard jobs in our society. Everyone bears a load.

While I have focused on release for ministers, the Sabbath-concept is for everyone. My undergraduate degree is in music education, specifically string instruments. Tuning the violins of beginning students is not exactly my idea of making music. Nor does teaching general music to eight graders satisfy my musical tastes. Other than a little student teaching, I never taught music in a school system. I don't envy school teachers today.

I have already described how my great grandfather and grandfather strained themselves with physical work; and how my father's health broke down on the road while driving a truck. As I observe truck drivers at my corporate chaplaincy job, I feel they are the most unappreciated servants in our society. After spending a lifetime behind the wheel of an eighteen wheeler, many die prematurely from the consequences of obesity. Typically only a handful of relatives and childhood friends show up at their funerals. Being on the road week after week limits their development of close friendships and diminishes most hometown relationships. Drivers of passenger cars do not appreciate having to share the roads with the big rigs. "You're going too fast; you're driving too slow; you're blocking the road—get out of my way!" When they need to stop they are told, "You can't park here." Yet it is the truck driver who often stops to help out a motorist with a broken-down car. The truth is everything we purchase in stores has been delivered by a truck even if it was loaded from a ship, train, or plane.

Likewise, it is not easy to be an executive or owner of a company. Many were surprised when I left for seminary instead of sliding into a position already made for me within the family company. It was not that difficult, given the call of God on my life and the fact that I had seen the strain of a family business from the inside. My Dad's life was honorable, but not easy.

> *God grant me the serenity to accept the things I cannot change; courage to change the things I can; and the wisdom to know the difference.*
>
> (Reinhold Niebuhr)

The hardest situation of all belongs to the single Mom who gets her children ready for daycare or school every morning. After she comes home from a long day at work the children are priority. She cooks supper, helps with homework, washes clothes, and gives baths. Life is tough!

Everyone has concerns to release. If we don't learn to release them, sooner or later we feel like life has been squeezed out of us by a boa constrictor. Bearing burdens of concern is a suffocating bondage.

Learning to release my concerns to the God I know as always good and great has freed me from many forms of bondage. Through much of my life I have been captive to worry and anxiety; I cannot manage either. I must release them. Release became a reality when I began practicing a weekly Sabbath. Doing so during daily quiet times did not satisfy. I needed more than drive-through devotionals to get to the core of what was making me anxious. I needed time to review my life after releasing my concerns, which I will cover in the next chapter. When I began entering Sabbath experiences I had no idea of how compatible a practice of release was with the Sabbath concept.

With pad and pen I would list all my concerns. Nothing was too small. Personal fears, family problems, ministry challenges were all recorded. Each time I would begin a sentence with the phrase, "I release to you, Lord…." Each act of release was an admission of my lack of control, ability, or power to do enough to solve any problem. Release became a form of relief, but not a form of irresponsibility. Marva J. Dawn, in her insightful book, *Keeping the Sabbath Wholly,* concurs that a weekly Sabbath practice is relief and not irresponsible.

> At this point you might be thinking that it doesn't do any good to set worries aside for just a day. If we merely run away from them, they will be there to bother us the day after the Sabbath. Before I began to practice Sabbath keeping seriously, I too thought that would be the case. On the contrary, I've discovered that the longer I enjoy Sabbaths, the very customs of that day give me not only refreshment, which makes the tension much less powerful in the days that follow, but also new perspectives, new priorities, and a new sense of God's presence, which all cause the tensions themselves to assume a less hostile shape during the week to come. The Sabbath is not a running away from problems, but the opportunity to receive grace to face them.[51]

Releasing my concerns to God has had untold positive effects on my life. I can relax and think more clearly. I can see a distinction between my part and God's part. In my journal, I record anything I could realistically do to help the situations I had released to the Lord. I would also state what only God could do as a prayer. For instance, I could comfort a person in the hospital with a visit, words, Scriptures, and prayer, but I could not heal anyone. That would be up to God. I would pray that he heal the person and use medical professionals as he saw fit, but I would not pretend to be more than I was—his humble and available servant. Much of worry is a matter of playing God, attempting to fill God's big role while neglecting my humble part.

Once anxieties are released, one is able to think objectively. A person can now distinguish between what is the responsibility of God and what is personal responsibility. A list of alternatives can be made for action. A prayer list can be made for intercession or supplication with thanksgiving: "Do not be anxious about anything, but in everything, by prayer and petition, with thanksgiving, present your requests to God. And the peace of God, which transcends all understanding, will guard your hearts and your minds in Christ Jesus" (Philippians 4:6-7).

Eventually I began to date the original release statements as well as identifiable answers to prayers. Some would call this a prayer list. But it was essential that I begin with the word *release*, because I was captive to my concerns. With the passing of years more time is spent listing answers than detailed concerns. God is so ready to respond to my needs when I am willing to release them to him.

Releasing my concerns has allowed me to take myself less seriously. There have been plenty of times when I have smiled about past anxieties because they were mere shadows of serious threats. Mark Twain said it well, "I have been through some terrible things in my life, some of which actually happened."

A REFLECTION OF REST

My great-grandfather Victor died broke but blessed. He was described as a calm man who had found peace with God and made peace with man. No one had to say, "God rest his soul" for he had already found rest.

Mathilda outlived Victor by thirty-two years and never remarried. I frequently visited my grandparents during my childhood, and on occasion Mathilda was with them. She was tall, thin, and frail. Her Swedish brogue and withered vocal cords made it almost impossible to understand her when she spoke. Half of what she said was probably in Swedish anyway. What I do remember is that she was a reflection of rest, sitting for hours in her rocking chair. Poor and fatherless in childhood, despised by her in-laws for marrying Victor, crossing the Atlantic in hope of a new home in the new land, logging, farming, raising eight children, suffering bankruptcy, Victor's death, and being a widow for thirty-two years was her life, all ninety-three years of it. Somehow she was able to release it all to God and reflect his rest.

Prayer

Lord, I release my many concerns to you, knowing that you care for me and can carry my burdens farther than I can. I trust you to do in and through my life what only you can do, as I trust you to show me my part and what I can do. In Jesus' name and for his sake I pray, Amen.

Questions to Ponder

1. Have I ever worked or worried myself into a physical, emotional, or mental breakdown?
2. Do I need to be released from any form of bondage?
3. Do I need to begin releasing my concerns right now?
4. Am I able to distinguish between my part and God's part in response to what concerns me?
5. When and where is my first or next Sabbath-rest for releasing my concerns?

See Appendix A, Part I for the exercise on releasing concerns.

CHAPTER EIGHT

SABBATH-REST,
A TIME TO REVIEW

Search me, O God, and know my heart; test me and know my anxious thoughts. See if there is any offensive way in me, and lead me in the way everlasting.

(Psalm 139:23-24)

When I was young, I set out to change the world. When I grew older, I perceived that this was too ambitious so I set out to change my state. This too, I realized as I grew older was too ambitious, so I set out to change my town. When I realized I could not even do this, I tried to change my family. Now as I am an old man, I know that I should have started with myself. If I had started with myself, maybe I would have succeeded in changing my family, the town or even the state—and who knows, maybe even the world!

(The words of an old Hasidic rabbi on his deathbed)[52]

The longer I live the harder it is to look in the mirror, so I spend less time doing it. Not that I was ever enamored by what I saw in years past. It's just that gray hair and wrinkles are reminders that time on earth is running out. There is more to do in less time.

There are more important things to do than waste my time gawking in the mirror. Mirrors are for models, actors, and actresses. I take a glance or two in the morning and move into the day's agenda. I am just not that concerned with appearance. Besides, if my hair is out of place, my wife is sure to tell me.

If I am honest with myself, I am not that comfortable around mirrors. I must admit that it is important to take a serious look in a mirror once in a while. Mirrors don't lie! The longer I stay away from mirrors, the easier it is to lie to myself. I can think that I am something I am not. In fact I really need more than a glance at a mirror in a dimly lit room. I need to examine the image in the mirror until I admit, *yep, those are real gray hairs coming out of my head. Aha, those are wrinkles under my eyes. Wow! When did my waist start to lap over like that?*

The epistle of James refers to the Word of God as a mirror and recommends that I do more than take a casual look into it:

> Therefore put away all filthiness and rampant wickedness and receive with meekness the implanted word, which is able to save your souls. [22] But be doers of the word, and not hearers only, deceiving yourselves. [23] For if anyone is a hearer of the word and not a doer, he is like a man who looks intently at his natural face in a mirror. [24] For he looks at himself and goes away and at once forgets what he was like. [25] But the one who looks into the perfect law, the law of liberty, and perseveres, being no hearer who forgets but a doer who acts, he will be blessed in his doing.
>
> (James 1: 21-25)

It takes courage to look at ourselves in the mirror of God's Word. The Pharisees found it easier to look at what was wrong with others than to look into God's Word with themselves in mind. Thus they drew these hard words from Jesus: "How can you say to your brother, 'Let me take the speck out of your eye,' when all the time there is a plank in your own eye? [5] You hypocrite, first take the plank out of your own eye, and then you will see clearly to remove the speck from your brother's eye" (Matthew 7:4-5). He also said, "Woe to you, teachers of the law and Pharisees, you hypocrites! You clean the outside of the cup and dish, but inside they are full of greed and self-indulgence. [26] Blind Pharisee! First clean the inside of the cup and dish, and then the outside also will be clean" (Matthew 23:25-26).

It actually takes humility more than courage to look in the mirror of God's Word. I was recently handed a powerful article on humility written by William P Farley. Farley views humility as the indispensable virtue. Humility permits other virtues to take root and grow.

> Humility is not self-hatred or lack of self-confidence. Rather, it is the ability to see yourself through God's eyes. A humble person increasingly

sees himself as he really is: "wretched, pitiful, poor, blind and naked" (Revelation 3:17). Ironically, such humility lays the foundation for contentment and healthy self-esteem.

In contrast, pride is spiritual blindness. Unfortunately, pride is also the sin to which we are most blind. In a demonic catch-22, pride causes us to chase our spiritual tails. I could not see my pride because I was full of it. Pride is a spiritual veil blinding us to the truth about ourselves.

Isaiah 66:2 says, "This is the one I esteem: he who is humble and contrite in spirit, and trembles at my word." There is an important progression here. Humility always metamorphoses into something more beautiful; it is the fountainhead of the other virtues. In this verse, we see how humility leads to real contrition and then deepens into trembling at God's Word. It sensitizes us to Scripture, motivating and equipping us to hear.[53]

Farley's definition of humility is worth repeating: humility is "the ability to see yourself through God's eyes." I must ask myself, *what does God see when he looks at me? What does God see without a mirror?* I must ask God to show me what I am like in his sight. Only as I am humbled or willingly humble myself will I have the courage to ask God to show me what he sees in my life.

Teacher and counselor Larry Crabb maintains that an inward look is a prerequisite to true spiritual freedom and growth. He also reminds us that there is a painful price to pay for such growth:

In His rebuke to the Pharisees, our Lord declares a principle that must guide all our efforts to change into the person God wants us to be. He made it clear that there is no place for pretense. We must come to grips with what's going on behind the whitewashed appearance of our life. It seems to be His teaching that we can't make it if we don't face all that we are. To look honestly at those parts of our experience we naturally deny is painful business, so painful that the analogy of death is not too strong. But to change according to Christ's instructions requires us to face all we prefer to deny. Real change requires an inside look."[54]

God invites us to take a look at ourselves as he sees us, even if it is painful. Bible characters like David willingly invited God to search them. Jeremiah called an entire nation to self-examination. "Search me, O God, and know my heart; test me and know my anxious thoughts. See if there is any offensive way in me, and lead me in the way everlasting" (Psalm

139:23-24). "Let us examine our ways and test them, and let us return to the LORD" (Lamentations 3:40).

Scripture implies that I need some kind of soul surgery from the Word of God: "For the word of God is living and active. Sharper than any double-edged sword, it penetrates even to dividing soul and spirit, joints and marrow; it judges the thoughts and attitudes of the heart" (Hebrews 4:12).

SABBATH-REST, A TIME TO REVIEW MY LIFE

In chapter seven I described the physical breakdown I endured at age thirty. Mandatory bed rest forced me to accept that if I didn't learn how to rest, I could work or worry myself to death. When I began to practice a form of Sabbath-rest, I began to release my concerns to the Lord on a weekly basis. Releasing my concerns naturally led to reviewing my life before him. I began to ask myself: *Is my manner of thought or behavior generating unnecessary concerns that are robbing me of joy and energy? Do I have dysfunctions which seem perfectly normal to me and my surroundings, that are grieving and quenching the Holy Spirit (I Thessalonians 5:19, Ephesians 4:30)?*

As I began to review my life, thoughts surfaced that I had long suppressed. I probably would not have faced them when I did had I not experienced physical and emotional exhaustion. Energy had been draining out of me like water gushing out of a bucket full of holes. I had to admit that I was not emotionally healthy. I was restless and driven. As I faced my drivenness, I began to go through an evaluation process similar to that described by Peter Scazzaro in his book, *The Emotionally Healthy Church*:

> I passed on to the leadership of our church a driving passion to grow bigger, better, and stronger every year. The pace was exhausting, much like my Dad's. I attributed it to the opportunities for God's kingdom to expand. In fact, I was seeking to find value and worth in the church, not in Christ. In the process I neglected the people closest to me—much like my father. [55]

Like Scazzero, I came to the realization that drivenness was a behavior that I had absorbed from the home where I grew up. My home was probably very similar to that of Peter's.

I come from a line of workaholics. My grandfather drove a bulldozer with cancer raging in his body at age sixty-eight. When he was too ill to work as a road construction contractor, he reverted to climbing onto his bulldozer pushing dirt around his property until cancer took him. My father ran a trucking business until his death at age eighty-five. For the last few years he was supposed to be on oxygen for pulmonary fibrosis, the same disease that took the life of Bill Bright, founder of Campus Crusade for Christ. However, Dad responded, "If I am on oxygen, I can't go to work. If I can't go to work, I won't be on oxygen." Eventually the oxygen tank went with him to work; but not until he was frequently found teetering on the top step all out of breath after climbing the stairs to his office.

I do not fault either my father or grandfather for the way they responded to life situations. Both of them tasted the deep poverty of the Great Depression. They were driven to work hard so I wouldn't have to eat beans and soda crackers three meals a day. But the day had come for me to discover a better way of life for myself and family.

I believe it takes spiritual discernment and courage from the Holy Spirit to sort out what to keep and what to discard when it comes to attitudes and behaviors from our parents and grandparents. There is a tendency to continually act as if our families were model families, not subject to analysis. Or there is the other extreme of ruthless rejection because we are appalled by our dysfunctional home life. The truth is we can all improve on our heritage, and wise parents are proud when we do.

I praise God for my family and the home where I grew up. I also thank God for the pilgrimage through which he has led me to discover Sabbath-rest as a means of sorting out and passing on what is worthy to the next generation. I must also praise God that I am not alone on this pilgrimage; others are on the path ahead of me: "Only through this commitment to reflect seriously on my family history in light of the values of the gospel have I been able to get off the 'fast track' of working and producing. Instead, slowly, I am learning to follow him in Sabbath rest, contentment, joy, peace (Romans 14:17), prayer, and reflection."[56]

Reviewing your life may be compared to peeling the layers of skin off an onion. You may be wondering: *where do I start?* The review process usually begins at a different place for each person. The Holy Spirit may lead you to a passage of Scripture that has been perplexing to you for some time.

Sabbath-rest is time set aside for intentionally pondering a verse or passage of Scripture with your life in mind. It may be a Scripture read in church, a sermon you heard on the radio, or a discussion among friends. You have put off the Holy Spirit while he has been tugging at your heart with a particular passage. But you said "later." Sabbath-rest is your appointment with God, a time to cease avoiding his prompting. It is the time you need if you are going to be serious about your relationship with God.

A more systematic approach to reviewing your life in light of God's Word is to examine various facets of your personality.

REVIEW YOUR LIFE BY EXAMINING YOUR ACTIONS

There are several avenues through which we can review our lives in the light of Scripture. Since behavior is much more visible than thoughts or feelings, it is a good place to begin. Our actions can be examined by others who can help in this process. Galatians 5:19-21 lists the deeds of the flesh by which our actions can be examined. A pound of flesh on a believer is capable of the same deviances as a pound of flesh on an unbeliever.

> Now the deeds of the flesh are evident, which are: immorality, impurity, sensuality, [20] idolatry, sorcery, enmities, strife, jealousy, outbursts of anger, disputes, dissensions, factions, [21] envying, drunkenness, carousing, and things like these, of which I forewarn you just as I have forewarned you that those who practice such things shall not inherit the kingdom of God.
>
> (Galatians 5:19-21, NAS)

Each one should test his own actions. Then he can take pride in himself without comparing himself to somebody else (Galatians 6:4).

REVIEW YOUR LIFE BY EXAMINING YOUR SPEECH

> Do not let any unwholesome talk come out of your mouths, but only what is helpful for building others up according to their needs, that it may benefit those who listen.
>
> (Ephesians 4:29)

Speech runs a close second to behavior as a means of reviewing our lives. The Word of God has much to say about the words that come out of our mouths. Once again James weighs in, this time with one of the heftiest warnings about the tongue:

> The tongue also is a fire, a world of evil among the parts of the body. It corrupts the whole person, sets the whole course of his life on fire, and is itself set on fire by hell. [7] All kinds of animals, birds, reptiles and creatures of the sea are being tamed and have been tamed by man, [8] but no man can tame the tongue. It is a restless evil, full of deadly poison.
>
> (James 3:6-8)

Psalms and Proverbs depict a sharp contrast between the speech of the wise and the speech of the foolish, that of the righteous and that of the wicked; they reinforce the truth that words reflect character. "The mouth of the righteous man utters wisdom, and his tongue speaks what is just " (Psalm 37:30). "Reckless words pierce like a sword, but the tongue of the wise brings healing" (Proverbs 12:18). "The tongue of the wise commends knowledge, but the mouth of the fool gushes folly" (Proverbs 15:2).

The words we speak are more than sounds and syllables. The words we speak expose the inner chambers of our hearts. Jesus said, "For out of the overflow of the heart the mouth speaks" (Matthew 12:34). The easiest way to find out what lurks in the deep, dark crevasses of our hearts is to listen closely to our words. We need to develop the art of listening to ourselves. We need to ask ourselves and others if we speak differently at church than at home or on the golf course. Wives and children are willing assistants if we are willing to ask, "Am I inconsistent?"

The book of James warns about the tongue: "With the tongue we praise our Lord and Father, and with it we curse men, who have been made in God's likeness. [10] Out of the same mouth come praise and cursing. My brothers, this should not be" (James 3:9-10).

Recently I was found to be inconsistent in my use of words. No, I did not cuss or curse. My weakness was off-color jokes on a four-day Canadian fishing trip among men who didn't mind, but prodded one another on with one silly story after another. For the want of laughter I contributed my share to the shades of discolored humor.

When I got home and entered my Sabbath time, I was convicted of my gross inconsistency. I had led in prayer, talked about Scripture on several occasions, and told stories with sensual overtones on other occasions. I humbled myself and apologized to several of my fishing buddies. Even more painful was the time I spent before God contemplating what must be in my heart. *Why do I find such stories funny? Is it just another convenient way of getting attention? Is it male chauvinism coming through? Can I honestly just pass it off on this sensuous culture that thrives on perverting what God has created as a sacred pleasure between husband and wife (Hebrews 13:4)?*

My words indicated there are plenty of fleshly notions left in me. The solution goes beyond watching my words. I must guard my heart. In the words of Solomon, "Above all else, guard your heart, for it is the wellspring of life" (Proverbs 4:23). I have begun to listen to myself more closely, realizing that my words portray my core being.

REVIEW YOUR LIFE BY EXAMINING YOUR ATTITUDES

Attitudes must also be evaluated. Attitudes can be negative such as selfishness and conceit, or positive such as humility and compassion for others. These contrasts of attitudes are obvious in this well-known passage exhorting believers to live out the attitudes of our Lord:

> Do nothing out of selfish ambition or vain conceit, but in humility consider others better than yourselves. [4] Each of you should look not only to your own interests, but also to the interests of others. [5] Your attitude should be the same as that of Christ Jesus: [6] Who, being in very nature God, did not consider equality with God something to be grasped, [7] but made himself nothing, taking the very nature of a servant, being made in human likeness.
>
> (Philippians 2:3-7)

A case can be made for right actions arising out of righteous attitudes. The fruit of the Spirit listed in Galatians chapter five appear to be more like attitudes than actions, implying that if our attitudes are righteous, right actions will follow: "But the fruit of the Spirit is love, joy, peace, patience, kindness, goodness, faithfulness, [23] gentleness and self-control. Against such things there is no law. [24] Those who belong to Christ Jesus have crucified the sinful nature with its passions and desires. [25] Since we live by the Spirit, let us keep in step with the Spirit" (Galatians 5:22-25).

Right attitudes are essential when it comes to giving to the Lord. Paul calls for willing and cheerful attitudes to accompany any financial gift: "For if the willingness is there, the gift is acceptable according to what one has, not according to what he does not have (II Corinthians 8:12)."Each man should give what he has decided in his heart to give, not reluctantly or under compulsion, for God loves a cheerful giver" (II Corinthians 9:7).

REVIEW YOUR LIFE BY EXAMINING YOUR EMOTIONS

Another gauge remains by which spiritual health can be measured. God has made human beings with a wide range of emotions. Emotions are windows into a person's life. Neil Anderson explains: "I believe that God has designed us in such a way that we can know on a moment-by-moment basis if our belief system is properly aligned with God's truth. God has established a feedback system which is designed to grab your attention so you can examine the validity of your goal. That system is your emotions."[57]

Anger is one of the most common emotions. Anger may be rooted in righteous causes like Jesus' display of anger when the money changers turned the temple court into a convenience store, robbing the Gentiles of an opportunity to draw near in prayer: "And as he taught them, he said, 'Is it not written: "My house will be called a house of prayer for all nations?" But you have made it "a den of robbers"'" (Mark 11:17).

In contrast anger can be triggered by inadequacy as in the case of Cain who killed his brother Abel (Geneses 4:1-15). Or a lack of trust as in the case of Moses who struck the rock when he was instructed to speak to the rock:

> He and Aaron gathered the assembly together in front of the rock and Moses said to them, "Listen, you rebels, must we bring you water out of this rock?" [11] Then Moses raised his arm and struck the rock twice with his staff. Water gushed out, and the community and their livestock drank. [12] But the LORD said to Moses and Aaron, "Because you did not trust in me enough to honor me as holy in the sight of the Israelites, you will not bring this community into the land I give them."
>
> (Numbers 20:10-12)

Moses had a tendency to take matters in his own hands. Early in life he killed an Egyptian in an impulsive attack against slave abuse in Egypt. In response to the Israelites' revelry he dashed the freshly engraved stone tablets of the Ten Commandments to the ground. I hesitate to speculate, but perhaps he would not have disqualified himself from entering the Promised Land had he traced his angry modes to his lack of trust in God to perform his will among his people.

I can certainly identify with Moses' fits of rage. I have been angry with people in various congregations for receiving grace while withholding it from others, for doubletalk, apathy, and a whole lot more. As I look back, God wanted me to trust him through such frustrations. When I did trust him, he showed up in marvelous ways. When I took matters into my own hands, I compounded problems, becoming my own worst enemy.

I can also identify with those whose limited trust produces worry. Worry and fear are very common emotions that cripple one's ability to accomplish the simplest tasks. Jesus had wonderful words for those whose fear exposed their feeble trust:

> "So do not worry, saying, 'What shall we eat?' or 'What shall we drink?' or 'What shall we wear?' [32] For the pagans run after all these things, and your

heavenly Father knows that you need them. [33] But seek first his kingdom and his righteousness, and all these things will be given to you as well. [34] Therefore do not worry about tomorrow, for tomorrow will worry about itself. Each day has enough trouble of its own."

(Matthew 6:31-34)

Jealousy is another emotion that commonly has its roots in a lack of trust. I remember on more then one occasion feeling jealous of pastors whose success in ministry was apparently far greater then mine. They had larger congregations, budgets, and buildings. As I walked through church facilities I sometimes felt jealousy welling up from within me. When I established a practice of Sabbath-rest, I began to process just what was going on when I entered those fine church edifices. Pondering the emotion in stillness before the Lord led to taking responsibility for my lack of trust in God's plan for my life.

Many negative emotions proceed from a lack of trust in God. We question God's goodness or ability to perform toward us. Each of us has to process our own emotions before the Lord. No one can do it for us. Failure to do so leaves us vulnerable to Satan's devious devices. "In your anger do not sin": Do not let the sun go down while you are still angry, and do not give the devil a foothold" (Ephesians 4:26-27). "See to it that no one misses the grace of God and that no bitter root grows up to cause trouble and defile many" (Hebrews 12:15).

If this sounds more like work than rest—it is! It is work that leads to rest. I recently made an appointment to see my chiropractor. Back pain and neck tightness had crept up my spine until I surrendered to getting help. After heat packs and a manipulation, the doctor ordered a massage. Moments later a massage specialist entered the room. She was a petite five foot two, possibly one hundred and five pounds. I volunteered that I once enjoyed a massage that was part of a vacation plan. She informed me that it was probably a relaxation message, designed to help me feel good at the time. I was about to receive a deep muscle massage, designed to help me feel better later. She was right about one thing: it didn't feel good at the time. It hurt! When she asked if the treatment was too much, I groaned, "I'm fine." My masculinity was not about to let me scream, "Enough!" Yet I pondered what it might be like to be tormented until I gave my torturers what they wanted. She was also right about making me feel better afterwards. The relief was definite. Even while it hurt, there was a sense of relief. The help I received was not cosmetic; it was real, lasting, and thorough.

> *No discipline seems pleasant at the time, but painful. Later on, however, it produces a harvest of righteousness and peace for those who have been trained by it.*
>
> *(Hebrews 12:11)*

I recommend being thorough when reviewing your life, even if it hurts. It is worth it. It is not temporary or cosmetic. It is deep therapy. It takes courage and humility to review your life. It is work that brings deep relief and the freedom to rest. I recommend being thorough even if it takes months of weekly Sabbath-rests before working through your actions, words, attitudes, and emotions.

While Sabbath-rest is of great value to all believers, it is very important that pastors and church leaders go through such a process of reviewing their lives before God. Peter Scazzero tells why: "Without doing the work of becoming aware of your feelings and actions, along with their impact on others, it is scarcely possible to enter deeply into the life experiences of other people. How can you enter someone else's world when you have not entered your own?"[58]

My pastor recently used an illustration in a sermon that compared reviewing our lives under the light of God's Word with examining a carpet under a black light. The illustration was originally submitted to *Preaching Today* by Stephen Kingsley of Craigmont, Idaho.

In our family carpet cleaning business we offered a special service for removing pet urine odors. To show potential customers their need for the service, I would darken the room and then turn on a powerful black light. The black light caused urine to glow brightly.

To the horror of the homeowners every drop and dribble could be seen, not only on the carpet, but usually on walls, drapes, furniture, and even on lamp shades. One homeowner begged me to shut off the light: "I can't bear to see anymore. I don't care what it costs. Please clean it up!" Another woman said, "I'll never be comfortable in my home again."

The offence was there all the time, but it was invisible until the right light exposed it. It would have been cruel to show customers the extent of their problem then say, "Too bad for you" and walk away. I brought the light so that they might desperately want my cleaning services.

In the same way, God shines the light of His commandments not just to make us feel guilty and leave us that way. He has a cleaning service to offer salvation through Jesus Christ.[59]

The courageous process of identifying sin in our lives necessitates another definite response known as repentance. Identifying sin without repenting is like sweeping the floor and not bending over with a dustpan and broom to pick up the dirt and throw it out. Repentance by definition requires a change of mind about sin. You and I are going to have to give up sin and do whatever is necessary to remove it from our lives. Without repenting we could feasibly enjoy reviewing our lives as we relive the sins of the past. Repentance agrees with God's opinion about sin, "It has to go!" I like Mark Buchanan's vivid description of repentance:

> Repentance is a ruthless dismantling of old ways of seeing and thinking, and then a diligent and vigilant building of new ones.
>
> Change begins with fresh eyes, in other words. It begins with an awakened imagination. You turn away, stubbornly and without apology, from that which formerly entranced you, and you turn toward that which you once avoided. You start to see what God sees, and as God sees it.[60]

Perhaps you think that reviewing your life and repenting of your sins in front of the mirror of God's Word will send you spinning into deep despair. You might think, *surely God will cast me out of his presence if I confess my sins and failures to him.* In all truth, standing before God stripped of your sin prepares you for his enormous embrace.

Lois and I maintain a close relationship with a particular family. Steve served as Elder Chairman at a church we once served until a job transfer occurred. Nancy now works as a marriage and family therapist. She counsels as one who has experienced God's love and embrace at the point of acknowledging sin:

> When we see in truth the reality of God's love for us, it then becomes possible to extend that same love toward others. The powerful, unconditional love of God becomes ours—ours to live in, and ours to give. We become free to love. This ability to love others can only happen when we no longer fear the truth about ourselves. God's love for me allowed me to look honestly at myself. Knowing that nothing could separate me from His love allowed me to look truthfully at my shortcomings and imperfections.[61]

A revelation of God's free grace gives us the courage to face the truth about ourselves. As we step out onto the tightrope of discovering the unpleasant things about ourselves, we have a safety net below, the Gospel of Jesus Christ.

(Peter Scazzero)[62]

The book of James speaks not only of the mirror of God's word, but of the gracious response of God: "Come near to God and he will come near to you" (James 4:8). Every time you dare to peel off a little more of the onion skin of denied sin, God will embrace you. I never felt really close to God until I dared to look into the mirror of God's Word and started peeling, confessing my sins after each layer. Contrary to my belief system, God did not torment me; he embraced me with the fullness of his love. His wrath is toward those who hide their sins and "suppress the truth in unrighteousness" (Romans 1:18, NASB), not toward those who come boldly before him seeking mercy. Hebrews chapter four describes God's readiness to grant mercy, while knowing everything about us:

Nothing in all creation is hidden from God's sight. Everything is uncovered and laid bare before the eyes of him to whom we must give account. [14] Therefore, since we have a great high priest who has gone through the heavens, Jesus the Son of God, let us hold firmly to the faith we profess. [15] For we do not have a high priest who is unable to sympathize with our weaknesses, but we have one who has been tempted in every way, just as we are—yet was without sin. [16] Let us then approach the throne of grace with confidence, so that we may receive mercy and find grace to help us in our time of need.

(Hebrew 4:13-16)

Sabbath-rest is a weekly appointment for such a merciful embrace. It feels so good to peel back the layers of dead skin, you won't want to stop. Without such Sabbath-rest appointments we may crave acceptance like children with rickets as described in Jim Smith's biography of Rich Mullins:

It is said that children with rickets "scratch lime from the walls." So, too, when we do not feel loved we "scratch acceptance from the walls." We will do anything to get it: climb the ladder of success, try to be funny, acquire possessions, alter our bodies, etc. If we are religious, this will often translate into becoming scrupulous. We will try to be perfect or saintly in order to find acceptance from God. Every attempt to find this acceptance in anything but God will eventually fail, and we will either have to deny the pain and try to ignore it or medicate it with a drink or a pill. But we must have it. The human soul cannot endure to be unloved.[63]

As I commune with God in Sabbath-rest, I am reassured of his unwavering love for me. When I neglect that cathedral of time, I begin to act like an unloved person. I seek attention from people and search for significance in sources that disappoint. Without intimate times with the Lord, I behave as unloved and driven. "Search me, O God, and know my heart; test me and know my anxious thoughts. See if there is any offensive way in me, and lead me in the way everlasting" (Psalm 139:23-24).

Prayer

Lord God Almighty, this day I present myself to you for review that I may please you fully. There are the sins that I know about and all the rest that you know about. I ask that you search out every corner and crevasse of my being and remove all that is offensive to you for your sake. I repent of all my sin giving it to you for disposal. Thank you, Lord Jesus, for paying the penalty for my sins by your death on the cross. I take up my cross and follow you anew and flee from the old. In Jesus' name and for his sake I pray, Amen.

Questions to Ponder

1. Do I stand in front of the mirror of God's Word on a regular basis?
2. Have I noticed family traits that have been passed on to me that need to be challenged and changed?
3. What is one trait in my life that I need to repent of?
4. Have I felt God's tender embrace lately?
5. When and where is my first or next Sabbath-rest for reviewing my life going to take place?

See Appendix A, Part II for the exercise on reviewing your life.

CHAPTER NINE

SABBATH-REST,
A TIME TO REMEMBER

Remember that you were slaves in Egypt and that the LORD your God brought you out of there with a mighty hand and an outstretched arm. Therefore the LORD your God has commanded you to observe the Sabbath day.

(Deuteronomy 5:15)

But God is the God of our yesterdays, and He allows the memory of them in order to turn the past into a ministry of spiritual culture for the future. God reminds us of the past lest we get into a shallow security in the present.[64]

(Oswald Chambers)

As I write this chapter a month has passed since Hurricane Katrina hit the gulf coasts of Louisiana and Mississippi, the worst natural disaster in United States history. The dead are still being counted and parents are still searching for their children. Over a thousand lives have been lost, and property damage totals billions of dollars. Charitable organizations are receiving large donations and collecting truckloads of tangible goods from around the country. Some foreign countries have also sent shiploads of goods to devastated locations. Human and material resources are headed down to New Orleans and other gulf cities like white blood cells attacking an infected laceration. Eventually the land will be healed and cities rebuilt. Most material possessions can be replaced, but many are lost forever.

Destroyed photo albums are possessions that cannot be replaced after the flood waters have receded. Those albums contained pictures of loved ones and friends who are no longer with those who now grieve. As one victim of Katrina said, "I do not even have one picture of my deceased mother."

Photo albums help families remember the good old days of being together with loved ones. Pictures of births, birthdays, graduations, weddings, family reunions, and little league teams help refresh the memories of those who view the pages.

Photo albums renew the joy of years gone by. Cheer percolates in the hearts of parents who gaze at pictures of their children when they were tiny. Children view pictures of the days when grandpa took them fishing and grandma baked cookies for them. With twinkling eyes grandparents gaze at snapshots of their teenage grandchildren courting prom dates.

> *The Bible serves as a photo album reminding the family of God of their spiritual heritage.*

There exists another photo album that cheers hearts generation after generation. The Bible serves as a photo album reminding God's family of their spiritual heritage. Like children surrounding the table where the photo album lies open, so one generation passes on memories of joy to the next. Psalm one hundred forty-five reminds all generations to pass on the joy of God's greatness and goodness:

> One generation will commend your works to another; they will tell of your mighty acts. [5] They will speak of the glorious splendor of your majesty, and I will meditate on your wonderful works. [6] They will tell of the power of your awesome works, and I will proclaim your great deeds.[7] They will celebrate your abundant goodness and joyfully sing of your righteousness.

The photo album begins with creation, "In the beginning God created the heavens and the earth" (Genesis 1:1). Creation provides a basis for a life of joy. It is good to be alive and enjoy all that surrounds me as a created being. Earth, water, and air flourish with life in harmony with their Maker. Scripture abounds with celebration, but never apart from the Creator. As I stand in awe of my Creator's majesty reflected in his artistry, Psalm nineteen comes to mind and expresses the joy in my heart:

> The heavens declare the glory of God; the skies proclaim the work of his hands. [2] Day after day they pour forth speech; night after night they display knowledge. [3] There is no speech or language where their voice is not heard. [4] Their voice goes out into all the earth, their words to the ends of the world. In the heavens he has pitched a tent for the sun, [5] which is like a bridegroom coming forth from his pavilion, like a champion rejoicing to run his course. [6] It rises at one end of the heavens and makes its circuit to the other; nothing is hidden from its heat.

Enjoying the many assets of creation without the Creator would deprive me of the full celebration of creation. As a painting reflects the artist, so creation reflects our Creator (Romans 1:18-24). An artist can exist without a painting, but no painting exists without an artist. So it is with creation. No Creator, no creation! Random chance does not stand a chance of making anything, much less organizing it. Knowing the Creator as I enjoy his creation augments the joy of life. Solomon settled his perplexing search for meaning by remembering his Creator in all facets of life. He urged the young in particular to remember their Creator early and often: "Remember your Creator in the days of your youth, before the days of trouble come and the years approach when you will say, 'I find no pleasure in them'"(Ecclesiastes 12:1).

Jonah tried to forget about God because He did not like the assignment God gave him. When he got literally *over his head* in circumstances, memories of God returned to his conscience.

> The engulfing waters threatened me, the deep surrounded me; seaweed was wrapped around my head. To the roots of the mountains I sank down; the earth beneath barred me in forever. But you brought my life up from the pit, O LORD my God. When my life was ebbing away, I remembered you, LORD, and my prayer rose to you, to your holy temple.
>
> (Jonah 2:5-7)

THE MAKING OF MEMORIES

Like Jonah I find that adversity not only stirs up memories, it also makes memories! Arguably the brain is the most amazing of all organs in the human body. Memory is perhaps the most fascinating function of all brain activity.

I must admit that I have become more forgetful with the passing of time. I first noticed it several years ago when our youngest son announced, "Dad remembers the things that happened long ago, but can't remember what just happened." Unfortunately I can relate to the humorous moments experienced by the following individual:

> A Harvard alumnus reports that he finds one of the most disturbing aspects of the passing years is his growing inability to recall vitally important information such as the Greek alphabet, the gross national product of Liberia, and where he put his slippers. This affliction becomes particularly pronounced whenever he goes upstairs to get something; half-way up he realizes he has no inkling as to what he was going upstairs to fetch, then he has to decide whether he should go back down stairs and try to remember what he needed, or to continue up and look around for something that wants bringing down. Unable to decide he resorts to sitting on the landing and sulking, only to discover that he has completely forgotten whether he was upstairs going down or downstairs going up.[65]

I have often wondered why it is so easy to remember some details and forget others. Psychologist and author Gary Collins provides an explanation in his book, *The Magnificent Mind*:

> Whenever the sense organs are stimulated they send electrical charges into the brain and on down the neuron pathways. If we don't pay attention to these stimulations, they fizzle out, usually within a few seconds....

> Some memories, however, do not fade. When short-term memories are mulled over, little growths appear at the synapses—those bridges between neurons. These growths remain as "long-term memories," even after the initial stimulation is gone.

> Someone has likened this to the influence of little streams of water running down a hillside. When the water stops, the little streams disappear. But if the water runs long enough, a small channel is cut out of the hillside and becomes a permanent memory of the water's original presence. In a similar way, long-term memories are created out of short-term memories if these keep flowing long enough.[66]

Repetition definitely enhances memory. Naturally I find it easier to remember the names of people I see on a regular basis versus people I see on occasion. As a pastor I found it difficult to remember the names of parishioners' relatives who visited only once or twice a year. If I want to remember a name, phone number, or formula, I must either use it often or intentionally repeat it until recall is a matter of reflex.

Another factor figures into recall. Memories stick when accompanied by emotions. For instance, I stand a better chance of remembering how to spell a word if I misspell it in public, like on a white board or overhead projector. While I do my best to avoid embarrassment, it has some redeeming value. I much prefer creating memories linked to positive emotions. Right now the fall colors in Minnesota are at their peak. Yellow birch trees, deep burgundy oaks leaves, and flaming red-orange maples make for an unforgettable walk with family, friends and certainly the Creator Redeemer. I am apt to remember conversations and thoughts in such a setting. Collins explains why:

Whenever we are emotionally aroused, there are chemical changes in the body, including the brain. Sometimes these chemical reactions stimulate long-term memory...

It has been known for many years that people and animals learn and form long-term memories better when they are in stimulating and enriched environments. The stimulated brain has more of the chemicals that are needed to change the neurons and help us form new memories.[67]

REMEMBERING GOD AS CREATOR

God engaged a means of grooving memories into minds which utilized both repetition and emotion. God in his foresight implemented repetition by establishing a day of the week for remembering his acts of creation and redemption. Week after week God's children gathered together turning short-term memories into long-term memories. It was so important the Father be remembered as the Mighty Creator that he established a day of the week for his children to open the photo album and view the many photos of his Creation. The Exodus reading of the Sabbath commandment reminded God's children that he was the Creator; and he established a healthy rhythm of work and rest:

Remember the Sabbath day by keeping it holy. [9] Six days you shall labor and do all your work, [10] but the seventh day is a Sabbath to the LORD your God. On it you shall not do any work, neither you, nor your son or daughter, nor your manservant or maidservant, nor your animals, nor the alien within your gates. [11] For in six days the LORD made the heavens and the earth, the sea, and all that is in them, but he rested on the seventh day. Therefore the LORD blessed the Sabbath day and made it holy.

(Exodus 20:8-11)

The Sabbath was not mundane but a pleasant relief from productive work which otherwise became laborious. It was a memory maker enriched with affirming emotions. Week after week this day was a celebration established as a lasting covenant: "The Israelites are to observe the Sabbath, celebrating it for the generations to come as a lasting covenant." (Exodus 31:16)

Sabbath celebrations were not as festive as the Passover, the Feast of Unleavened Bread, the Feast of Weeks, and the Feast of Tabernacles, which were celebrated annually (Deuteronomy 16:1,16). Weekly Sabbaths were quiet celebrations which reminded participants that they had permission and power to cease both business and busyness. Sabbaths celebrated internal and external rest, something that separated them from the unbelieving ranks.

The weekly celebration was a reminder that God was their Creator. It was a day God's children could lay aside their own work and recognize the awesome work of the One who created all. It was to be a day for gathering around the photo album and remembering their Creator. As God had originally paused to rest and recognize the goodness of what he had created, his children were to follow his example. They were to celebrate the joy of being created by him and for him. They were to rest from their own work and recognize God's handiwork.

God is not the only one seen working in this photo album. We see ourselves working with the abilities God has given us. We are to not only remember the works of God but to remember that it was God who created us with skills and the ability to make a living. "But remember the LORD your God, for it is he who gives you the ability to produce wealth, and so confirms his covenant, which he swore to your forefathers, as it is today" (Deuteronomy 8:18).

With every stroke of a brush the painter is to remember that it is God who has given the ability to paint. With the close of every deal the salesperson is to remember that it is God who has given the ability to sell. With the review of every account the accountant is to remember that it is God who has given the ability to keep a ledger. With every opportunity to stand in front of a class the teacher is to remember that it is God who has given the ability to teach. With every swing of a hammer the carpenter is to remember that it is God who has given the ability to build homes.

SELF-FORGETFULNESS

The great personal benefit of remembering God is self-forgetfulness. To remember God is to be released from consuming self-thoughts. When I remember God for a full moment I lose myself in him. Thinking *God* is such a big thought that it leaves little room for ruminating about me. To remember God is to be consumed with his majesty. It doesn't matter if my self-thoughts are positive or negative; it is a relief to be enamored with God and not myself.

I had the privilege of hearing John Piper make one of his radically true statements about the Gospel, "God came in Jesus Christ in order to liberate you from your love affair with a carnival image that makes you look great." He went on to unveil the value of self-forgetfulness:

> The highest moments of joy are not the times I have liked myself or liked what I have done, but when I have forgotten myself in delight of God in the service of other.

> Self-forgetfulness is the most wonderful gift in the world, not self-esteem. Self-forgetfulness is the most wonderful gift in the world. No buddy goes to the Grand Canyon to increase his self-esteem. We go to the Grand Canyon because we might be given the gift for a few minutes to forget that we are big and feel the bigness of something outside of ourselves, which is just a little tiny image of God.[68]

REMEMBERING GOD AS REDEEMER

There is much more in this family photo album called the Bible. God our Father is seen not only as a Mighty Creator; he is also pictured as a Merciful Redeemer (Isaiah 44:24). That means that as a Father he does not turn his back on his children when they get into trouble or go astray. As Redeemer he rescues his children, even if the redemption cost is very high requiring immense sacrifice.

Both accounts of the fourth commandment begin with the command–Remember!

Pages and pages of this photo album remind us that he is a Merciful Redeemer. The most prominent picture of redemption in the Old Testament is that of the exodus from Egypt. "Therefore, say to the Israelites: 'I am the LORD, and I will bring you out from under the yoke of the Egyptians. I will free you from being slaves to them, and I will redeem you with an outstretched arm and with mighty acts of judgment'" (Exodus 6:6).

It was so important that the Father be remembered as the Merciful Redeemer that he set aside a day for all of his children to open the photo album and view the act of redemption at least once a week. Once again the Sabbath was designed to turn short-term memories into long-term memories through repetition and emotion.

Both accounts of the fourth commandment begin with the command, *Remember!* The Sabbath was a day to remember that God is the Mighty Creator and Merciful Redeemer. The Exodus view of the fourth commandment emphasizes God as Creator. The Deuteronomy perspective on the Sabbath commandment reminded God's children that he was the Merciful Redeemer who delivered them from Egypt: "Remember that you were slaves in Egypt and that the LORD your God brought you out of there with a mighty hand and an outstretched arm. Therefore the LORD your God has commanded you to observe the Sabbath day" (Deuteronomy 5:15). The Israelites were commanded to set aside a day each week to remember the mighty and merciful works of God while resting from their labor.

The Sabbath is associated with the act of remembering. The Sabbath is a weekly reminder of the two major themes of this family photo album. First, God knows that I am prone to forget if time is not set aside to recall and consider again and again that he made the universe and everything in it. Second, he cared enough to rescue me when I went astray.

The Sabbath was a celebration of God's mighty acts of creation and his merciful acts of redemption. The photos of God's redemption, the release of his children from the Egyptian captivity, picture just the beginning of his redeeming acts. The photos of the Redeemer would become clearer as the cost of redemption became higher. The Father's one-of-a-kind Son would be the sacrificial price of redeeming his wayward children. These photos would be terrifying to ponder. The Prophet Isaiah described the content of these photos before they were taken:

See, my servant will act wisely; he will be raised and lifted up and highly exalted. [14] Just as there were many who were appalled at him—his appearance was so disfigured beyond that of any man and his form marred beyond human likeness—[15] so will he sprinkle many nations, and kings will shut their mouths because of him. For what they were not told, they will see, and what they have not heard, they will understand.

(Isaiah 52:13-15)

He was despised and rejected by men, a man of sorrows, and familiar with suffering. Like one from whom men hide their faces he was despised, and we esteemed him not. [4] Surely he took up our infirmities and carried our sorrows, yet we considered him stricken by God, smitten by him, and afflicted. [5] But he was pierced for our transgressions, he was crushed for our iniquities; the punishment that brought us peace was upon him, and by his wounds we are healed. [6] We all, like sheep, have gone astray, each of us has turned to his own way; and the LORD has laid on him the iniquity of us all.

(Isaiah 53:3-6)

The prophet made it clear that the Redeemer would suffer a gruesome death for guilty sinners. His act of redemption would be unforgettable. Yet those he died for would need reminding (Psalm 106:2, Hosea 13:6).

What the prophets revealed would come true as the pages of the photo album were turned. Photos of the Redeemer himself are viewed. Every dreadful word of the prophets would be confirmed by the lips of the Redeemer himself: "Jesus took the twelve aside and told them, 'We are going up to Jerusalem, and everything that is written by the prophets about the Son of Man will be fulfilled. [32] He will be handed over to the Gentiles. They will mock him, insult him, spit on him, flog him and kill him. [33] On the third day he will rise again'" (Luke 18:31-33).

As pages are turned to the unjust trial, the mocking, and flogging, parents hold their breath thinking, *perhaps we shouldn't let the children see the next pages. Young minds shouldn't be scared by vivid pictures of the shredded body of the flogged and crucified.* Breathless they refrain from intruding, remembering that each must look at the bleeding Redeemer until he or she is pierced by the reality that he was scarred for the sins of each child and adult. They may weep, and sleepless nights may come until they say, "My Redeemer and God" (Zechariah 12:10).

I clearly remember the day that I was pierced through with the realization that it was for me he was tormented to death. At age twelve I received Christ, having a simple understanding that Christ died to save me from my sins. At age eighteen I absorbed with emotional impact the reality that he, the Righteous, was pierced through for me, the guilty. I had to look at

Christ's contorted body until I realized my sins were so deadly that it took such an agonizing death to forgive them. Hide their young faces as we may, the whole family, young and old alike, must look at these dreadful pages until they all say, "My Redeemer and God."

Thankfully that is not the last page of the photo album. While the crucifixion is to be remembered, it is not the last scene to be remembered. Christ rose again victorious over death, the grave, and our sin. His death and resurrection conquered our worst enemies and fears. The pictures of the empty tomb with angels surrounding it tell the story:

> On the first day of the week, very early in the morning, the women took the spices they had prepared and went to the tomb. [2] They found the stone rolled away from the tomb, [3] but when they entered, they did not find the body of the Lord Jesus. [4] While they were wondering about this, suddenly two men in clothes that gleamed like lightning stood beside them. [5] In their fright the women bowed down with their faces to the ground, but the men said to them, "Why do you look for the living among the dead? [6] He is not here; he has risen! Remember how he told you, while he was still with you in Galilee: [7] 'The Son of Man must be delivered into the hands of sinful men, be crucified and on the third day be raised again.'"[8] Then they remembered his words.
>
> (Luke 24:1-8)

Christ's numerous appearances to his surprised followers conclude the Redeemer's first coming to earth. Every remembrance of his victory over death would bring joy to first century believers: "When he was at the table with them, he took bread, gave thanks, broke it and began to give it to them. [31] Then their eyes were opened and they recognized him, and he disappeared from their sight. [32] They asked each other, "Were not our hearts burning within us while he talked with us on the road and opened the Scriptures to us?" (Luke 24:30-32).

The resurrection of Jesus Christ deserved a new page in the photo album and a new day for remembering the most powerful demonstration of life since God breathed into man. The resurrection made such an impact on those who witnessed the risen Lord that a new day of the week was assigned for remembering his victory. Since it was the first day of the week that Jesus, the Redeemer, rose from the dead, the first day would be set aside for public worship of the risen Redeemer.

> *It is not the day of the week that matters, but the way of life that counts.*

While there is no New Testament command equivalent to the Old Testament, "Keep the Sabbath," there is significant evidence that Sunday became the day when Christians gathered in memory of the resurrection. The early church shifted from meeting on the Sabbath, the seventh day of the week, to Sunday, the first day of the week. Sunday ultimately became known as The Lord's Day.

I have already noted that the resurrection took place on the first day of the week (Matthew 28:1; Mark 16:2, 9; Luke 24:1; John 20:1). Furthermore the Gospels make a point of mentioning it was on the first day of the week that Jesus later appeared to the disciples: "On the evening of that first day of the week, when the disciples were together, with the doors locked for fear of the Jews, Jesus came and stood among them and said, 'Peace be with you!'" (John 20:19).

Likewise, the book of Acts and First Corinthians make the point that the early church met together on the first day of the week: "On the first day of the week we came together to break bread. Paul spoke to the people and, because he intended to leave the next day, kept on talking until midnight" (Acts 20:7). "On the first day of every week, each one of you should set aside a sum of money in keeping with his income, saving it up, so that when I come no collections will have to be made" (1 Corinthians 16:2).

It is apparent that by the end of the first century AD when John penned Revelation that the first day of the week had become known as The Lord's Day. "On the Lord's Day I was in the Spirit, and I heard behind me a loud voice like a trumpet" (Revelation 1:10).

While I am persuaded that Sunday is the intended day for Christians to gather for worship, I have concluded that I should not be judgmental toward those who choose another day for public worship. I say this for the following reasons:

- There is no commandment in the New Testament to worship on Sunday.
- The fourth commandment is the only one of the ten that is not repeated as a commandment in the New Testament.

- Holy days are a shadow of things to come and not reason to judge one another. Paul addresses those with condescending attitudes regarding holy days in the following manner: "Therefore do not let anyone judge you by what you eat or drink, or with regard to a religious festival, a New Moon celebration or a Sabbath day. These are a shadow of the things that were to come; the reality, however, is found in Christ" (Colossians 2:16-17).
- Sabbath, Sunday, or any other religious observance is by no means a way of gaining salvation or sanctification. It is, however, a means of remembering one's relationship with Christ.
- Observance of the Sabbath or Sunday must never be put above Christ. Christ is the fulfillment of the law (Matthew 5:17), indicating that we become better law keepers as he, the Law Giver, lives within us.

The Sabbath, in concept, is a gift more than a commandment. Jesus said, "The Sabbath was made for man, not man for the Sabbath" (Mark 2:27).

"The Sabbath was made for man" communicates that the Sabbath was a gift for weary man. The Sabbath was designed to refresh man as modeled by God: "It is a sign between me and the children of Israel forever: for in six days Jehovah made heaven and earth, and on the seventh day he rested, and was refreshed" (Exodus 31:17 NASB).

Finally Jesus Christ, the Lord of the Sabbath, is to be the focus of the Christian life. No practice is to take precedence over him: "So the Son of Man is Lord even of the Sabbath" (Mark 2:28).

THE DAY ENHANCES THE WAY OF LIFE

Having retreated from being emphatic about the day for public worship, I remain passionate about remembering our Lord in all of his grace towards us. Without designating a day the Apostle Paul commands believers to, "Remember Jesus Christ, raised from the dead, descended from David. This is my gospel, for which I am suffering even to the point of being chained like a criminal" (II Timothy 2:8-9).

It is not the day of your week that matters, but the way of life that counts. The day enhances the way of life! The day makes the way more attainable, providing a means of remembering the risen Creator Redeemer. My observation and experience convince me that a person needs to be intentional about recalling what is worth remembering. The word *intentionality* mandates setting aside a time and place to open the photo album of remembrances.

By the end of the three-step process one is inclined to experience great freedom in speaking with God. Burdens have been cast upon the Lord and direction has been determined. One feels free to express themselves in the way God has gifted them. A pianist may go to the piano and an artist may go to his or her canvas. If time permits, a round of golf or a fishing trip may top off your praise experience.

In his book, *Working the Angles,* Eugene H. Peterson comments regarding the combination of playing and praying in Psalm ninety-two: "It is good to give thanks to Yahweh, to play in honor of your name, Most High" (Psalm 92:1; Jerusalem Bible).

> What is it like to pray? To play? Puritan Sabbaths that eliminated play were a disaster. Secular Sabbaths that eliminate prayer are worse. Sabbath-keeping involves both playing and praying. The activities are alike enough to share the same day and different enough to require the other for a complementary wholeness.[69]

A stroll through a park may be desirable. Observing creation is my favorite activity. Andrew Murray's thoughts on Psalm 104:27-28 have helped me understand the connection between observing creatures of nature and waiting on God: "These all look to you to give them their food at the proper time. When you give it to them, they gather it up; when you open your hand, they are satisfied with good things" (Psalm 104:27-28).

> As we read this psalm, and learn to look upon all life in Nature as continually maintained by God Himself, waiting on God will be seen to be the very necessity of our being. As we think of the young lions and the ravens crying to Him, of the birds and the fishes and every insect waiting on Him, till He gives them their meat in due season, we shall see that it is the very nature and glory of God that He is a God who is to be waited on. Every thought of what Nature is, and what God is, will give new force to the call: "Wait thou only upon God." What the universe and the animal creation does unconsciously, God's people are to do intelligently and voluntarily. Man is to be the interpreter of Nature. He is to prove that there is nothing nobler or more blessed in the exercise of our free will than to use it in waiting upon God.[70]

In similar fashion Jonathan Edwards "had an extraordinary love for the glory of God in nature."[71] John Piper has researched Edwards for years and notes that, "The good effects of this love on his capacity to delight in the greatness of God and on the imagery of his preaching were tremendous."[72]

> Once as I rode into the woods for my health in 1737, having alighted from my horse in a retired place, as my manner commonly has been, to walk for divine contemplation and prayer, I had a view, that for me was extraordinary, of the glory of the Son of God, as Mediator between God an man, and his wonderful, great, full, pure and sweet grace and love and meek, gentle condescension...which continued, as near as I can judge, about an hour; which kept me the greater part of the time in a flood of tears, and weeping aloud."[73]

I am persuaded that the best of life is spent outdoors. Men were not made to sit in cubicles and work for hours without windows. My observation is that women do a bit better with enclosures, but both men and women need to experience the great outdoors on a regular basis. That is why it is so important to enjoy a weekly Sabbath away from the common enclosures of work and home.

I have gone for long walks usually once a week for years in rural and suburban settings. When Minnesota snowfall prohibits walking, I cross-country ski. Other times I have found that gazing outdoors through a window in a safe, distraction-free building or stationary car satisfies. There is plenty to ponder if we open the shades to see that we are surrounded by the glory of God.

The biggest challenge to walking through parks or gawking through windows is the assault of guilt. For years I fought the whispers from my workaholic background, *this is such a waste of time, how unproductive.* Only after years of noting improved productivity, better perspective, and power from on high, did I learn to rebuke the whisper.

My discovery of the benefits of contemplative walks parallels that of David Hansen's prayer walks:

> Initially I didn't know the long-term benefits of taking these prayer walks, but now I do. Lest this sound all that "spiritual" an exercise, often I just *see* in a new way the light playing on a tree trunk, the colorful lichen on a boulder helping to break it down into soil over the years, inviting the natural world to help me empty myself so that God can fill me with his

presence, his agenda for me. Often these are times when I feel so loved by him.[74]

What I once considered to be a waste of time has become a great source of strength. The following poem recorded in Tim Hansel's book, *When I Relax I Feel Guilty*, expresses my experience:

I wasted an hour one morning beside a mountain stream,
I seized a cloud from the sky above and fashioned myself a dream,
In the hush of the early twilight, far from the haunts of men,
I wasted a summer evening, and fashioned my dream again.
Wasted? Perhaps. Folks say so who never have walked with God,
When lanes are purple with lilacs or yellow with goldenrod.
But I have found strength for my labors in that one short evening hour.
I have found joy and contentment; I have found peace and power.
My dreaming has left me a treasure, a hope that is strong and true.
From wasted hours I have built my life and found my faith anew.[75]

THE PARABLE OF THE JEWELER

Once upon a time there lived a jeweler who handled diamonds on a daily basis. Some of them were splendid selections from his personal collection which he had purchased over the years. Others belonged to customers who came into his store to have them cleaned, appraised, and placed in settings. Occasionally a customer came in with a fine diamond worth thousands of dollars; but most of these diamonds were more valuable as keepsakes than monetary possessions. These keepsakes brought to mind precious memories of those who had given them as wedding bands, anniversaries, and other momentous occasions.

Day after day the jeweler examined diamonds under special light and a magnifying glass. None of these diamonds possessed perfection, including those in his personal collection. Then one day he came across a diamond that was perfect. No matter how many times he turned it in the light he could not find a single shadow or imperfection. It was flawless. He immediately fell in love with this diamond. He sold his entire collection in order to purchase that one diamond.

Day after day he continued to view diamonds as customers and merchants visited the store. But none of them presented a diamond comparable to the one he kept in his safe. It was matchless.

At least once a week when the store was closed and he was all alone he opened his safe and viewed the perfect diamond. He discovered great pleasure in holding the diamond in his hand and gently turning it in the light. That one diamond reminded him that the perfect exists. That one diamond made the monotony of viewing flawed diamonds worth it. That one diamond made him a better jeweler because it provided a standard by which he could measure all diamonds. Because of that single diamond the jeweler kept his jewelry store open for years; it gave the jeweler future hope.

I am not a jeweler. Nor am I in the diamond business. The few diamonds Lois and I possess are keepsakes. As a minister, I am in the people business. Like it or not, I have to evaluate people for character, giftedness, leadership, and passion. I have yet to meet face to face a perfect person and just by reading this book you already know that I am not perfect. People disappoint us. I know that I have personally disappointed others. Working with people can be very discouraging. At times working with my own imperfections is more than I can bear.

There is one exception to all these imperfect people. As I read the gospel accounts of Jesus, the Old Testament prophecies and the New Testament epistles, I must conclude that Jesus Christ is that one perfect person who has set foot on planet earth. He is my perfect diamond. As I get alone with him, I am encouraged to know that the perfect does exist and I can work with all the other diamonds in the rough which will disappoint me. I take heart regarding my own flaws knowing that he is alive within me and refining me from the inside out. There will come a day when I am perfected along with all others throughout all time who bow to receive him (Philippians 1:6). No diamond has the ability to perfect other diamonds. Jesus Christ is able to perfect you and me as we place our faith, hope, and love in him.

Sabbath-rest is like that weekly visit to the safe, when for a prolonged time in the quietness of our hearts we review the diamond. Sabbath-rest reminds us that the perfect does exist. A prolonged look brings Christ to the foreground of our minds so that we can live and work with all the other diamonds in the rough.

How long has it been since you opened the safe and viewed the perfect diamond, Jesus Christ?

Prayer

Jesus, my Lord, you are worthy of my total focus and devotion every day of the week. As you cleared a segment of your eternal existence to come to earth and die for me in demonstration of your love toward me, so I clear a segment of my week to remember that you are my Creator and Redeemer forevermore. This I do as a demonstration of my love for you.

In Jesus' name and for his sake I pray, Amen.

Questions to Ponder

1. What passages of Scripture has God fused into my memory bank which daily keeps him before me?
2. What memories are in my photo album of times with God?
3. Am I engaged in making lasting memories by entering Sabbath-rest repeatedly and with emotion?
4. What activities best help me remember and enjoy God?
5. When and where is my first or next Sabbath-rest for remembering my God going to take place?

See Appendix A, Part III for the exercise on remembering God.

CHAPTER TEN

SABBATH-REST,
A TIME TO LOOK FORWARD

There remains, then, a Sabbath-rest for the people of God; for anyone who enters God's rest also rests from his own work, just as God did from his.

(Hebrews 4:9-10)

This last Sabbath Liturgy is to help train your restless heart heavenward, and it borrows from the logic of "how much more." If this meal with friends and family is rich, *how much more* the banquet of the great King? If resting in this patch of sunlight is refreshing, *how much more* in the place where God and the Lamb shine brighter than any sun? If love making with my spouse is blissful, *how much more* what no eye has seen and no ear heard but which God prepares for those he loves?[76]

(Mark Buchanan)

I have a glorious homesickness for heaven, a penetrating and piercing ache.

(Joni Eareckson Tada)

Like a fine diamond, Sabbath-rest deserves another look. Another turn under the light unleashes a new world of beauty. Thus far we have discovered that Sabbath-rest provides a time to release our concerns, review our lives, and remember our God. As we turn the diamond again another facet is unveiled. Sabbath-rest opens a window to the future. It has eschatological significance projecting our thoughts into the future. While our bodies rest from work, our minds review the hope of final rest from toil, when all consequences of the curse are removed from the believer. Hope is a priceless commodity.

HOPE VERSUS PROVISIONAL EXISTENCE

Ever since visiting the Holocaust Museum in Israel I have paid particular attention to the perspective of those who have endured horrific suffering. I would not go so far as to say that suffering is a complete test for truth. Suffering, however, is a reliable refiner of truth, siphoning off the deceptions of pleasure.

Several years ago I became familiar with Viktor Frankl through his book, *Man's Search for Meaning*. Frankl was a Jewish psychiatrist who lived to tell about his experiences during World War II at Auschwitz, a Nazi death camp. He witnessed a marked difference between prisoners who maintained hope beyond a *provisional existence* within the camp and those who had abandoned hope:

> A man who could not see the end of his "provisional existence" was not able to aim at an ultimate goal in life. He ceased living for the future, in contrast to a man in normal life. Therefore the whole structure on his inner life changed: signs of decay set in which we know from other areas of life. The unemployed worker, for example, is in a similar position. His existence has become provisional and in a certain sense he cannot live for the future or aim at a goal.[77]

> Woe to him who saw no more sense in his life, no aim, no purpose, and therefore no point in carrying on. He was lost."[78]

One does not have to face a holocaust to lose hope. I have a friend who serves as a chaplain in a nursing home. Every day he observes a distinct difference in the attitudes of residents. There are those who with the passing of years focus on their eternal home with God in heaven. They also have a growing interest in future generations and jump at every opportunity to encourage those who may follow them in their hope. In contrast there are those who live from one doctor appointment to the next. Their conversations center on their medications and who is going to pay for their prescription drugs. With the passing of time their focus becomes increasingly short-sighted. These residents no longer live from day to day, but meal to meal, even pill to pill. This is a provisional existence.

Provisional existence reminds me of a baseball player who hopes to get on base with a bunt. Not a bad idea if he is a good bunter, fast, and the infield is playing back. But this ballplayer is bunting because he has lost confidence in getting on base any other way. He no longer looks out over the fence to hit a homerun. Nor does he notice how the outfielders are playing that he might hit one in the gap for a double or possibly a triple. His focus is so short-sighted that he only notices the first fifty feet of infield grass. He has choked up on the bat so far that there is more wood behind his hands than in front of them. Provisional existence tends to choke up on life until there is nothing left for which to live.

In the comfort of my own home and country I can slither into a provisional existence. All I have to do is abandon a future perspective. All I have to do is start living from one vacation to the next, or one home improvement project to the next, or one oil change to the next. A life of prosperity and pleasure can become as void of future hope as a life of poverty. All I have to do is work or play focusing on temporal pleasures or pains. All I have to do is revert to former ways of thinking, or go with the flow of current trends of hopelessness. All I have to do is devalue the source of hope and set him aside. That is what the early Hebrew Christians did, making it necessary for God to set forth the book of Hebrews.

Hebrews is a book of hope written to a people who were losing confidence in their hope and did not know it. They underestimated the value of Christ and failed to cling to him as their hope. For this reason the author repeatedly confronted them with the supremacy of Christ as the ultimate source of hope.

> *Paul, an apostle of Christ Jesus by the command of God our Savior and of Christ Jesus our hope.*
>
> *(I Timothy 1:1)*

In the past God spoke to our forefathers through the prophets at many times and in various ways, [2] but in these last days he has spoken to us by his Son, whom he appointed heir of all things, and through whom he made the universe. [3] The Son is the radiance of God's glory and the exact representation of his being, sustaining all things by his powerful word. After he had provided purification for sins, he sat down at the right hand of the Majesty in heaven. [4] So he became as much superior to the angels as the name he has inherited is superior to theirs.

(Hebrews 1:1-4)

But Christ is faithful as a son over God's house. And we are his house, if we hold on to our courage and the hope of which we boast.

(Hebrews 3:6)

We want each of you to show this same diligence to the very end, in order to make your hope sure.

(Hebrews 6:11)

God did this so that, by two unchangeable things in which it is impossible for God to lie, we who have fled to take hold of the hope offered to us may be greatly encouraged. We have this hope as an anchor for the soul, firm and secure. It enters the inner sanctuary behind the curtain.

(Hebrews 6:18-19)

The former regulation is set aside because it was weak and useless (for the law made nothing perfect), and a better hope is introduced, by which we draw near to God.

(Hebrews 7:18, 19)

Let us hold unswervingly to the hope we profess, for he who promised is faithful.

(Hebrews 10:23)

Jesus Christ is the same yesterday and today and forever.

(Hebrews 13:8)

Hope was not a new concept to the Hebrew Christians. God has always given his people hope. God provided the nation of Israel with two assurances which allowed them to survive and thrive throughout history. By faith they were to enter the Promised Land and in faithfulness they were to enter the Sabbath. The Promised Land and the Sabbath provided rest on earth while reflecting eternal rest.

ETERNAL REST REFLECTED THROUGH THE PROMISED LAND

God portrays his offer of eternal hope through the Promised Land. The creation narrative in Genesis one clearly depicts God as the Creator of all. As Creator, God is also the Owner. The Psalmist David declares this very thought, "The earth is the Lord's and everything in it, the world, and all who live in it" (Psalm 24:1). John Sailhamer states that the writer's intention is to declare that the one who made the land is its rightful owner and that as owner he is justified in giving the land to Israel to possess:

> What, then, does Genesis 1:1-2:4a tell us about the land? It tells us that God is its owner. He created and prepared the land, and He can give it to whomever He chooses (Jeremiah 27:5). In the ancient world, and in our own, the right to own land and grant it to others formed the basis of an ordered society. The author of the Pentateuch, then, is quick to point out that the promise of the land to Israel, made effective in the Sinai covenant, was in every way a right justly belonging to God.[79]

In the fifth book of the Pentateuch, Moses makes clear what he has suggested in Genesis. Namely, that it is the Lord who has given the Promised Land to Israel. "The LORD your God has given you this land to take possession of it" (Deuteronomy 3:18).

OWNERSHIP AND REST

Owning property assures one of some degree of rest. Lois and I have been fortunate to own a home in most places throughout our journey together. As newlyweds we rented a one bedroom basement apartment from an elderly woman who had grown up in the home. The house was full of memories, especially of her parents who were deceased. For obvious reasons she was quite protective of the property. If our old car left oil spots on the driveway, we were sure to hear about it. She was sensitive to the volume dial on our stereo and scrutinized who visited the apartment. As soon as possible we found a way to own our own home.

During seminary we rented an apartment. There we quickly found ourselves to be noise sensitive. We could not control the noises of those in apartments on each side and above us. It was not so much the loud music that annoyed us as the fighting that alarmed us. We found it necessary to guard our two-year-old son from older children on the playground. When our rent was increased by twenty percent, owning a home began to look really attractive.

For three years our family of four lived in a church parsonage. It was a beautiful setting surrounded by tall pines and a golden meadow, located just a few miles away from several clear blue lakes. The parsonage was a nice enough home. The only problem was that it shared a driveway with the church facility. We were witnesses to everything that went on at church. Like it or not we couldn't get away from the hustle and bustle of church life. Furthermore, the key to the church door hung on a nail near the front doorbell of the parsonage. If church members didn't have a key, they came to our door to get one; and if the key was missing, they were likely to ring our door asking for our keys. The church playground equipment was on the parsonage lawn, making it convenient for children to come to our home to use the bathroom. Adults also showed up on our step wanting impromptu advice or counseling at their convenience. Try as we did to graciously establish boundaries, it was hard to relax at home. While we cherish many memories of that congregation, parsonage living is not one of them.

All of these rental homes were adequate. They just lacked one thing, a sense of rest. Ownership has its problems as well; if you own it, you fix it! However, owning gives one a sense of boundaries and greater control over what takes place on the premises. Rest to a greater degree comes with ownership. Ownership of land and the rest that accompanies it compels a nomadic people all the more to enter the Promised Land.

> *The Promised Land signified a place where God and man were united in rest.*

From the day God called Abraham from his homeland until Joshua crossed the Jordan River, Israel wandered from place to place and experienced frequent wars with those who did not like squatting nations. While Abraham, Isaac, and Jacob spent time in the Promised Land, the land was occupied by the Canaanites during their lifetimes. Famine drove the patriarchs out of the land, causing each to spend lengthy periods of time in Egypt. Egypt was anything but a resting place for the generations of Hebrews who endured four hundred years of slavery. Occupation of the Promised Land would have promptly followed the Exodus from Egypt had it not been for a failure to believe the God who promised the land. Thus an entire generation wandered outside of the land without the rest God intended for them to enjoy.

THE LAND OF REST

Jacob's request is the first time the Promised Land is associated with rest, "But when I rest with my fathers, carry me out of Egypt and bury me where they are buried" (Genesis 47:30). Later the land offered rest from war and enemies: "But you will cross the Jordan and settle in the land the LORD your God is giving you as an inheritance, and he will give you rest from all your enemies around you so that you will live in safety" (Deuteronomy 12:10; 25:19).

As Joshua begins the conquest, the Promised Land is clearly associated with the rest given Israel by the hand of God:

> "Remember the command that Moses the servant of the LORD gave you: 'The LORD your God is giving you rest and has granted you this land.' Your wives, your children and your livestock may stay in the land that Moses gave you east of the Jordan, but all your fighting men, fully armed, must cross over ahead of your brothers. You are to help your brothers until the LORD gives them rest, as he has done for you, and until they too have taken possession of the land that the LORD your God is giving them. After that, you may go back and occupy your own land, which Moses the servant of the LORD gave you east of the Jordan toward the sunrise."
>
> (Joshua 1:13-15)

> So Joshua took the entire land, just as the LORD had directed Moses, and he gave it as an inheritance to Israel according to their tribal divisions. Then the land had rest from war.
>
> (Joshua 11:23)

The Promised Land was not only a resting place for man; it was a place of rest for God, not that God ever gets weary and needs rest like man (Isaiah 40:28). The Promised Land signified a place where God and man were united in rest. A.T. Lincoln explains:

> In Deuteronomy, since Israel was to find rest from all its enemies in the land of its inheritance (12:10; 25:19 cf. also 3:20), the land itself can be called their resting place (12:9). In addition we find that God Himself has His resting place in the land, and especially in His sanctuary at Zion. This is particularly clear in Ps. 132:7-8, 13-14; Is. 66:1. In other places these two motifs are combined so that the resting place of the people is also the resting place of God.
>
> (Deuteronomy 12:9,11; I Chronicles 23:25; II Chronicles 6:41)[80]

THE LAND OF REST ENTERED BY FAITH

Inasmuch as the Promised Land represents a place of rest, the land portrays God's invitation for man to enter into his rest. In Psalm ninety-five the Psalmist refers to the generation of Israel that wandered in the desert outside the Promised Land for forty years as those who will not enter God's rest. The root cause of the lockout was failure to believe in God's goodness and greatness after witnessing both divine characteristics throughout the exodus from Egypt.

> The LORD said to Moses, "How long will these people treat me with contempt? How long will they refuse to believe in me, in spite of all the miraculous signs I have performed among them?"
>
> (Numbers 14:11)

> Today, if you hear his voice, [8] do not harden your hearts as you did at Meribah, as you did that day at Massah in the desert, [9] where your fathers tested and tried me, though they had seen what I did. [10] For forty years I was angry with that generation; I said, "They are a people whose hearts go astray, and they have not known my ways." [11] So I declared on oath in my anger, "They shall never enter my rest."
>
> (Psalm 95:7-11)

Like heaven, the eternal resting place, the Promised Land was a resting place for those who believed in the One True God. James M. Boice speaks of the land as a symbol of heaven: "When God led Israel out of Egypt into the wilderness in their days of wandering He had a goal to bring them into the Promised Land. It was to be a place where they would find rest from their wanderings. It was a symbol of heaven."[81]

Consistent with Psalm ninety-five the writer to the Hebrews states that the heavenly Promised Land is entered by faith. He is quick to point out that the absence of belief was the reason the Israelites were forbidden to enter the earthly Promised Land: "And to whom did God swear that they would never enter his rest if not to those who disobeyed? So we see that they were not able to enter, because of their unbelief" (Hebrews 3:18-19).

He goes on to emphatically state that the faith which was needed to enter the Promised Land is also necessary to enter his rest: "Therefore, since the promise of entering his rest still stands, let us be careful that none of you be found to have fallen short of it. For we also had the gospel preached to us, just as they did; but the message they heard was of no value to them, because those who heard did not combine it with faith" (Hebrew 4:1-2).

Lincoln observes that the phrase, *enter that rest* (Hebrews 4:3) is to be taken as a true present and not simply viewed as having future force: "The Greek text means neither that they are certain to enter, nor that they will enter, but that they are already in the process of entering."[82]

Faith in the Provider brings the benefits of heavenly rest to believers before they reach heaven. This same writer assures his readers that the land was not the final intended rest, since Joshua, who led the people into the land, spoke "about another day" (Hebrews 4:8, Joshua 22:4).

The author skillfully weaves together the provision of rest through the Promised Land with the concept of Sabbath-rest:

ETERNAL REST REFLECTED THROUGH THE SABBATH

Ownership of land provides a partial solution to the problem of restlessness. As a property owner I may actually rest less than if I am a visitor, renter, or squatter on someone else's land. Without designated times for rest, caring, repairing, storing, and cleaning what I own becomes a restless proposition.

Owning land without knowing how to rest in the land is a recipe for fatigue. For that reason I believe God presented time as a provision for rest before presenting space as a provision for rest. God demonstrated the practice of rest before making any reference to a land of rest (Genesis 2:1-3).

Rest as time has provided greater hope of rest for the multitudes who never become land owners. Rest as time proved to be more durable and versatile than rest as space throughout Hebrew history. Abraham Heschel makes this very point regarding the Sabbath in Jewish history: "The Sabbaths are our great cathedrals; and our Holy of Holies is a shrine that neither the Romans nor the Germans were able to burn."[83]

Time has been a constant companion in the lives of nomadic peoples for centuries and modern man for decades. The businessman who has learned the value of rest can enjoy an hour while waiting for his next flight at an airport. A housewife can close the door on napping children and absorb moments of rest.

Sabbath-rest reminds us to rest in God's finished work of salvation.

In an attempt to rekindle future hope, the author of Hebrews now reaches back in history to the creation narrative and pulls out the oldest concept of rest, the Sabbath. At the completion of creation God modeled rest on the seventh day.

> For somewhere he has spoken about the seventh day in these words: "And on the seventh day God rested from all his work." [5] And again in the passage above he says, "They shall never enter my rest." [6] It still remains that some will enter that rest, and those who formerly had the gospel preached to them did not go in, because of their disobedience. [7] Therefore God again set a certain day, calling it Today, when a long time later he spoke through David, as was said before: "Today, if you hear his voice, do not harden your hearts." [8] For if Joshua had given them rest, God would not have spoken later about another day. [9] There remains, then, a Sabbath-rest for the people of God; [10] for anyone who enters God's rest also rests from his own work, just as God did from his.
>
> (Hebrews 4:4-10)

Sabbath-rest, as used in verses nine and ten, addresses the most significant aspect of rest—salvation. Sabbath-rest delivers us from the notion that we can work off the penalty of sin or work for the rewards of eternal life. Sabbath-rest reminds us to rest in God's finished work of salvation. While the greatest benefits of salvation will be enjoyed in heaven for eternity, resting in the gift of God's finished work of salvation is enjoyed by believers while they are living on earth.

The weekly practice of Sabbath-rest signifies the believer has ceased striving for salvation and has entered into God's rest. It is a reminder to the believer and a witness to the unbeliever of God's offer of salvation. The entire context of Hebrews begs us to conclude that the rest is salvation through Christ, "the author and perfecter of our faith" (Hebrew 12:2).

Heaven is, therefore, the intended place of rest suggested through the Sabbath and portrayed through the land. Lincoln observes correctly that the rest which the writer of Hebrews refers to is associated with the heavenly Promised Land:

> It seems very likely that being acquainted with such a tradition the writer of Hebrews views "rest" as an eschatological resting place with associations with the heavenly promised land, the heavenly Jerusalem, and the heavenly sanctuary. This view is confirmed by the frequency of these items in Hebrews (cf. the heavenly sanctuary 6:19-20; 8:2; 9:11, 23-24;

10:19, the city that is to come, the heavenly Jerusalem 11:10,16; 12:22; 13:14, and the heavenly promised land 11:14ff.)[84]

"There remains, then, a Sabbath-rest for the people of God" (verse nine) indicates the Sabbath is not merely a thing of the past but has future significance for those who believe. Old Testament scholar John Sailhamer suggests the writer of the Pentateuch has included the initial statement of God's rest to indicate there is a future rest for the believer:

> If, as we have earlier suggested, the author's intention was to point to the past as a picture of the future, then the emphasis on God's "rest" forms an important part of the author's understanding of what lies in the future. At important points along the way, the author will return to the theme of God's "rest" as a reminder of what yet lies ahead (Hebrews 2:15; 5:29; 8:4; 19:16; Exodus 20:11; Deuteronomy 5:14; 12:10; 25; 29). Later biblical writers continued to see a parallel between God's "rest" in creation and the future "rest" that awaits the faithful.
> (Psalm 95:11; Hebrews 3:11)[85]

Sailhamer is not alone in stating the past is a picture of the future. Commentators Keil and Delitzsh likewise note that the Sabbath has a future aspect:

> To this rest the resting of God points forward; and to this rest, this divine Sabbath (Hebrews 4:9), shall the whole world, especially man, the head of the earthly creation, eventually come...In connection with Hebrews 4, some of the fathers have called attention to the fact, that the account of the seventh day is not summed up, like the others, with the formula "evening was and morning was."[86]

The Sabbath in time and the land in space were like pieces of heaven. They were samples to keep the people of God looking forward and seeking for the Sabbath-rest of heaven. God served a portion of the week and a portion of land as appetizers to arouse a craving for the rest that does not end. His intent reaches beyond mere satisfaction of human temporal needs to communicate that there is more to be found where rest in time and rest in space came from. Ben Patterson illustrates the focus which the Sabbath specifically provides: "The Sabbath is therefore a window to the future. It points to the time when God will make sense of this mess. It tells us that there is more than just the inexorable march of time. It reminds us that there is meaning to our lives beyond the rat race."[87]

SABBATH-REST BOLSTERS LONG RANGE HOPE

Sabbath-rest provides a weekly opportunity to refresh my long-range hopes. Short-range hopes pertain to my earthly existence such as: *I hope I don't ever have cancer, a stroke, or a heart attack, at least not until I am very old. I also hope that I never have a serious car accident, or have to file for bankruptcy, nor do I want any of these hardships to happen to my children, grandchildren or friends.* Long-range hopes pertain to eternity and my relationship to God. Long-range hope makes any short-term disappointments tolerable.

I have met believers who in my mind were *so heavenly minded they are no earthly good.* However, I have met more believers who are *so earthly minded they are no heavenly good.* The former specialize in spiritual clichés, but rarely engage in projects requiring tenacity. The latter devote themselves to tasks tenaciously until they work themselves into a tizzy. They typically become agitated with those who refuse to join them in the tasks at hand. They are also prone to bury themselves in responsibilities until depressed. Yet other earthly minded people are so preoccupied with this world's goods and pleasures that heaven has no place in their leisure driven minds.

Obviously balance is needed. God wants me and you to be responsible on earth while headed for heaven (1 Thessalonians 4:11; 2 Thessalonians 3:6-8). He wants us to be heavenly minded so that we radiate with hope despite earthly troubles. He wants us to be ready to give an answer to anyone who asks us about our hope (I Peter 3:15).

While the Christian life benefits the believer in numerous ways, the eternal benefits far outweigh the earthly benefits. The Apostle Paul made this clear on a number of occasions: "I consider that our present sufferings are not worth comparing with the glory that will be revealed in us" (Romans 8:18). "If only for this life we have hope in Christ, we are to be pitied more than all men" (I Corinthians 15:19).

I feel that an emphasis on eternity is greatly needed in this age of immediate gratification. My hope is to be a long-range hope, so that I do not despair when materialism disappoints or life in this body diminishes.

Growing old is an American obsession. While impoverished countries despair over food shortages, contaminated water, and civil wars, Americans dread the aging process. This phobia starts somewhere around age thirty. Most athletes recognize that they have physically passed their prime and must resort to experience, intelligence, and hard work if they are going to compete with emerging young athletes.

Graying hair, hair loss, wrinkles, muscle loss, slowing of body and mind begin by age forty. Unless extra measures that tone up or cover up are applied, aging is obvious by age fifty. Slowing the aging process through diets, workout routines, various applications to hair and skin employ many people. Retarding the aging process is big business. Try as we may to overcome aging, it is a losing battle. Eventually time wins over the best of efforts and products. The best that friends and physicians can tell us is that we are well preserved for our age. For the next thirty years a no-win battle is fought and lost. Premature death is the alternative.

When I finally admitted that it was a losing battle, I could laugh about the aging process. Some of the funniest jokes are about growing old. For instance I just received the following in an email:

GREAT TRUTHS ABOUT GROWING OLD

- Forget the health food; I need all the preservatives I can get.
- When you fall down, you wonder what else you can do while you're down there.
- You're getting old when you get the same sensation from a rocking chair that you once got from a roller coaster.
- Time may be a great healer, but it's a lousy beautician.
- Wisdom comes with age, but sometimes age comes alone.

Sabbath-rest allows me to live light and laugh much.

Better to laugh than cry. Laughter about old age can be an attempt to deny old age. It can also be a response of hope. People of hope don't need to deny anything. They can age with honor! The Psalmist declares the righteous as fruitful in old age:

> The righteous will flourish like a palm tree, they will grow like a cedar of Lebanon; planted in the house of the LORD, they will flourish in the courts of our God. They will still bear fruit in old age, they will stay fresh

and green, proclaiming, "The LORD is upright; he is my Rock, and there is no wickedness in him."

(Psalm 92:12-15)

The Apostle Paul spoke of the changing of the garb, "When the perishable has been clothed with the imperishable, and the mortal with immortality" (I Corinthians 15:54). Believers have a much greater hope than the reversal of the aging process or returning to youth. The bodies of those who are in Christ will be changed into imperishable immortal bodies, ageless bodies, never to age again. That is what I ought to think about as I face new limitation with the passing of time. As I think about the immortal man I am able to laugh and even mock my fading flesh. Paul goes on to actually mock death:

> For the perishable must clothe itself with the imperishable, and the mortal with immortality. Then the saying that is written will come true: "Death has been swallowed up in victory." [55] "Where, O death, is your victory? Where, O death, is your sting?" [56] The sting of death is sin, and the power of sin is the law. [57] But thanks be to God! He gives us the victory through our Lord Jesus Christ.
>
> (I Corinthians 15:53-55)

I believe God plants some believers in our midst who have a profound hunger for heaven. Every day they entertain thoughts of heaven and crave the fruition of their faith. Most of these people have experienced losses that generate their passion for heaven. Some have lost loved ones. My perception is the death of children creates the most acute awareness of heaven. Pastor Erwin Lutzer of Moody Church in Chicago cites an illustration from James Vernon McGee that has helped me understand God's purpose in permitting the death of small children:

> ...when a shepherd seeks to lead his sheep to better grass up the winding, thorny mountain paths, he often finds that the sheep will not follow him. They fear the unknown ridges and the steep rocks. The shepherd will then reach into the flock and take a little lamb on one arm and another on his other arm. Then he starts up the precipitous pathway. Soon the two mother sheep begin to follow, and afterward the entire flock. Thus they ascend the tortuous path to greener pastures.
>
> So it is with the Good Shepherd. Sometimes He reaches into the flock and takes a lamb to Himself. He uses the experience to lead His people,

to lift them to new heights of commitment as they follow the little lamb all the way home.[88]

Faithful Christians who live with severe handicaps serve as God's instruments of future hope. While they may be physically challenged, they encourage us to look beyond earthly delights and develop an appetite for heaven. Since her diving accident in 1967, which left her paralyzed from the shoulders down, Joni Eareckson Tada, has challenged millions with her hunger for heaven:

> I have a glorious homesickness for heaven, a penetrating and piercing ache. I'm a stranger in a strange land. A displaced person with a fervent and passionate pain that is, oh, so satisfying. The groans are a blessing. What a sweetness to feel homesick for heaven for, "a longing fulfilled is sweet to the soul" (Proverbs 13:19).

> Father, I miss you. I miss a closeness to you that is tangible. I long for the righteousness of heaven. Focus my eyes of faith. Bring heaven forward into a vivid reality in my heart and mind that will spur me on to righteous living now.[89]

I have found that a weekly Sabbath-rest is one of the best remedies for a provisional existence. Before I started the practice I despaired in the midst of what I perceived to be one hopeless situation after another. I found myself living from one Sunday sermon to the next, one board meeting to the next, and one pastoral visit to the next. As my eternal perspective diminished, I felt like life was being drained from me.

Today Sabbath-rest provides a means to go to God with my situations. Sabbath-rest opens the windows of future hope. This rest allows me to live light and laugh much. Resting in God's completed salvation and continual care feeds a robust hope! "And hope does not disappoint us, because God has poured out his love into our hearts by the Holy Spirit, whom he has given us" (Romans 5:5).

Prayer

Dear Lord, I enter a weekly Sabbath-rest as a reminder of the eternal rest you have purchased for me and all who rest in your work of eternal salvation. In Jesus' name and for his sake I pray, Amen.

Questions to Ponder

1. Have I been living a provisional existence? If so, how?
2. Has owning property been a hassle or a restful experience?
3. What is my favorite Scripture verse pertaining to heaven?
4. When was the last time I seriously thought about heaven?
5. When will I contemplate heaven next?

Appendix B has been provided as an exercise for looking forward.

Part III

PLEASING GOD, AT REST AT WORK AND LIFE

HOW CAN I REST WHILE ENGAGED IN WORK AND LIFE?

When I speak of *rest at work*, by no means do I suggest that we sack-out, slough-off, or catch-up on much needed sleep while on the job. By rest at work I mean being at ease on the job because we have discovered the combination which unlocks rest for our lives.

Sabbath keeping is a means of establishing a restful center around which all of the demands of life revolve. If I cannot be a restful person apart from the stresses of the job, it is highly unlikely that I will be at rest on the job. These final five chapters address topics related to life and work. They suggest answers to the basic question, *how can I be at rest while engaged in work and the responsibilities of life?*

Chapter eleven recommends that we all live and work lighter by coming to Jesus and learning from him. Chapter twelve encourages us to be as intentional about our private times with God as we are with our public times on the job and life in general. Chapter thirteen provides a guide to satisfaction, security, and success beyond what any job can provide. Chapter fourteen addresses our need to forgive as forgiven. Unforgiveness creates restlessness in the workplace and beyond. Chapter fifteen, the finale, identifies the essential role rest plays in spiritual revival, something needed at every workplace and in every community.

May God be pleased as we learn the art being at rest at work and life.

CHAPTER ELEVEN

TAKING A LOAD OFF
AS GOD INTENDS

Come to me, all you who are weary and burdened, and I will give you rest. Take my yoke upon you and learn from me, for I am gentle and humble in heart, and you will find rest for your souls. For my yoke is easy and my burden is light.

(Matthew 11:28-30)

Come to me. Get away with me and you'll recover your life. I'll show you how to take a real rest. Walk with me and work with me—watch how I do it. Learn the unforced rhythms of grace. I won't lay anything heavy or ill-fitting on you. Keep company with me and you'll learn to live freely and lightly.

(Matthew 11:28-30, *The Message*)

Self-realization leads to the enthronement of work; whereas the saint enthrones Jesus Christ in his work.[90]

(Oswald Chambers)

I once read of a pastor in the Philippians who was on his way to the market. He noticed an elderly man carrying an enormous load on his back, so he stopped and asked the man if he wanted to ride in his wagon. With a grin the old man accepted the offer. After driving a few minutes the pastor looked to see how his passenger was doing. To his surprise the man was riding but had not removed his load from his back.

I am afraid that is a picture of many Christians. While they are on their way to heaven, they are not experiencing the full relief of rest. They are in the wagon for the ride but are still under their burdens. Most believers have not taken a load off as God intends.

Since receiving Christ as my Savior I have consistently trusted his offer of rest for eternal life. I understood at an early age that I could not earn salvation and I certainly did not deserve it. However, when it came to my lifestyle I labored like rest was a forbidden fruit. My belief system contended with the rhythm of rest and work Jesus offers. I had a long way to go before living like Jesus' offer was for me during my days on earth.

While I memorized Matthew 11:28-30 at a young age, quoted it often, and hung it on the wall, I did not live like it was part of my belief system. While Jesus said, "Come to me and I will give you rest" my belief system whispered something else: *Come to Jesus and he'll give you work, a job, a broken heart, church conflict, disappointment, and burnout.*

I now have opportunity to come alongside of fellow pastors and church leaders and have observed that their belief systems are similar to mine. Their lives are out of step with Jesus' rhythm of rest and work. Many have come to the Sabbath retreats that Lois and I facilitate, wondering how they can synchronize life with Jesus' offer of rest. I believe the answer resides in Jesus' invitation to come to Him: "Come to me, all you who are weary and burdened, and I will give you rest. Take my yoke upon you and learn from me, for I am gentle and humble in heart, and you will find rest for your souls. For my yoke is easy and my burden is light" (Matthew 11:28-30).

"Taking a Load Off" as God Intends Requires that I Accept Christ's Offer of Rest from Work.

Rest from My Work

For the first ten years of weekly Sabbaths I learned how to rest from work. This required a lot of unlearning. I had to accept that it was all right to rest. "Come to me, all you who are weary and burdened, and I will give you rest," took years to unpack.

Recognizing My Condition

The first thing I had to do in coming to Jesus was recognize my condition. He summons all *who are weary and burdened.* That was me and occasionally I am still that way. The difference is, I respond more quickly to the word *come*.

Sometimes I am weary because of physical exertion or simply working too many hours for too many days in a row. While physical exertion and long days make me weary, emotional weariness taxes my energy more severely. Life and death issues, extensive conflict, increased discouragement—all stretch the emotions. Once emotional weariness becomes impacted, it becomes extremely difficult to extract.

Likewise burdens are both physical and emotional. To carry a heavy load is physically very strenuous. I know of a young man named Dan who is headed for Iraq. A heavy duty machinegun nicknamed *The Saw* has been assigned to him. In addition to the weight of the machinegun, he is equipped with approximately sixty pounds of gear including a thirty-five pound armored vest. That adds up to one serious physical burden. Of greater concern are the emotional burdens he bears. Dan has left behind a lovely wife and three precious children. Two years ago he purchased an insurance business. Now he is not home to work his business. If his employees don't work hard and make wise decisions, he may come home to a bankrupt business. Given where he is going, Dan cannot afford to be distracted by either physical or emotional burdens. I praise God that Dan is aware of his vulnerability and knows how to come to Jesus with his numerous burdens. He takes Jesus' offer of rest seriously.

Legalistic religious observances, such as those imposed by the religious leaders of Jesus' day, also qualify as burdens. Jesus' words offer splendid relief compared to the burdensome demands imposed on the masses by the religious régime of his time. Jesus exposed their game plan as scandalous: "Jesus replied, 'You experts in the law, woe to you, because you load people down with burdens they can hardly carry, and you yourselves will not lift one finger to help them'" (Luke 11:46). Then Jesus offered the divine plan of salvation, which begins by simply coming to him as we are. When it comes to salvation from our sins and the wrath of God toward sins, Jesus came to take the load off of us. The load is our sins and the very notion that we can dig our way out of our sinful nature. We must give up the burden of earning our salvation. If we could earn salvation from our sins, the death of Christ would be unnecessary. Jesus bore a load that we could not bear.

RECOGNIZING MY NEED FOR RECOVERY

I cannot think of a more powerful statement on rest than the Savior of the world saying, "Come to me, all you who are weary and burdened, and I will give you rest." However, I must do more than recognize my weary and burdened condition. That's the diagnosis. Coming to Jesus necessitates that I recognize my need for recovery. That's change. I think Eugene Peterson has captured the essence of Jesus' offer in *The Message*: "Get away with me and you'll recover your life."

Most people preempt the recovery process by hiding behind their talents. I work with pastors who are in recovery from various forms of personal and ministry failure. The more talented the minister the less he is likely to stay with the recovery process. Recovery requires the hard work of humility.

Recovery takes time. After growing up in Egypt for forty years Moses spent another forty years in the wilderness. Perhaps it took that long to recover from the Egyptian culture ingrained in him. The Apostle Paul drove himself to be among the most religious of the Pharisees. After his conversion he lived in seclusion for most of the next fourteen years. Perhaps it took him that long to take the Pharisee out of him. I praise God that Jesus did not just call us to a diagnosis, he said, *come and I will bring you through a recovery.*

WELCOMING JESUS AS MY TRAINER

Jesus does better than prescribe a recovery program for us. He goes through it with us as our trainer. Millions of people spend hundreds and even thousands of dollars annually on exercise equipment. The problem with exercise equipment at home is that it seldom gets used. Sooner or later most who are serious about fitness join a fitness club. Those who are really committed to fitness hire a personal trainer to count repetitions and see that the right exercises are done correctly. The trainer cheers the client into doing more reps than would be done without the trainer. If I am going to make progress in recovery, I need to recognize my need for a trainer. Jesus is that trainer.

Coming to Jesus necessitates that I welcome him as my trainer. I need to learn how to rest by observing the Master. *The Message* translation of the Bible by Eugene Peterson brings home this emphasis: "I'll show you how to take a real rest. Walk with me and work with me—watch how I do it. Learn the unforced rhythms of grace." I best learn how to rest from my work by reading and rereading the gospels. As Corrie ten Boom often said:

> Look around and be distressed.
> Look inside and be depressed.
> Look at Jesus and be at rest.[91]

Jesus doesn't just show us the equipment we need for recovery; he works out with us encouraging us all the way. I have asked myself, *why should Jesus care if I recover from the weariness and burdens I have loaded on myself by my own sin and restless reactions? I have gotten so out of shape I must be repulsive to him.* Grace does not stop with salvation; Christ salvages all that is worth recovering. Furthermore, my recovery is free to me. That's grace. The only thing we have to do is come.

There is no recovery without accepting Christ's invitation to come. It should be the easiest thing to do; yet I have to ask myself, *why is it so difficult to come to Jesus? Why do I insist on untangling the snares I have fallen into? Why is coming to Jesus the thing I consider last after trying everything else?*

Nearly a century ago Oswald Chambers answered my questions. In order to come to Jesus I have to give up denial. When I come to Jesus I must no longer deny that I am weary and burdened. I must no longer ignore my need for recovery. I must no longer refuse the trainer who guides me into rest. Coming to Jesus means I have to be real. Chambers said, "If you want to know how real you are, test yourself by these words—'Come unto Me.' In every degree in which you are not real, you will dispute rather than come, you will quibble rather than come the last lap of unutterable foolishness—'Just as I am.'"[92]

God intends for you to unload your work completely on a regular basis. He intends for you to rest burden-free. No more riding on the wagon with your load still on your back and calling it rest. God wants you to learn how to unload.

Humility is a prerequisite to taking off the load as God intends. Once again Corrie ten Boom comes through with a word picture that tells us exactly what we need to do to unload: "As a camel kneels before his master to have him remove his burden at the end of the day, so kneel each night and let the Master take your burden."[93]

The Lord, our trainer and Master, will not use a stepladder to remove our burdens. He will wait until we humble ourselves into a kneeling position. If we cannot humble ourselves in private before our Master so we can rest from our work, it is highly improbable that we will ever learn to rest at work before our superiors and peers.

"TAKING A LOAD OFF" AS GOD INTENDS REQUIRES THAT I ACCEPT CHRIST'S OFFER OF REST AT MY WORK

"Take my yoke upon you and learn from me, for I am gentle and humble at heart, and you will find rest for your souls. For my yoke is easy and my burden is light" (Matthew 11:30).

After spending approximately ten years learning how to rest from work, I invested another ten years learning how to rest at my work. It was all about taking the theology of rest from the resting place to the workplace. Phrase by phrase Jesus shows the way. The place to begin is with his yoke.

A yoke is an ancient device universally used by all cultures that use work animals. As a work device a yoke makes labor easier for a team of horses or oxen. In fact it is the tool that turns a pair of animals into a team. With the yoke the load is distributed more evenly.

The yoke facilitates training as a more experienced work animal is joined or yoked with an inexperienced animal. The younger beast lunges forward at the start of the day fighting against the resistance of the weighty load. By the end of the day he moves only at the crack of the whip. The young horse's gait changes as he works beside the experienced horse that pulls with a steady stream of energy throughout the day. In time teamwork becomes companionship.

Jesus makes reference to a yoke as an invitation to join him in a working relationship. From that day forward our work changes.

In the past I worked alone without being yoked to a mature team worker. After accepting Jesus' invitation, I had someone with whom to share the burden evenly. He taught me how to avoid getting lathered up over *small stuff*. In time I learned that it is all *small stuff*. What began as teamwork became a companionship that will outlast the very ancient ground we plow together. Once again Peterson has caught the essence of this working companionship in *The Message*: "Walk with me and work with me—watch how I do it. Learn the unforced rhythms of grace. I won't lay anything heavy or ill-fitting on you. Keep company with me and you'll learn to live freely and lightly."

Resting at Work Requires that I Change Masters

Having identified the yoke as an instrument of work, I must now determine who is going to be in charge. I must ask myself, *who is going to take the lead? Am I going to let someone else tell me what to do? Where to go? How to behave?*

First of all, resting at work requires that I change masters. Jesus said, "Take my yoke upon you and learn from me." He is the instructor. I am the student. That means I am no longer in charge regardless of my title or how many people report to me. I am to learn from him and work for him above anyone else. Paul expressed this sentiment: "Whatever you do, work at it with all your heart, as working for the Lord, not for men, since you know that you will receive an inheritance from the Lord as a reward. It is the Lord Christ you are serving" (Colossians 3:23, 24).

Second, resting at work requires that I change agendas. A yoke is fitted according to a prescribed work agenda. Jesus said, "For my yoke is easy and my burden is light." I must note that he said "My yoke." I am to accept the yoke of his making—not necessarily the one I would make or choose for myself. While I may favor the yoke of my choice and fear the yoke of his choice, his yoke is a right fit for me. After trying both on, I discovered the yoke of his choice was best for me.

It is a matter of trust: do I really believe that Christ—the one who made me, saved me, and called me into his service—knows what is best for me? Eugene Peterson translates:

> *Learn the unforced rhythms of grace.*
> *I won't lay anything heavy or ill-fitting on you.*

In early life I feared what God might choose for me. I figured that he would force some rhythm on me to which I could not keep step, some job that I could not do and it would be awkward and embarrassing. I thought he would burden me with something awful, like being a minister or missionary. What I did not understand was that he would change me so I would fit into that specific agenda he had designed for me.

I've now been a minister for nearly thirty years. I have served on mission boards and made numerous mission trips. The very things I once dreaded have given me great joy. Not until I fully surrendered my life to God and trusted him as good and able, did I experience the good fit of his plan for my life. His agendas are right for each of us, never ill-fitting.

In contrast the agendas we choose for ourselves or that others impose on us are usually ill-fitting. Sometimes even those who love us impose agendas that are ill-fitting. I experienced this as my business-minded father planned for each of his children to take an active role in the family business. His agenda fit my older brother very well. Today he serves as president of the companies Dad established. But business was not my forte.

Art, music, people were my interests. Dad tried to cultivate the few business genes that resided in me by bringing me to his office and to the trucking sheds when I was a child. When I was old enough to work he provided jobs in the business, but it didn't take. My mother finally whispered in Dad's ear, *I don't think Jim is interested in business.*

When Dad accepted the idea that I was headed for seminary, he was very supportive of God's agenda for my life. When I became a pastor of a local church he was always quick to introduce his son as a pastor. I thank God for an understanding Christian father and mother.

Dad was delighted when our oldest son majored in business, married a certified public accountant, and began working in the family company. Lois and I were also pleased knowing that business fit him well.

Sometimes those we serve impose agendas that are ill-fitting. I have witnessed well-meaning parishioners place agendas on ministers that are ill-fitting. Such agendas are imposed in the form of symbols. David Hansen identifies this phenomenon:

> People want symbols of God. People want their ideas of God reflected back to them. People want their ideal parental figure symbolized for them. People revere symbols; people will pay for symbols, die for symbols, kill for symbols. The greatest, most continuous pressure in the ministry is to symbolize back to people what they already believe about God. In other words, the greatest constant pressure in the ministry is to become an idol.[94]

If a minister is not secure in God's agenda, he or she may succumb to imposed symbols which vary greatly and often conflict with one another. After attempting to wear them all, he or she screams in frustration, *I cannot possibly please everyone!* Truer words were never spoken. Hansen suggests that pastors are to be parables of Jesus Christ:

> Being a parable of Jesus Christ is an exceedingly powerful pastoral role. Parables change people's minds. As a parable of Jesus, the pastor has power, because the pastor is the well-known figure juxtaposed to the

less-known figure: Jesus Christ. Through their life, pastors can radically alter the understanding of who Jesus is. A parable doesn't mirror back what is already believed, but challenges current belief, expanding and exploring what was thought to be true. Pastors who are parables of Jesus Christ change people's minds about Christ and bring the real Christ to people.[95]

Sometimes those who serve us impose ill-fitting yokes on us. Well-intentioned ministers are also guilty of placing ill-fitting yokes on their parishioners. Regimented programs are easy to adopt, but their implementation seldom fits everyone. Those for whom such programs are ill-fitting are often made to feel uncomfortable because they do not jump into the endorsed yoke. God is far more creative than ministers. Often the most creative programs are homegrown in specific local churches and communities where laymen are permitted to utilize their unique gifts as God intends.

Sometimes we place ill-fitting yokes on ourselves. Perfectionism is an example. Preaching got easier for me once I gave myself permission to make mistakes. Prior to that time I would fixate on my mistakes. If I stumbled on a word, got tongue-tied, or lost my train of thought, it would grate within me the rest of the sermon, the rest of the day, and sometimes the rest of the week. Thus I was less aware of God and the people to whom I was speaking. I was self-possessed with perfectionism. As the yoke of perfectionism rubbed me raw, figuratively speaking, I eventually gave it up allowing myself to be human. God alone is perfect! I appreciate what Alan Loy McGinnis has to say about perfectionism: "Human beings can achieve remarkable things, but in God's eyes and by God's standards we are simply not perfectible, and the sooner we can relax with that truth, the more confident we will be."[96] While we will not obtain perfection on earth, God will complete to perfection what he has begun in us through Jesus Christ (Philippians 1:6, Hebrews 11:40).

Comparisons are also examples of ill-fitting yokes. You cannot be the best you can be while comparing yourself to someone else. God didn't intend for you to be a clone of someone else. If you succeed at becoming someone else, then something very important is missing from God's plan—you!

Observing others to improve your own game plan and abilities is commendable as long as you do not try to be who they are. Young ballplayers in any sport watch their sports heroes or heroines to improve their own skills; but when they start to walk like them, chew gum like them, and spit like them, comparison has become idolatry.

Another self-imposed, ill-fitting yoke is prideful ambition. Such an ambition was present among the disciples:

> Then James and John, the sons of Zebedee, came to him. "Teacher," they said, "we want you to do for us whatever we ask." [36] "What do you want me to do for you?" he asked. [37] They replied, "Let one of us sit at your right and the other at your left in your glory." [38] "You don't know what you are asking," Jesus said. "Can you drink the cup I drink or be baptized with the baptism I am baptized with?" [39] "We can," they answered. Jesus said to them, "You will drink the cup I drink and be baptized with the baptism I am baptized with, [40] but to sit at my right or left is not for me to grant. These places belong to those for whom they have been prepared." [41] When the ten heard about this, they became indignant with James and John.
>
> (Mark 10:35-41)

Given Jesus' response, John and James had no idea what they were asking. Greatness in the Kingdom equaled great suffering; the cup Jesus referred to was the cup of God's wrath toward man's sin. Jesus alone could consume that cup and satisfy the wrath of God. The disciples would drink the benefits of Jesus' act of drinking the cup.

John and James' ambition caused great turmoil among the other disciples, probably because they had the same aspirations for themselves. The seed of distrust had sprouted and was fed by the competitive spirit within each one of them. Such desires were perfectly acceptable by the ways of the world in the first century, just as they are in the twenty-first century. This was an excellent opportunity for Jesus to compare the Kingdom of man with the Kingdom of God.

> Jesus called them together and said, "You know that those who are regarded as rulers of the Gentiles lord it over them, and their high officials exercise authority over them. [43] Not so with you. Instead, whoever wants to become great among you must be your servant, [44] and whoever wants to be first must be slave of all. [45] For even the Son of Man did not come to be served, but to serve, and to give his life as a ransom for many."
>
> (Mark 10:35-45)

Greatness does exist in the Kingdom of God, but you would not recognize it by the way God's great ones achieve it. Those who will sit on the right and left of Jesus will have worn the garb of servanthood before they are awarded royal robes.

One can achieve greatness in various realms of life by selfish ambition. Even if he or she achieves the goal in focus, the price is high. Like the disciples he or she will arouse competitive spirits in others. Competition has its good and bad side—good in that it motivates others to achieve, bad because realms of trust are strained. Students and workers are now wondering who will undercut them while stopping at nothing to get to the top. As friendships depart one becomes isolated from others. Selfish ambition becomes lonely and ill-fitting.

Arrogant ambitions also change one's relationship with God. Like John and James, one begins to beg God to assist on this journey of self-exaltation. Human success easily becomes the idol to which God himself is asked to worship. Much of what is ill-fitting is self-imposed.

Grandiose expectations for ourselves prove to be ill-fitting and make us weary. Baruch was Jeremiah's scribe. After he had recorded the words of Isaiah's prophesy on a long scroll, evil King Jehoiakim had the scroll burned. When the word of the Lord came to Baruch through Jeremiah instructing him to record the entire scroll again, Baruch complained having become weary of the task (Jeremiah 36:23). The word of the Lord came through Jeremiah saying:

> You said, "Woe to me! The LORD has added sorrow to my pain; I am worn out with groaning and find no rest." [4] The LORD said, "Say this to him: 'This is what the LORD says: I will overthrow what I have built and uproot what I have planted, throughout the land. [5] Should you then seek great things for yourself? Seek them not. For I will bring disaster on all people, declares the LORD, but wherever you go I will let you escape with your life."
>
> (Jeremiah. 45:1-5)

Like Baruch I have been caught groaning about the laborious work of God. I have had to eat my bitter words, for it was not God who made his work heavy. It was my seeking great things for myself that weighed me down. God's work is light when we go about it resting and rejoicing in his protection and provision.

As long as you have the tiniest bit of spiritual impertinence, it will always reveal itself in the fact that you are expecting God to tell you to do a big thing, and all He is telling you to do is to "come."

(Oswald Chambers)

Desiring an enviable position, important role, or big task proves to be ill-fitting as well. Can you change jobs, accept a promotion, or step into a position of greater responsibility? Yes, as long as you are consecrated to God.

Years ago a college student handed me a book by Francis Schaeffer. I have referred myself and others to *No Little People* time and again. Schaeffer expounds: "There are no little people and no big people in the true spiritual sense, only consecrated and unconsecrated people. As there are no little people in God's sight, so there are no little places."[97]

There was a time when I seriously questioned whether or not I was in the right place. The inner turmoil was resolved after I took a quote from the book, had a plaque made, and hung it on the wall above my desk.

To be wholly committed to God in the place where God wants him—this is the creature glorified.

(*Francis A. Schaeffer*)

Frances Schaeffer advocated that a person not seek promotion in the workplace but be *extruded* by the influence of others and circumstances God provides:

> Jesus commands Christians to seek consciously the lowest room. All of us—pastors, teachers, professional religious workers and nonprofessional included—are tempted to say, "I will take the larger place because it will give me more influence for Jesus Christ." Both individual Christians and Christian organizations fall prey to the temptation of rationalizing this way as we build bigger and bigger empires. But according to the Scripture this is backwards: we should consciously take the lowest place unless the Lord Himself extrudes us into a great one.

> The word extrude is important here. To be extruded is to be forced out under pressure into a desired shape. Picture a huge press jamming soft metal at high pressure through a die, so that the metal comes out in a certain shape. This is the way of the Christian: he should choose the lesser place until God extrudes him into a position of more responsibility and authority.

> Let me suggest two reasons why we ought not grasp the larger place. First, we should seek the lowest place because there it is easier to be quiet before the face of the Lord....

The second reason why we should not seek the larger place is that if we deliberately and egotistically lay hold on leadership, wanting the drums to beat and the trumpets to blow, then we are not qualified for Christian leadership.[98]

Matt Hasselbeck made it to the Super Bowl in 2006 as the quarterback of the Seattle Seahawks. He played well enough to be the MVP of the game, had the Seahawks won. The day after the Super Bowl I was with a group of pastors and one of them shared that Matt was in his youth group several years ago. He followed Matt's progress through college and into the pros. As a backup quarterback it was assumed that Matt would be in the face of the coaches showing off his abilities in the hope that they would conclude he was better than the starter. In fact he was until he learned a better way. After an interview with Matt, Associated Press Sports Writer Gregg Bell reported:

> Even the teams that know Hasselbeck don't know how he got here.... They don't know how Hasselbeck went from a sixth-round draft choice in 1998 to a self-described arrogant know-it-all in 2001. Then, from Seattle fill-in in 2002 to quiet excellence in 2005.
>
> He's the NFC's leading passer and will start the Pro Bowl. He has 24 touchdown passes, only nine interceptions and a career-high 66 percent completion rate. And the top-seeded Seahawks are a franchise-best 13-3.
>
> "It's very easy for me—I'm not a good listener—to say, 'Yeah, yeah. I got it.' But you don't really got it," is how Hasselbeck explained his first seasons with Seattle coach Mike Holmgren.
>
> "Some of it is arrogance ... (then) I did a better job of being a little more humble and really being more coachable."[99]

Once Matt figured out that arrogance was getting him nowhere, he began to improve and so did his team. The rest is history. One might say that Matt was extruded into the Super Bowl.

I have observed employees in more conventional occupations receive promotions repeatedly as they concentrated on doing their best work for their employer and peers. These employees developed trust with a servant attitude instead of suspicion with self-serving ambitions. Known for their hard work and lack of contentious relationships, they make excellent team workers cooperating with both their superiors and peers. Success catches them without their pursuing it.

Third, resting at work requires that I change values. Values such as gentleness and humility are close to his heart. "...for I am gentle and humble at heart." Jesus' heart reflects who he is. There is no discrepancy between what he values and his heart. They are one and the same.

Our Master invites us to look into his heart and value what he values. A look into our Master's heart indicates that he is gentle. Gentleness is not to be considered a weakness. Gentleness is strength under control. A tame horse is not to be considered weak because it is under control. In fact the well-fed and cared-for tame horse is apt to be stronger than the wild horse. The compliant animal is obviously more useful to its master. The horse or ox which accepts its master's control and purpose sweats less and rests more than the one which resists its master's control. The resistant work animal is a waste of strength. Christ does not call us to be a waste of strength. He was completely under his Father's control. He invites us to accept not only his yoke but his heart. Gentleness is a heart value of Christ.

Another look into my Master's heart reveals that he is humble. Humility is not measured by my opinion of myself; rather it is a matter of God's opinion of me and my willingness to accept what God says about me.

If I am going to accept Christ's heart values, I want to know what gentleness and humility look like lest I deceive myself into thinking I am gentle and humble when I am not. Note the following contrasts between pride and humility supported by Scripture.

Pride measures itself by sacrifices made for God. Humility desires to be with God.

> With what shall I come before the LORD and bow down before the exalted God? Shall I come before him with burnt offerings, with calves a year old? [7] Will the LORD be pleased with thousands of rams, with ten thousand rivers of oil? Shall I offer my firstborn for my transgression, the fruit of my body for the sin of my soul? [8] He has showed you, O man, what is good. And what does the LORD require of you? To act justly and to love mercy and to walk humbly with your God.
>
> (Micah 6:6-8)

Pride tends to rejoice in sensation. Humility rejoices in essentials.

> Then the seventy returned with joy, saying, "Lord, even the demons are subject to us in Your name." [18] And He said to them, "I saw Satan fall like lightning from heaven. [19] "Behold, I give you the authority to trample on serpents and scorpions, and over all the power of the enemy, and nothing

shall by any means hurt you. [20] "Nevertheless do not rejoice in this, that the spirits are subject to you, but rather rejoice because your names are written in heaven."

(Luke 11:17-20)

Pride rejects instruction. Humility accepts learning opportunities.

I will instruct you and teach you in the way you should go; I will counsel you and watch over you. [9] Do not be like the horse or the mule, which have no understanding but must be controlled by bit and bridle or they will not come to you. [10] Many are the woes of the wicked, but the LORD's unfailing love surrounds the man who trusts in him. [11] Rejoice in the LORD and be glad, you righteous; sing, all you who are upright in heart!

(Psalm 32:8-11)

Opportunistic pride looks for promotions that exalt self. Humility recognizes that God exalts (Psalm 75:6-7). In the *Search for the Excellent Leader* video series, Howard Hendricks was asked a question from a student, "How do you manage to stay humble after so many years of being in demand as professor, speaker and author?"

After the chuckles faded Hendricks replied, "Every once in a while in west Texas you might find a turtle on top of a fence post. In which case, you know that it didn't get there on its own."[100]

Everyone got the message; being humble recognizes that you got a lift from someone whose abilities are far beyond your own.

Peter instructs believers of all ages to humble themselves: "Young men, in the same way be submissive to those who are older. All of you, clothe yourselves with humility toward one another, because, 'God opposes the proud but gives grace to the humble.' Humble yourselves, therefore, under God's mighty hand, that he may lift you up in due time" (I Peter 5:5-6).

It is a universal truth that God resists the proud. There is nothing we have that we have not received from our Maker. Humility belongs in our department. Promotion belongs in God's department. We are to embrace humility and serve. God is far better equipped to exalt any of us. The yoke of self-exaltation may feel good for a while, but wears heavy before long.

Not even the perfect all-powerful Son of God took on the yoke of self-exaltation. His job was to serve. The Father's job was to exalt him. Paul says He is our model.

Each of you should look not only to your own interests, but also to the interests of others. [5] Your attitude should be the same as that of Christ Jesus: [6] Who, being in very nature God, did not consider equality with God something to be grasped, [7] but made himself nothing, taking the very nature of a servant, being made in human likeness. [8] And being found in appearance as a man, he humbled himself and became obedient to death–even death on a cross!" Therefore God exalted him to the highest place and gave him the name that is above every name, [10] that at the name of Jesus every knee should bow, in heaven and on earth and under the earth, [11] and every tongue confess that Jesus Christ is Lord, to the glory of God the Father.

(Philippians 2:4-8)

Jesus came from heavenly fellowship with the Father to serve the lowest human being who ever lived by dying for the sins of the world. No man will ever humble himself to the extent that Jesus humbled himself. Servant was his title. Dying was his calling. No man will ever be exalted from such depths to such heights. That was the Father's job. Jesus has lived in the lowest valleys and the highest peaks. Jesus took care of the valleys and the Father took him to the peaks.

Humility is the indispensable virtue. Humility is the yoke under which we can rest at work. That is the yoke Jesus invites us to take. That is the restful yoke we are to put on and never take off at work, home, or away. It is the yoke of humility that is the light yoke. Humility is God's well-fitting agenda. If we will take care of business in the valleys where we live and work, God will take us to the peaks. If we attempt to switch roles with God, our yoke will prove to be most ill-fitting.

Jesus invites us to lighten up! Take a load off and let God do the lifting. That is the yoke that allows you to take a load off and live light. That is the agenda that grants you rest while working. "For my yoke is easy and my burden is light" (Matthew 11:30).

There exists another key to living light and laughing much. We must narrow our focus without narrowing our minds. The only way we can do that is by focusing on that which is bigger than all outdoors. Os Guinness has defined this focus as living for the Audience of One:

A life lived listening to the decisive call of God is a life lived before one audience that trumps all others—The Audience of One....

That is why Christ-centered heroism does not need to be noticed or publicized. The greatest deeds are done before the Audience of One, and that is enough. Those who are seen and sung by the Audience of One can afford to be careless about lesser audiences.[101]

Living for the Audience of One has been my quest since age eighteen. In all honesty it has been a descending journey that has felt like an uphill battle. One by one I have had to unload audiences. Parents, peers, professors, and parishioners are no longer subjects before whom I perform. The process of shedding audiences has intensified with the transitions of life.

> *The saint who is intimate with Jesus will never leave impressions of himself, but only the impression that Jesus is having unhindered way, because the last abyss of his nature has been satisfied by Jesus. The only impression left by such a life is that of the strong calm sanity that Our Lord gives to those who are intimate with Him.*
>
> *(Oswald Chambers)*

When I accepted the positions in which I now serve as a resource to pastor and chaplain of a family business, I had to resign my position as a senior pastor. After serving as a pastor for twenty-five years, I no longer was surrounded by a congregation. My office went back into our home as it was after seminary when I started out as a church planting pastor. I become Jim to most people, as few would call me pastor. There would be no weddings, baptisms, or child dedications to conduct. Seldom would I preach on a Sunday morning. Being a pastor without a church can be a rather naked and chilling experience. The most instructive Scripture during this transition to which I believe the Lord directed me was Genesis 5:24: "Enoch walked with God; then he was no more, because God took him away. "I soaked in this verse for about three months.

Enoch had no church, no nation to lead. Enoch wrote no books of the Bible. He was not a prophet, priest or king. He possessed one role and identity. Enoch walked with God. I heard the still small voice of God whisper, "Jim, would it be enough for you to walk with me the rest of your life?" The longer I deliberated the more I realized that it was an insult for God

Almighty to have to ask the question. I wondered *why wouldn't I jump at the opportunity to walk with God as my single focus letting every other ambition or opportunity slither away? Yes, Lord, that is more than I could ask or think of doing.*

I now live lighter and laugh more often in my new servant roles. I still work long hours. In fact I feel like a minnow in an ocean of human need at both jobs. More than ever I am able to rest from work and at work.

Prayer:

Dear Lord Jesus, you rested with me when I was restless with self-interest until I found my rest in you. You have walked with me when I was burdened with selfish ambition and collapsed under the weight of my own ill-fitting yoke. Now I walk with you much lighter. Under your yoke it is much easier to keep step with you. In Jesus name and for his sake I pray, Amen.

Questions to Ponder

1. What comes to mind when I hear the words "Come to Jesus" (work, surrender, rest, etc.)?
2. How am I like or unlike the man who got on the wagon and did not remove the pack from his back?
3. Have I made my workload heavier than necessary with pride, perfectionism, etc.?
4. What have I gleaned from this chapter that would help me rest at work?

CHAPTER TWELVE

COMMUTING
BETWEEN TWO POLES,
PRIVATE LIFE AND PUBLIC LIFE

Then, because so many people were coming and going that they did not even have a chance to eat, he said to them, "Come with me by yourselves to a quiet place and get some rest."

(Mark 6:31)

When we are able to recognize the poles between which we move and develop sensitivity for this inner field of tension, then we no longer have to feel lost and can begin to discern the direction in which we want to move.[102]

(Henri Nouwen)

Millions of Americans commute to and from work every day regardless of increasing distances and rising fuel prices. By commuting one can receive the benefits of a better paying job in the city and go home to some semblance of small town living. On the way, work progress and productivity consume the commuter's agenda. On the commute home the rewards of rest and relaxation await him or her.

There are three scenarios that commuters hope to avoid. Most try to dodge work projects that hold them captive at the end of the day. If long days go on for weeks at a time, the commuter begins to wonder if it pays to commute. In such situations he or she misses supper, time with his or her spouse, tucking children in bed, and necessary rest. Such workers may elect to get a hotel downtown or sleep on the couch at the office. Regrettably he or she is stuck at the work end of the commute.

The second scenario finds the worker stuck at the home end of the commute. At first this may appear to be ideal. Catching up on home improvement projects, extra time with spouse and children may seem like utopia. However, if one hasn't elected to be at home, being at the home end of the commute for a prolonged period of time usually means something has gone wrong. The worker may be laid off, unemployed, fired, or seriously ill.

In chapter seven I referred to a time when I was desperately ill with hepatitis. There were weeks when it looked doubtful that I was going to recover. While my commute at the time was a walk from the second floor bedroom to a walkout basement office, I was too ill to make the commute and the office desk collected dust. Unlike the temporary relief of canceling appointments for a few days because of the flu, these were dreaded days of bewilderment. I found myself begging God for a recovery so I could return to serving as a pastor.

I have watched a number of men endure prolonged periods of unemployment. I enjoyed a wonderful friendship with a hardworking Christian neighbor for thirteen years. Twice during those years I watched him agonize through prolonged unemployment. As I drove off to work, he stayed home making phone calls and sending emails hoping that one of them would lead to a new suitable job. Being stuck at home under such circumstances is devastating, especially for men. I've found that men wear their jobs like women wear their homes. Unemployment for most men is a naked embarrassment.

The third situation the commuter tries to avoid is being stuck between work and home. One dreads being late for work because of a traffic jam, bad weather, mechanical failure, accident, illness, or crime. It is just as frustrating to be sitting on the shoulder of the road, stalled, during the drive home, especially when loved ones eagerly await your arrival and you are ready to relax for the evening or weekend. Being stuck at one end or in the middle of a commute is exasperating.

THE COMMUTE TO AND FROM SABBATH-REST

Sabbath-rest works much the same as commuting to work and from work. In both situations the commuter is intentional about rest and work. Both require direction and movement, the main difference is that Sabbath-rest is more of a state of mind than a destination.

> *It is my conviction that the most effective servants of God are able to travel freely and often between two equally profound poles of truth—rest and responsibility.*

Physicist Neils Bohr has said, "The opposite of a true statement is a false statement, but the opposite of a profound truth can be another profound truth."[103] Throughout these chapters I have attempted to point out that Sabbath-rest is a profound truth originating from God. The same God presented another profound truth, an active life of responsibility. Rest must always be viewed in the context of responsibility. It is my conviction that the most effective servants of God are able to travel freely and often between two equally profound poles of truth—rest and responsibility. They refuse to abuse prolonged periods of rest by using them as an escape from responsible activity, nor do they bury themselves in perpetual activity as an escape from reality. Parker J. Palmer asserts in his book, *The Active Life,* that both contemplation and action should open our minds to reality, not illusion.

No action will have lasting effects if it is inconsistent with reality. Ultimately, action will help to reveal what the reality is, if we pay attention to its outcomes. These are the crucial links between action and contemplation, for the function of contemplation in all its forms is to penetrate illusion and help us to touch reality.[104]

It is an unfortunate reality that most people are stuck at either pole or are stalled somewhere between contemplation and activity. Palmer asserts that, "A tug-of-war between active and contemplative life has gone on for a long time in the Western world."[105]

People caught in the gap between monastic values and the demands of active life sometimes simply abandon the spiritual quest. And people who follow a spirituality that does not always respect the energies of actions are sometimes led into passivity and withdrawal, into a diminishment of their own spirits.[106]

> ### Commuting Between Two Poles
>
> *Private Life* _____ *Public Life*

Commuting between two poles—private life and public life—requires that one not abuse either rest or activity. In her book, *Between Walden and the Whirlwind,* Jean Fleming presents a well-balanced statement on the subject of solitude and service:

> In Christianity, service and solitude are inseparable. God's kingdom is best advanced when they are joined—each stimulating the other to new depths. Walden becomes a stagnant pond without the outflow of service. And serving apart from still moments listening to and drawing strength from God produces a destructive, continual whirlwind. Although service and solitude may be thought of as separate poles in the Christian experience, they are the aggregate of God's intention. Like solitude, service is essential to spiritual health."[107]

REST ABUSE

There is a danger in building a strong argument for any single truth; followers may become eccentrics whose lives are badly out of balance. In my attempt to break out of the workaholic trap in a performance-oriented world, I fear that some readers may abuse rest. For several years I have pondered the question, *what are the signs of rest abuse?* When rest moves from retreat to escape, it ceases to be totally constructive. A retreat is always entered with an awareness that one must return to an active life of responsibility. Escape is the voice of false hope which whispers, *just bail out of the active life and all of its demands.*

Contemplation, prayer, and rest must never become an escape from reality, relationships, or responsibilities. In contrast to ancient eastern religions or the modern New Age movement, no aspect of true Christianity is an escape from reality. The disciplines of the true spiritual life are tools which enable one to face the hardships of reality with new strength. Rest is for renewal, not direct flight to some Nirvana.

ACTIVITY ABUSE

While rest abuse is a problem for some people, others topple in the direction of activity abuse. Parker Palmer describes the abuses of activity:

> But the active life also carries a curse. Many of us know what it is to live lives not of action but of frenzy, to go from day to day exhausted and unfulfilled by our attempts to work, create, and care. Many of us know

the violence of active life, violence we sometimes inflict on ourselves and sometimes inflict on our world.[108]

I was first introduced to a contemporary use of the Sabbath concept by Gordon MacDonald. His description of the weary workaholic caught my attention, and the very thought of Sabbath-rest calmed me from the inside out. MacDonald illustrated the negative impact of an overactive life by depicting what some Florida residents saw one morning as they looked outside their apartment windows:

> The ground beneath the street in front of their building had literally collapsed, creating a massive depression that Floridians call a sinkhole. Tumbling into the ever-deepening pit were automobiles, pavement, sidewalks, and lawn furniture. The building itself would obviously be next to go. Sinkholes occur, scientists say, when underground streams drain away during seasons of drought, causing the ground at the surface to lose its underlying support.[109]

MacDonald goes on to say that many people experience a sinkhole syndrome because they neglect the *private world*. A frantic pace and external pressures can cause a person to feel like the outer world is caving in on him or her.

JESUS LIVED AN ACTIVE LIFE

A casual reading of Luke chapter four reveals that Jesus lived an active life. For one reason or another people lined up to see Jesus. No surprise since Jesus was the most important person to ever walk planet earth. He was the Messiah, the link between man and God, and the world depended on him. God the Father counted on him to accomplish a one-of-a-kind mission. Jesus could not afford to experience a sinkhole syndrome. No man has ever been in more demand than our Lord. More than once I have asked, *what would Jesus do in this situation or ministry opportunity?* More than once I have found out what he would do by reading the Gospels.

WE NEED OUR LORD'S PRIVATE LIFE TO CARRY OUT OUR LORD'S PUBLIC MINISTRY

This chapter is designed to bring context to our discussion of rest and balance to the work-rest rhythm of our lives. I believe balance is best achieved by observing our Lord's life.

Our Lord did more than keep the Sabbath. He embodied the Sabbath. He demonstrated the true purpose of the Sabbath by balancing rest and work. Many passages within the Gospels communicate the secret of our Lord's stamina. His private life was the key to his public ministry. We need our Lord's private life to carry out our Lord's public ministry.

On one occasion Jesus stressed the importance of utilizing opportunities to work. "As long as it is day, we must do the work of him who sent me. Night is coming, when no one can work" (John 9:4). On another he said to his disciples when the crowds were pressing them, "Come with me by yourselves to a quiet place and get some rest" (Mark 6:31). His example throughout the Gospels exhibits how to commute between two poles. One pole represents rest, retreat, contemplation, prayer and private life, while the other signifies activity, work, interaction, purpose, direction and public life.

COMMUTING BETWEEN TWO POLES
PRIVATE LIFE AND POPULARITY

As a person with a workaholic ancestry and a compulsion for accomplishment, I have gradually become aware of the daily pressures that bend me in the direction of work and the persuasions that compel me to get stuck at the work end of the commute. The first persuasion may be categorized as a desire for popularity. I must admit that I am tempted to sacrifice private life on the altar of popularity. Not that I hunted for opportunities to be on stage while people cheered. It was simply about pleasing people.

Years ago I was confronted with the realization that I wanted to be liked by people. That may sound rather benign on the surface; it was certainly healthier than wanting people to hate me. However, I tended to please people in order to avoid rejection. For me pleasing people translated into working longer and resting less in an attempt to make people like me, an endless and in many cases impossible task.

As I read the following passage I grappled with the fact that Jesus was not governed by popularity:

When the sun was setting, the people brought to Jesus all who had various kinds of sickness, and laying his hands on each one, he healed them. [41] Moreover, demons came out of many people, shouting, "You are the Son of God!" But he rebuked them and would not allow them to speak, because they knew he was the Christ. At daybreak Jesus went out to a solitary place. The people were looking for him and when they came to where he was, they tried to keep him from leaving them. [43] But he said, "I must preach the good news of the kingdom of God to the other towns also, because that is why I was sent."

(Luke 4:40-43)

The setting of the sun on the Sabbath meant the sick could now be carried to Jesus for healing. From various diseases to demonic possession Jesus healed them all. Given his effectiveness, I get the picture that they would have broken down a gate in order to see Jesus. But Jesus did not deal with them impersonally, like they were some sort of mob. He did not just wave his arm and all were healed. Instead he personally placed his hands on each one.

Personal ministry is especially exhausting. I have wondered, *would I have exhausted all my energy by milking the opportunity for all it was worth; or would I have done as Jesus did and broken loose from the crowd in order to replenish spiritual strength and seek new direction?* Jesus sought strength and direction from his Father as he "went out to a solitary place."

Solitude costs! Running off to some solitary place looks like political suicide to the person seeking popularity: *You don't run from a captive audience!* Most celebrities are careful not to turn their backs on crowds for fear of losing their hard-earned fame. Crowds of people are impatient; they are not kept waiting very long before departing in search of another sensation.

However, addiction to a public arena also costs! Eugene Peterson exposes the deception of crowd pleasing:

> Any part of our lives that is turned over to the crowd makes it and us worse. The larger the crowd, the smaller our lives. Pliny the Elder once said that the Romans, when they couldn't make a building beautiful, made it big. The practice continues to be popular: If we can't do it well, we make it larger. We add dollars to our income, rooms to our houses, activities to our schedules, appointments to our calendars. And the quality of life diminishes with each addition.
>
> On the other hand, every time that we retrieve a part of our life from the crowd and respond to God's call to us, we are that much more ourselves, more human. Every time we reject the habits of the crowd and practice the disciplines of faith, we become a little more alive.[110]

Our Lord lived above any urge to be popular. Personal glory was among the many privileges he left in heaven when he came to earth. Philippians two indicates the issue of earthly popularity was settled long before his coming as "He emptied Himself "(Philippians 2:7, NASB), and "made himself of no reputation" (Philippians 2:7, KJV). Popularity is an issue that I must settle deep within the attitudes and appetites of my heart. Paul exhorts, "Your attitude should be the same as that of Christ Jesus" (Philippians 2:4).

I must also deal with the desire to help every person and reconcile with the disappointment of not being able to help everyone. Our Lord lived above the desire to complete everything in his earthly ministry. Upon emptying himself to become man, as a man he became limited in time and space. This meant that there were times when he had to choose between people and prayer. He had to give up the dream of healing every person during his earthly ministry. The Gospels do not indicate that Jesus met every human need in even one city. Jesus would not attempt to heal every blind man, but enough so the public got the message that *Jesus cares!*

While Luke chapter four does not specifically state what Jesus did in solitude, chapter five gives us a pretty good idea: "But Jesus often withdrew to lonely places and prayed" (Luke 5:16).

Jesus taught his disciples to pray in private, "But when you pray, go into your room, close the door and pray to your Father, who is unseen. Then your Father, who sees what is done in secret, will reward you" (Matthew 6:6). His practice of prayer taught them, "as God is unseen, you must be unseen if you wish to find Him."[111] In his book, *A Center of Quiet*, David Runcorn has helped me appreciate the value of praying in solitude. He equates private prayer to punctuation. Just as commas and periods give meaning and flow to writing, solitude and prayer give direction to my life:

> Punctuation is a helpful way of thinking about Jesus' relationship with silence and solitude. Jesus punctuated his life with silence and solitude. His times alone were the commas, pauses and full stops in the story of his life. They gave the rest of his life its structure, direction and balance. His words and his works were born out of those hours of silent waiting upon God.[112]

It appears that our Lord received both the direction and courage to pull away from the expectations of the crowd. He emphatically replied, "I must preach the good news of the kingdom of God to the other towns also, because that is why I was sent" (Luke 4:43). The narrative implies there is an association between prayer and direction. Ministry was defined and redirected after a private session of prayer. It was not about the needs of a single village, nor was it purely about physical needs. The Gospel message extended beyond the physical realm.

Private prayer seems like such a waste of time when I am surrounded by needy people. *I will just fall farther behind if I pause to pray.* That's how I think. In reality God is always ahead of us and prayer is the only way to catch up with his plan and will for our lives.

There is a paradox regarding prayer. I have discovered that it is necessary to slow down to pray. By doing so I connect with the God who created light-speed. An illustration from outer space may shed some light on this confusing concept:

> Astronaut Michael Collins has described the problem of two orbiting space vehicles trying to link up with each other. Unlike the rendezvous of two airplanes refueling, the vehicle behind will only go into a higher orbit if it speeds up. The ship's commander must resist all natural instincts and slow down, dropping his craft into a lower orbit. This enables him to catch up and maneuver into position.[113]

To get ahead in my spiritual life I must slow down and wait on God. There is no substitute for waiting on God, the source of all life and energy.

PRIVATE LIFE AND PRODUCTIVITY

Bottom-line productivity continues to drive industrialized nations. How much? How many? How far? How short of a time period? These are the questions that dominate business transactions. More-for-less is the focus of the twenty-first century. However, productivity without boundaries produces short-sighted plans that yield long-term disasters.

Our firstborn son, Scott, is the safety director for a large trucking company. The days when trucking was as simple as *get a load and go* are long gone. Everyone wants their product delivered *yesterday*, with the guarantee that freeways and highways are safe *twenty-four-seven*. The push to deliver a product on time is complicated by numerous regulations, especially safety regulations. No wonder a single accident involving a truck can bankrupt an entire company and destroy the lives of entire families. Life is not totally about productivity; it never has been!

If our Lord were to be graded at the end of his life by modern standards of productivity, his marks would be less than superior. Most of his time was spent with twelve disciples whose personal track records were less than spectacular. From a historical perspective Christ must have done something right; after all, who in the literate world has not heard of Christianity?

Philosopher William James affirmed "that the great use of one's life is to spend it for something that will outlast it, for the value of life is computed not by its duration but by its donation."[114] Jesus Christ is a perfect portrayal of this statement. Without conducting fulltime ministry for more than three years, his teachings were transmitted from generation to generation. Without traveling one hundred miles from home, his ministry had universal impact. Without achieving a formal education, volumes have been written about him.

Jesus Christ depicts quality. The total of all human existence does not equal the quality of his one life. No eloquence of speech has surpassed the excellence of his sayings. No sacrifice approaches the contribution of his sufferings. Besides the perfection of Jesus as a person, there is another factor that must be considered significant to his productivity.

The selection of a workforce is vital to productivity. Jesus would select disciples to be with him and spread his ministry. His selection would be validated in history, for those few disciples would bear the responsibility of proclaiming the Gospel to the world.

Before making this monumental decision, Jesus labored intentionally in private conversation with his and our Heavenly Father:

> One of those days Jesus went out to a mountainside to pray, and spent the night praying to God. [13] When morning came, he called his disciples to him and chose twelve of them, whom he also designated apostles: [14] Simon (whom he named Peter), his brother Andrew, James, John, Philip, Bartholomew, [15] Matthew, Thomas, James son of Alphaeus, Simon who was called the Zealot, [16] Judas son of James, and Judas Iscariot, who became a traitor.
>
> (Luke 6:12-16)

My flesh says to me, *prayer seems like an unwise use of time when so much depends on the selection of individuals.* I must question myself, *is that what I would have done when so much rested on the selection of these individuals? Wouldn't it be wise to interview a few more just in case there was a better choice out there? Perhaps a few more questions to the current nominees will reveal something that I have overlooked regarding these potential disciples. Surely there are more tests that we can run on them.* I must admit that I am tempted to sacrifice private life on the altar of productivity.

The Master Plan of Evangelism by Robert Coleman has remained for decades as a classic regarding Christ's plan to bring Christianity to the world. He has identified that Christ provided no back-up plan if his disciples failed. His initial selection must be right. Coleman comments on the selection process of the original disciples: "The initial objective of Jesus' plan was to enlist men who could bear witness to His life and carry on His work after He returned to the Father…. There is no evidence of haste in the selection of these disciples; just determination."[115]

While a detailed account of that prayer was not provided in the narrative, I am led to believe that Jesus must have cleared each name with the Father. Jesus, the Son of God, said, "By myself I can do nothing; I judge only as I hear, and my judgment is just, for I seek not to please myself but him who sent me" (John 5:30). Each disciple was carefully selected. Not even Judas was a mistake.

While taking Doctor of Ministry classes at Trinity Evangelical Divinity School, I had a conversation with Robert Coleman. The topic was discipleship.

"Unlike Jesus I have never had twelve disciples at a time," I confessed.

He commented, "Jesus had twelve, and within that group he had three that were closer to him. He also had Judas; and that too was good."

I nodded knowing that he was referring to Judas' betrayal of Jesus which led to the crucifixion and our redemption. Silenced by the profundity of the thought, I walked away. I have pondered Coleman's comment many times since. Judas was no mistake. A betrayer in the midst was God's plan and Jesus knew it. Numerous texts indicate that Jesus had more than a background check on Judas; he knew what Judas would eventually do: "Then Jesus replied, 'Have I not chosen you, the Twelve? Yet one of you is a devil!'" (John 6:70). "While I was with them, I protected them and kept them safe by that name you gave me. None has been lost except the one doomed to destruction so that Scripture would be fulfilled" (John 17:12).

Having served on several church/denominational nominating and search committees, I am sad to say that for some on those committees prayer was like a set of bookends. Prayer simply provided a means of getting meetings started and adjourned; but was not valued as an essential part of the process. Meeting agendas consisted of proceeding through prescribed checklists designed to separate the qualified from the unqualified. Despite the use of strategic checklists, selections often boiled down to whom the committee knew. The outcome produced a list of recycled leaders and little thought toward the development of future leaders.

However, sometimes there were people on the committees for whom prayer proved to be an important part of the selection process. For such individuals no checklist or personal knowledge was conclusive evidence for accepting or rejecting anyone. To the frustration of others, prayer was not only asking but waiting on God for answers. Sometimes answers showed up as a hesitation toward someone who appeared to be well qualified. At other times it provided assurance regarding a person who was not particularly impressive. There was no urgency to produce a list for these people until they had thoroughly prayed.

Sometimes I was that person who had thoroughly prayed and received either reluctance or a confirmation from above. It was a thrill to observe new leaders surprising congregations with their capabilities and fresh ideas.

Other times I was in a hurry to produce a list of nominees to meet election deadlines. Rushing on without prayer often proved disastrous. Putting productivity before prayer is often unproductive and sometimes disastrous. I would agree with the statement: *bad character shows up at the worst time.*

If it would have been presumptuous for the Son of God to select disciples without first communicating with his Heavenly Father, it would be incredibly presumptuous for me to attempt to be productive without interacting with my Heavenly Father. In his book, *The Grand Essentials,* Ben Patterson correctly includes prayer as a daily essential:

> That is why it is so important to begin the day with prayer. It is presumptuous to begin any other way! As workers, it is our first responsibility to check in with the boss and get in tune with what he has been doing while we slept and what he requires of us while we are awake. To just get up and rush into the day is to presume that we are the ones who are in charge of our lives and our work.[116]

As a reminder to myself and all who read my e-mails, I have selected Productive Rest (*productiverest@*) as my email address. I thoroughly believe that Sabbath-rest is highly productive. Functioning without such rest proves unproductive. If life were a sprint, working without rest might be both productive and survivable. Since life is a marathon, rest is essential to thriving productively. Rest and rise to work productively!

Thomas Merton unearthed a poem of Chuang Tzu, a fourth-century B.C. Chinese Taoist teacher which illustrates the necessity of solitude prior to decision making and seasons of productivity:

"THE WOODCARVER"

Khing, the master carver, made a bell stand
Of precious wood. When it was finished,
All who saw it were astounded. They said it must be
The work of spirits.
The prince of Lu said to the master carver:

"What is your secret?"

Khing replied: "I am only a workman:
I have no secret. There is only this:
When I began to think about the work you commanded
I guarded my spirit, did not expend it
On trifles, that were not to the point.
I fasted in order to set
My heart at rest.
Three days fasting, I had forgotten gain and success.
After five days
I had forgotten praise or criticism.
After seven days
I had forgotten my body
With all its limbs.

By this time all thought of your Highness
And of the court had faded away.
All that might distract me from the work
Had vanished.
I was collected in the single thought
Of the bell stand.

Then I went to the forest
To see the trees in their own natural state.
When the right tree appeared before my eyes,
The bell stand also appeared in it, clearly, beyond doubt.

All I had to do was to put forth my hand
And begin.

If I had not met this particular tree
There would have been
No bell stand at all.
What happened?
My own collected thought
Encountered the hidden potential in the wood;
From this life encounter came the work
Which you ascribe to the spirits."[117]

While Christianity is not to be confused with ancient Taoism, the ancient Taoist has identified some universal truths regarding solitude as it relates to productivity. Not just any wood will do, not just any tree will do. The person who produces quality work conditions himself or herself for the task by removing distractions and seeking to find the right material for the right job.

What is applicable to wood is also valuable in the realm of humanity. In order to produce the desired result there must be respect for the grain and the bent of personhood. All too often leaders fail to produce because they force a rigid job description on a person without consideration of personality, desires, or gifts. The effective leader takes into consideration not only the job but the person for the job. This consideration requires time alone with the true and living God who is equally interested in both task and worker.

Perpetual motion is not the key to productivity. Bill Hybels, in his timely book *Too Busy Not to Pray*, stresses the need to balance productivity with privacy and prayer:

If we are involved in the marketplace, we are trained to believe that time is money. That's why we talk about managing time, using it efficiently and profitably, and—as a result of our concern—dealing with time pressures.

Cram more in. Start earlier. Work later. Take work home. Dictate on the commuter train. Make phone calls in the car. Use a laptop computer in airports. Schedule breakfasts, lunches and dinners for profit. Performance, performance, performance—it's the key to promotion, to compensation increase, to power....

No one can become an authentic Christian on a steady diet of activity. Power comes out of stillness; strength comes out of solitude. Decisions that change the entire course of your life come out of the Holy of Holies, your times of stillness before God.[118]

PRIVATE LIFE AND PRESSURE

Tucked away between the steep mountains of northern Idaho rests a small manufacturing plant with a big assignment. What is designed and built there is extremely high performance, able to carry fuel and cargo more than its weight, and able to both land and take off loaded within a stretch of 1,000 feet of unpaved runway. The Kodiak is a single engine turbo jet designed to replace less effective aircraft and advance mission aviation world-wide. To date only two exist. One is used as a demonstrator, the other for testing. The FAA tests materials, design, and performance in circumstances far beyond what the aircraft is likely to endure in any flight or landing situation. These tests are performed in private so that when the Kodiak performs its public service, the outcome is trustworthy, not disastrous.

The airline industry spends millions of dollars on simulators designed to test and train pilots. These pilots experience bad weather, mechanical failures, and their own pilot error in private, to produce right responses in public service with passengers in the air and populations below. Private aviation training is designed to prevent public disaster.

I believe God intends believers to experience immense pressure in private so they generate right responses in public. It is better to be stress tested in the Lord's quiet presence than to react irresponsibly in public. The Bible is full of examples of both. Luke's Gospel provides the most vivid example of a private meeting under pressure.

> Jesus went out as usual to the Mount of Olives, and his disciples followed him. [40] On reaching the place, he said to them, "Pray that you will not fall into temptation." [41] He withdrew about a stone's throw beyond them, knelt down and prayed, [42] "Father, if you are willing, take this cup from me; yet not my will, but yours be done." [43] An angel from heaven appeared to him and strengthened him. [44] And being in anguish, he prayed more earnestly, and his sweat was like drops of blood falling to the ground. [45] When he rose from prayer and went back to the disciples, he found them asleep, exhausted from sorrow. [46] "Why are you sleeping?" he asked them. "Get up and pray so that you will not fall into temptation."
>
> (Luke 22:39-46)

It was the hour of our Lord's greatest temptation. Luke, the physician, indicates that Jesus' anguish was so acute that the corpuscles in his head broke causing blood to drip like sweat. Jesus was about to experience an agony far beyond physical suffering on the cross. The cross was not the subject of prayer. His prayer was about the *cup*. In the Old Testament this cup symbolized the wrath of God toward man's sins (Psalm 11:6; Isaiah 51:17; Ezekiel 23:33).[119]

Jesus was about to consume the cup that contained the wrath of God toward human sin. The cross was man's tool of wrath toward criminals. The cup was God's instrument of wrath toward sinners. He would suffer the penalty due our sins so we wouldn't have to.

He was about to perform a ministry that would prove him absolutely worthy of eternal popularity. Without this service he would never produce one Christian. Without a cross-bearing Savior all ministry would provide nothing but temporary relief, and his disciples would have nothing to proclaim. It all rested on Jesus.

As was his habit, Jesus went to the Mount of Olives, which overlooked the city of his atoning death. Jesus settled the matter of the cross in private at Gethsemane, so that he just had to endure the events when they happened. While my immediate response says, *that is one big "just,"* I am reminded that indecision heaps more anguish on stressful situations. Without pre-determining your response, the reactions of others as well as your own are uncertain. Jesus wrestled with the dread of it all in private. When it came time to face the cross and jeering crowds, Jesus had been there in private with his Heavenly Father.

Prayer equalizes pressure. The following illustration by Jay Kessler has helped me understand the power of private prayer:

> A bathysphere is a miniature submarine used to explore the ocean floor in places where the water pressure would crush a conventional submarine like an aluminum can. Bathyspheres compensate for the pressure with plate steel several inches thick. Yet fish remain supple and free at the bottom of the ocean where the water pressure is great. How? They compensate for the outside pressure by equalizing the pressure within themselves. Jesus was equalizing the pressure produced by His public life with an intense private life. You can't meet the pressures of public life if you are always in public.[120]

In prayer Jesus was tuning his will to the Father's will much like a concert violinist tunes his instrument before a concert. First the musician tunes his A string to a standard A 440 (440 vibrations per second). Then he tunes the other three strings to the A string. The sound of a violin being tuned can be quite annoying. But he goes through this agony before thousands because he knows that an out-of-tune string can tarnish if not ruin his performance. Our Lord was making sure his will was tuned to the perfect standard of his Father's will before performing his greatest concert on the cross.

J. Oswald Sanders has experienced one of the most profound truths about prayer: "I have found that a great deal of the praying has to do with getting my mind in the place where I have a real preference for the will of God above everything else."[121]

His will was in harmony with his Father's and his body was strengthened by an angel. Once the subject of will was settled within himself, he was free to settle the issue of sin, of which he had none. He simply arose from prayer and acted in obedience. I am so glad that he prayed that night.

FAILING TO HANDLE PRESSURE IN PRIVATE

An example of failure to handle pressure in private that ended up in public embarrassment took place that same evening. Realizing that his crucifixion would put great pressure on his disciples, Jesus urged them to pray. "Get up and pray so that you will not fall into temptation." That evening the disciples were tempted to exercise both fight and flight. As a lead disciple, Peter would yield to both. Immediately after the prayer meeting in the garden he would slice off the servant of the high priest's ear (Luke 22:50, John 18:10), and he managed to deny his Lord three times before sunrise (Luke 22:60).

Moses must have also regretted his failure to work through pressure in private. Most of the time Moses handled the magnitude of his leadership position in private with God. His relationship with God was so intimate that it was said of him, "The LORD would speak to Moses face-to-face, as a man speaks with his friend" (Exodus 33:11). However, Moses allowed his anger towards the complaining Israelites to get the best of him. Moses struck the rock and publicly dishonored the Lord.

He and Aaron gathered the assembly together in front of the rock and Moses said to them, "Listen, you rebels, must we bring you water out of this rock?" But the LORD said to Moses and Aaron, "Because you did not trust in me enough to honor me as holy in the sight of the Israelites, you will not bring this community into the land I give them."

(Numbers 20:10-12)

As long as Moses processed the pressure of leading that ungrateful nation with the Lord Almighty in private he responded honorably. Unfortunately there were a few occasions where Moses got stuck on the public end of the commute. His loss was great!

I must admit that I am tempted to sacrifice private life on the altar of pressure. There are times when pressure isolates me from God, driving me away from where the stress tests ought to be performed. It may seem like a harmless sin that everyone will understand; but if I slight time in private because I am under pressure, I am likely to make mistakes that are impossible to correct. A sarcastic remark, an angry tone, an ignored opportunity to respond as Christ's shepherd, are just a few outcomes of unprocessed stress.

I recall attending a meeting for church elders four days after returning from a three-week short-term missions trip in Russia. Still suffering from jet lag, I was trying to dig my way out of an avalanche of ministry challenges that had accumulated while I was gone. But that was not the worst of it. After reading a certain report I was angry. Before the trip I had forewarned leaders that a certain situation would occur if we did not take action. Nothing had been done. I expressed my anger in my own report, but denied being angry at the meeting. After a long discussion a veteran elder asked, "Jim, would you like to collect your report and remove it from the record?" I said, "Yes, I would."

I had reason to be angry but not in the way I expressed it. Had I held my peace until I had processed my anger with the Lord in private, I would not have strained my relationships with the leaders I loved. Apologies may smooth over poor responses, but fail to reverse words and actions that should have been filtered in private.

I believe God allows temptations to come to us in private so that we can process them with him and work out a godly way of escape. Private time with him is often the escape Paul introduced in II Corinthians 10:13: "No temptation has seized you except what is common to man. And God is faithful; he will not let you be tempted beyond what you can bear. But when you are tempted, he will also provide a way out so that you can stand up under it."

Somewhere in my Christian development I was told to suppress tempting thoughts when they came to my mind in private. I have found that it is better to process them with God in private. The process is usually working through a series of questions, such as: *What triggered this thought? Where did it come from? Why am I tempted in this particular way? What would be the outcome and cost of carrying out such a thought? What is my way of escape if I am ever presented with such a tempting situation? What boundaries must I establish to prevent failure at the point of temptation?* In this way, I "take captive every thought to make it obedient to Christ" (II Corinthians 10:5).

When such temptations actually present themselves in public, I have already taken the way of escape the Lord provided in private. It is like I have already been there and foreseen the outcome of carrying through with the temptation. Having wrestled with it in private, I am not taken by surprise so as to react unaware of the consequences. I like what Corrie ten Boom, a survivor of the Holocaust, said about temptations: "When temptation knocks I ask Jesus to open the door." Jesus knows how to slam the door on temptation.

SUMMARY

Before every takeoff of a commercial flight, a flight attendant announces where the emergency exits are in the event of an emergency. It is easy to ignore her rehearsed monologue and to just continue to read, daydream, or converse with the person next to you. If we ever need to use an emergency exit, we will be glad for every moment we listened to her instructions, thus avoiding panic and potential harm.

Perhaps the greatest temptation we face is the temptation to ignore private moments which prepare us for making right decisions in public. It can be said that we fail temptations in private before we fail them in public. It is the neglect of preparation in private that leads to catastrophe. Author and Pastor Ron Mehl reminds us that respecting Sabbath-rest will always be a battle:

> But please remember this: the path to Sabbath rest will always be a contested path. Haven't you ever wondered why it seems so incredibly difficult to find these times with God in our life? Why it seems like such a chore to simply pick up your Bible or get down on your knees to pray? The enemy knows this path to the Sabbath will lead you to rest and righteousness and perspective and a reordering of your priorities. And Satan will try

to thwart you. He doesn't want you to find that path. Never doubt it! He has a thousand ways to sidetrack and divert you.

Satan knows that if he keeps us striving in our own strength, the joy and sense of purpose in our lives will drain like oil out of a quarter-sized hole in your car's oil pan.[122]

Prayer

Lord Jesus, I praise you for leaving your example as I commute between work and rest. You flowed easily between the two without being uptight with rest because of tasks undone, or frustrated with work because of much needed rest. You never got burned-out or broken down in the pursuit of your global mission for eternity. Your example will help me finish well. In Jesus' name and for his sake I pray, Amen.

Questions to Ponder

1. Am I stuck at one end or the other, or in the middle of my commute between work and rest?
2. Have I learned to equalize the pressures of life with rest?
3. What mistakes have I made in public because I refused to rest in private?

CHAPTER THIRTEEN

THE TWENTY-THIRD PSALM, A RECIPE FOR REST

[1]The LORD is my shepherd, I shall not be in want.
   [2]He makes me lie down in green pastures,
he leads me beside quiet waters,
   [3] he restores my soul.
He guides me in paths of righteousness,
   for his name's sake.
[4] Even though I walk
   through the valley of the shadow of death,
I will fear no evil,
   for you are with me;
your rod and your staff,
   they comfort me.

[5] You prepare a table before me
   in the presence of my enemies.
You anoint my head with oil;
   my cup overflows.
[6] Surely goodness and love will follow me
   all the days of my life,
And I will dwell in the house of the LORD
   forever.

(Psalm 23)

One of the great revelations of the heart of God given to us by Christ is that of Himself as our Shepherd. He has the same identical sensations of anxiety, concern and compassion for cast men and women as I had for cast sheep.[123]

(Phillip Keller)

Life really is an unpredictable tragedy that provides no rest apart from confidence in God's kind intentions toward us.[124]

(Larry Crabb)

The Twenty-Third Psalm and The Lord's Prayer preside as the most recited passages of the Bible. Many church attendees can quote the entire Psalm from memory. Most people born in the United States can quote the first verse without hesitation. Movies depicting graveside funerals often include the reading of the Psalm by a clergyman.

Familiar as it is, few lives reflect the tranquility portrayed in this landmark passage of Scripture. In fact many, including those who quote it best, live lives that look like anything but the original Twenty-Third Psalm. Several years ago I came across a rewrite of Psalm twenty-three that best reflected my life:

THE WORKAHOLIC'S 23RD PSALM
BY EDWARD J. VASICEK

The Lord is my foreman, I shall not rest.
He makes me mow down the green pastures.
He leads me to generators beside rapid waters. He wears out my soul.
He shoves me to conferences for my schedule's sake.
Even though I walk through the valley of relaxation,
I fear no chance of rest; for my feelings of guilt, they haunt me.
Thou dost prepare a work table before me,
In the presence of my comrades.
Thou hast filled my mind with worry; my workload overflows.
Surely busyness and pressure will follow me, all the days of my life,
And I will run to and fro in the house of the Lord forever.[125]

I have found it helpful to circle those words and phrases that reflect my own driven behavior. Years ago I was hit the hardest by the heart of this Psalm rewrite, "I fear no chance of rest; for my feelings of guilt, they haunt me." Ironing out those feelings of guilt has gone a long way toward alleviating workaholic tendencies. I have also asked others, such as my wife, to identify the words and phrases that describe me. In an effort to live by the true Twenty-Third Psalm, I invited those who loved me to be brutally honest about how my life mimicked *The Workaholics Twenty-Third Psalm*. If your ego can endure such a critique, ask your teenagers to scrutinize your life in light of this Twenty-Third Psalm makeover.

Driven-ness isn't necessarily about work. Life goals or leisure apart from work can drive me from quiet waters. It may be other people with their expectations that drive me out of green pastures, or self-imposed ideals that keep me in a panic mode. It could even be a distorted view of God that makes the psalm rewrite fit. That is why it is so important to understand and live by the inspired Twenty-Third Psalm. In order to do so I must know the shepherd who wrote the original Psalm and the Shepherd who inspired it.

DAVID UNDERSTOOD SHEEP!

He chose David his servant and took him from the sheep pens;
From tending the sheep he brought him
To be the shepherd of his people Jacob, of Israel his inheritance.
And David shepherded them with integrity of heart;
With skillful hands he led them.

(Psalm 78:70-72)

It is obvious from Psalm seventy-eight and other passages of Scripture that David spent time with sheep before becoming a leader of people. The text implies that the skills applied to shepherding sheep are transferable to leading people. If I understand sheep, I am apt to have a greater under-standing of how God views people.

Sheep are rather defenseless animals. They have no meat-shredding teeth, no flesh-tearing claws. They are not swift afoot, nor particularly bright. I don't know of any athletic teams that claim sheep as their mascot, with the possible exception of one. You have heard of the Chicago Bears, the Detroit Lions, the Carolina Panthers, the Philadelphia Eagles, and the Minnesota Timberwolves. Teams tend to choose intimidating meat eaters as their mascots. There is one team that utilizes a member of the sheep family as its mascot—the St. Louis Rams. You have heard of the *Rams*, but never the *Lambs*. Imagine the headline: *Lambs Play Lions*. Worse yet, imagine the outcome.

The Lord does not pamper our egos with the shepherd-sheep analogy. If left out unattended in the wilderness by ourselves, we are apt to become lamb chops or road kill. When David said, "The Lord is my Shepherd" he was admitting that he, David, was a defenseless, dependent creature. In the Gospels Jesus described people without a shepherd as vulnerable and defenseless.

> *When He saw the crowds, He had compassion on them, because they were harassed and helpless, like sheep without a shepherd.*
>
> *(Matthew 9:36)*

Having a shepherd is essential to my survival. Embracing the Lord as my Shepherd is vital to my temporal and eternal wellbeing. I cannot truly rest until I honestly say, "The Lord is my Shepherd." The Twenty-Third Psalm is a recipe for rest, the deep rest for which we yearn. In order to experience true rest I must receive three ingredients provided by the Good Shepherd. The first ingredient is satisfaction.

THE LORD IS MY SATISFACTION!

The LORD is my shepherd, I shall not be in want.
He makes me lie down in green pastures,
He leads me beside quiet waters,
He restores my soul.
He guides me in paths of righteousness for his name's sake.
(Psalm 23:1-3)

Everyone seeks satisfaction from something or someone. David discovered that the Lord was the key to satisfaction; as a shepherd he wanted nothing more. Most of us go on a journey of self-satisfaction before making David's discovery. My journey took a turn in the right direction thanks to the help of a much-needed friend.

I was a seminary grad, a pastor, a successful church planter with a church building, a growing congregation, a beautiful wife, and a nice family with two boys. Yet, I was restless. An older gentleman who could see my condition invited me to study the Bible with him. I thought to myself, *I'll show him how to study the Bible; after all I am a pastor, seminar grad, soon to begin a doctoral program.* When he turned to The Twenty-Third Psalm, I thought to myself, *this is almost an insult. What kind of spiritual baby pabulum is he feeding me? I have known this passage since childhood.*

Then he read, "The Lord is my Shepherd, I shall not want," and stopped. I thought to myself. *Come on, read on!* But he didn't. The silence revealed that he had something I didn't have. I knew Jesus as my Savior for eternal life, but I didn't know him as my Shepherd. I didn't know him as my Satisfier. I was craving and crawling inside. I wanted to escape, but had to face the fact that I was seeking satisfaction outside of the Shepherd. Things, titles, degrees, achievements, honors were my pursuits. These were not evil in themselves; they just couldn't satisfy the tremendous need I had for a Shepherd who satisfies.

In the weeks that followed I discovered how the Good Shepherd satisfies, "He makes me lie down in green pastures." It takes a lot to get sheep to lie down. They have to feel safe from outside threats and inner flock tensions. They have to be *debugged.* They have to feed on green pastures. In human terms he satisfies my immediate and eternal needs. But some people and sheep alike simply refuse to lie down on their own. If left to themselves, restlessness will turn into a deep and dangerous fatigue. I know because I was once one of them. Pastor and author Ron Mehl's commentary kindly addresses this problem:

> He *makes* you to lie down! If you don't lie down and rest, if you don't seek out those quiet pastures and still waters with your Shepherd, it's not beyond Him to make you. You say, "Well, I don't believe God would do that." Then you don't understand His Father love! If you're not going to slowdown and rest, then look around at the circumstances of your life and find out why you're in the condition you're in. Maybe He loves you more than you think.

> Please note that the phrase "He makes me lie down" comes before the words "He restores my soul." It is as we enter into His rest that we experience His wonderful healing touch on our lives. Restoration is neither quick nor cheap.[126]

Furthermore, the Good Shepherd leads beside quiet waters. Not whitewater rapids. Not stagnant puddles. He selects streams that are just right for me. He knows what I can handle. Restlessness tends to refuse a challenge on one hand or impulsively take on too much on the other. When rightly satisfied I can identify those challenges that fit me with the courage to take the next step.

"He restores my soul" literally means he turns back the soul to an original state of wellness. The implication is the soul or personhood has been wounded in some way. He mends my soul. I began a midlife journey of restoration. Embarrassing situations of the past had left my soul scarred leaving me with a void of confidence and a tentative nature. My family and community experience was far from atrocious or abusive. It is probable that we all have wounds of the soul no matter how *normal* our environment has been.

Do you have a need for mending of the soul because of some past memories or literal scars that remain? Perhaps the wounds are so deep that you feel like damaged goods or a wasted product. It is time to open those wounds because there is a Good Shepherd who heals them.

Phillip Keller wrote a classic on the Twenty-Third Psalm, *A Shepherd Looks at Psalm 23*. This book has helped me understand the Psalm more than any other. Most memorable was Keller's first-hand experience of restoring a *cast* sheep:

> A "cast" sheep is a very pathetic sight. Lying on its back, its feet in the air, it flays away frantically struggling to stand up, without success. Sometimes it will bleat a little for help, but generally it lies there lashing about in frightened frustration....
>
> As soon as I reached the cast ewe my very first impulse was to pick it up. Tenderly I would roll the sheep over on its side. This would relieve the pressure of gases in the rumen. If she had been down for long I would have to lift her onto her feet. Then straddling the sheep with my legs I would hold her erect, rubbing her limbs to restore the circulation to her legs. This often took quite a little time. When the sheep started to walk again she often just stumbled, staggered and collapsed in a heap once more.
>
> All the time I worked on the cast sheep I would talk to it gently, "When are you going to learn to stand on your own feet?"—"I'm so glad I found you in time—you rascal!"
>
> And so the conversation would go. Always couched in language that combined tenderness and rebuke, compassion and correction.
>
> Little by little the sheep would regain its equilibrium. It would start to walk steadily and surely. By and by it would dash away to rejoin the others, set free from its fears and frustrations, given another chance to live a little longer....
>
> Many people have the idea that when a child of God falls, when he is frustrated and helpless in a spiritual dilemma, God becomes disgusted, fed-up and even furious with him. This simply is not so.

One of the great revelations of the heart of God given to us by Christ is that of Himself as our Shepherd. He has the same identical sensations of anxiety, concern and compassion for cast men and women as I had for cast sheep. This is precisely why He looked on people with such pathos and compassion. It explains His magnanimous dealing with down-and-out individuals for whom even human society had no use. It reveals why He wept over those who spurned His affection. It discloses the depth of His understanding of undone people to whom He came eagerly and quickly, ready to help, to save, to restore.[127]

"He guides me in paths of righteousness." In other words he is entirely trustworthy. I can trust my entire soul, mind, and body to him. No matter how traumatized I have been by past experiences, I can trust him. Trust is essential to life; without it I am destined for a lonely, fear-ridden existence.

Several years ago I made a house call on a family that had visited the church I was serving at the time. There seemed to be considerable openness to the Good News that Jesus died for our sins so that we could be received into heaven when we die. When I asked the couple if they would like to ask Christ to forgive their sins and receive him as Lord and Savior, tears welled up in the young woman's eyes. She wanted forgiveness and eternal life but had a problem with Jesus. He was a man. She had been abused by a man, none other than the father she trusted. Receiving Christ sounded so intrusive. In time she did invite Christ to be her Lord and Savior. It was the beginning of a healing trust relationship that she would never regret. When she received Christ she began to trust others again.

The prepositional phrase *for his name's sake* rescues us from slithering into the pit of self-focus. Dissatisfaction comes as we seek to satisfy ourselves. As strange as it may sound, seeking to satisfy self leaves us less satisfied. As a child of the sixties I have experienced the impact of the *me generation* that has bred great dissatisfaction. My personal experience is that it's extremely difficult to wean a person off of a constant diet of *have it your way*. Satisfaction comes as I live for someone bigger than myself. A journey down the paths of righteousness begins as I acknowledge that every phrase of Psalm Twenty-Three begins with the word he—not me, myself, or I.

Once again the theme of pleasing God has surfaced. Paths of righteousness are not only satisfying and best for me, they are pleasing to God. Author and counselor Larry Crabb has given himself to pleasing God and understanding the human need for God. He has captured the essence of satisfaction in God when he writes: "God's position seems to be that we will not properly value the good things of life until first we value Him...." [128]

You may have received Jesus Christ as your Savior, but have you received him as your Shepherd who satisfies? You cannot rest without the satisfaction he provides.

THE LORD IS MY SECURITY!

Even though I walk through the valley of the shadow of death,
I will fear no evil, for you are with me;
Your rod and your staff, they comfort me.
You prepare a table before me in the presence of my enemies.
(Psalm 23:4-5a)

Security is the second ingredient in the recipe for rest. Ever since the devastation of September 11, 2001, Americans have felt insecure about everything from airlines to airwaves. Just as Americans thought themselves insolated from the tragedies of other nations, an invasion beyond the imaginations of Hollywood shattered the security of the most secure. Before 9/11 the average American living in the States couldn't have cared less about National Security and was sure to complain about the ridiculous security measures at airports. Not any longer! Security has become a national obsession and rightfully so.

The relationship between security and rest was experienced by all the Americans who tossed and turned sleepless on their beds as the tragedy flooded the media. The same interruption of rest was experienced for months by those who witnessed deaths first-hand. I have joined the millions who have asked, *is there such a thing as personal security in the shadow of melting skyscrapers and national insecurity?*

Psalm Twenty-Three presents the reality of security in the midst of danger. David presents three vivid portraits of security in verses four and five. The first is that of walking in the midst of deadly danger, "Even though I walk through the valley of the shadow of death." Valleys are places of death for sheep. There is thick foliage and plenty of rocky ledges where sheep eaters can hide. Valleys are full of shadows much of the day and darkness falls early in the evening. Yet our Good Shepherd leads us through them, not around them. Walking through them with the Shepherd communicates that there is a state of security. I am to walk, not run as if frightened. The lion roars as a means of stampeding and scattering the flock. Panic-stricken sheep that leave the path and lose their way are easy prey for a host of predators.

Nor am I to stop, permitting myself the opportunity to dabble in dark shadowy places. The valley of the shadow of death connotes evil. "I will fear no evil," does not mean that evil is not present; it simply means that I need not fear in the midst of it. The fact that our Shepherd leads through shadowy places is not license to stop and ponder evil things with intrigue. Walk! Don't run! Don't dabble!

The key to being secure in dangerous places and not fearing evil is a matter of focus. "I will fear no evil, for you are with me." It is not where you are but who is with you that makes you secure. And when the day comes that death knocks on life's door, we will find that it is only a shadow and a valley through which we must pass. We will not pass through it alone for he has been there and will walk through it with us. Fear no evil no matter where he leads.

The second portrait of security depicts instruments of comfort and correction: "Your rod and your staff, they comfort me." A rod was used to fight off animals that would try to devour the flock. Sheep are comforted knowing that the shepherd brought his rod with him.

But it is also a comfort to know the shepherd would use the rod on the sheep if necessary. Sometimes sheep bully or butt one another. While they are defenseless against other animals, they tend to take cheap shots at one another. There is a comfort in knowing the Shepherd will discipline fellow sheep. There is even security in knowing the Good Shepherd will use the rod on me for my own safety and development. As Walter Henrichsen says, "The purpose of accountability is to protect you from yourself."[129] If I get out of hand and begin to stray, he will confront and correct me as firmly as I choose necessary.

I will long remember the day I made a real estate decision that I was not sure I should make. I thought to myself, *if it is wrong, God will correct me*. It was wrong and God's correction went on for about five years. But it was a very valuable path-changing correction, which altered my way of thinking. Thank God he uses the rod on me!

The staff is a long stick with a hook on the end of it. It is used to lift out the lamb that has had the misfortune of falling into leg-breaking crevasses or crags where it will starve to death. Sheep are comforted by such an instrument because it serves as an extension of the loving shepherd's strong merciful arm.

The third portrait of security is one of dining in the presence of enemies: "You prepare a table before me in the presence of my enemies." High plateaus on which sheep graze are sometimes referred to as tables. Imagine a flock of sheep grazing on a high plateau surrounded by wolves and mountain lions. That is the picture that is presented.

Tables are used by human beings for many purposes, but are universally used as places where food is served. Imagine going to a fine restaurant with a loved one and being seated comfortably at a table. Just as you begin to scan the menu, your eyes glance over the top of the menu and catch a glimpse of a familiar face. It's not just any face. It's that person who opposes you. This person has caused you great pain and is sitting just two tables away. He or she has betrayed you in some way. It's your ex-boyfriend, ex-girlfriend, ex-boss who just fired you, or ex-employee who slandered you. Emotions of insecurity churn within you like sour milk. You can feel the sweat roll down your spine.

Our Lord was very aware that Judas would ultimately betray him; yet Jesus dined frequently with Judas. That is the picture of security the Lord modeled for us and wants us to emulate because he has said; "Never will I leave you; never will I forsake you" (Hebrews 13:5).

U.S. Navy Chaplain Lt. Carey H. Cash titled his book about the first days of the war in Iraq *A Table in the Presence*. What David spoke of three thousand years ago, Cash and the troops he accompanied experienced first hand in March of 2003.

> The "table" that David spoke about, the "table" that David longed for in the presence of his enemies, was the table of God's presence. It amounted to a feast of spiritual strength and friendship that no degree of danger and no amount of evil could infringe upon....
>
> The irony, the paradox, the bright contradiction was obvious to all of us. We'd been given a mission to tear down and destroy, to go into the teeth of enemy territory and wage war. And yet in those quiet moments of silence and prayer, we had also been given a blessing. We had been invited to a table hosted by God's empowering presence, to taste of the miraculous power that only He could offer. Indeed, it was a most unexpected feast.[130]

In each portrait David is saying, "The Lord is my security!" You know Jesus, the Good Shepherd, as your Savior, but do you know him as your Shepherd? Do you know him as your security? You cannot rest without the security he provides.

THE LORD IS MY SUCCESS!

You prepare a table before me in the presence of my enemies.
You anoint my head with oil; my cup overflows.
Surely goodness and love will follow me all the days of my life,
And I will dwell in the house of the LORD forever.

(Psalm 23:5-6)

Success is the third ingredient for rest. Success is something everyone wants but few can define. Once again David's definition comes in word pictures. "You prepare a table before me in the presence of my enemies" not only depicts security but success. A well-prepared table overflowing with food is a symbol of prosperity; such is the case with the first reference to a table in Scripture: "When portions were served to them from Joseph's table, Benjamin's portion was five times as much as anyone else's. So they feasted and drank freely with him" (Genesis 43:34).

I must confess that I have had trouble getting over, under, or around the table when it comes to the word *success*. God's view of success has more to do with relationships than the typical *plenty to eat, plenty to have, and plenty to do* definitions.

True lasting success is *striking oil in your relationship with God.* In the oil industry, striking oil is an expression of great success. All the drilling through the earth's crust has finally paid off. When you strike oil you finally have a product of great worth, especially with today's rising fuel prices.

Instead of crude oil, it was olive oil and other plant extracts that were valued in ancient times. Plant products released pleasant fragrances and were used for medicinal purposes. Oil was applied to sheep for healing sores and keeping bugs away. Oil was applied to people for some of the same reasons. But one application was very special. The anointing of oil applied to kings, priests, and prophets was symbolic of their special positions and relationships with God. Thus the phrase "You anoint my head with oil" represented a very favorable and honorable occasion. It was an indication of success in a relationship with God. It is written of David, "So Samuel took the horn of oil and anointed him in the presence of his brothers, and from that day on the Spirit of the LORD came upon David in power" (I Samuel 16:13). Oil was symbolic of the Holy Spirit who was given to God's appointed leaders for the purpose of drawing a whole nation closer to God. David himself wrote about the symbolic value of oil in reference to Aaron the priest: "How good and pleasant it is when brothers live together in unity! ² It is like precious oil poured on the head, running down on the beard, running down on Aaron's beard, down upon the collar of his robes" (Psalm 133:1-2).

In the New Testament all believers have access to the same fullness of the Holy Spirit. Therefore every believer may be rich in his or her relationship with God, "For we were all baptized by one Spirit into one body—whether Jews or Greeks, slave or free—and we were all given the one Spirit to drink" (I Corinthians 12:13). If that is the case, all who believe in and follow the Good Shepherd can be successful by God's definition. We can all experience what David experienced when he said in Psalm twenty-three, "My cup overflows." We can each *strike oil* in our relationship with God.

God's definition of success begins with knowing him. In God's opinion knowing him is superior to wisdom, strength, or wealth. In God's opinion knowing him is something to boast about:

> Let not the wise man boast of his wisdom or the strong man boast of his strength or the rich man boast of his riches, ²⁴ but let him who boasts boast about this: that he understands and knows me, that I am the LORD, who exercises kindness, justice and righteousness on earth, for in these I delight," declares the LORD.
>
> (Jeremiah 9:23-24)

Success grows as we learn that God loves us. In God's dictionary knowing you are loved is success. Effort invested in knowing God pays great dividends as we discover God passionately pursues us. Verse seven says, "Surely goodness and love will follow me all the days of my life." *Follow me* could be translated pursue, chase, or overtake. Eugene Peterson captures the essence of the word in *The Message*: "Your beauty and love chase after me every day of my life." David's thought is: *I can't get away from the love and kindness of God. Everywhere I turn it is there, over and over, again and again.* Now *that's* success!

I have to admit through much of life I have pursed love instead of living like God's love was pursuing me. I thought that if I accomplished something noticeable people would love me. If I had a certain talent or ability, then people would notice, respect, and love me. Gradually, I have come to understand that God's love is not earned. When you cease doing things in order to be loved, you will discover God's love is pursuing you until it overwhelms you. That is win/win surrender. God's love is not something you have to hunt for. God hunts you with goodness.

Are you working so hard at something in order to be loved by people? Have you ever thought: *once I get rich people will love me?* No they won't; they will just want your money. *Once I get that position, that honor, once I win at something, then they will love me.* Perhaps! More likely they will just envy you.

True success realizes that God loves you even in your humanly unlovable state. Among the many passages of Scripture that communicate God's love, I treasure Romans 5:8, "But (God) demonstrates his own love for us in this: While we were still sinners, Christ died for us" (Romans 5:8). You no longer have to pursue another activity or opportunity in hopes of being loved by God. He loves you now as you are. Open yourself to his love now. That is the success you are looking for.

Success grows immensely when we know where we are going. David said, "And I will dwell in the house of the LORD forever." The only physical house of the Lord David knew in his lifetime was the tabernacle. It was not very large and much of it was off limits to all except the priests. Like a child in a museum David was not apt to do any running in the tabernacle. While he desired to build the temple, that task belonged to his son, Solomon. David never witnessed the building of the temple in Jerusalem. When David speaks of dwelling in the house of the Lord forever, he must be speaking of heaven. He declares with great certainty that heaven is his eternal home. An eternal home in heaven was more than a wish; it was a certainty and confidence. Success is knowing you are headed for heaven, the dwelling place of God.

Do you know where you are going when you die? Knowing all the earthly pleasures of this life cannot take away the pain of not being certain of eternal life. Jesus, the Good Shepherd, said, "I tell you the truth, he who believes has everlasting life" (John 6:47).

By now I hope you know the Good Shepherd as your Shepherd. But do you really know the Good Shepherd as your Savior? Jesus Christ is the Shepherd David claimed to know as his satisfaction, security, and success. Jesus said:

> I have come that they may have life, and have it to the full. I am the good shepherd. The good shepherd lays down his life for the sheep.
> (John 10:10-11)

My sheep listen to my voice; I know them, and they follow me. [28] I give them eternal life, and they shall never perish; no one can snatch them out of my hand.

(John 10:27-28)

Having a Savior is actually a greater need than satisfaction, security, or success. You simply cannot leave this life without the one-and-only Savior. If you have any doubt about Christ being your Savior, invite him right now to be your Savior that you may know him as the one who saves you from the eternal consequences of your sins.

Prayers

I receive you, Lord Jesus Christ, as my Savior. I ask you to forgive my sins for which you have died. Come into my life that I might have eternal life from this day forward, Amen.

Perhaps you have known The Good Shepherd as your Savior but have never humbled yourself and given up the independent lifestyle. This prayer is for you:

I receive you, Lord Jesus, as my Shepherd. I have known you as my Savior but have acted independent of you. I have sought satisfaction, security, and success apart from you. I have not accepted the fact that I am a dependent, defenseless creature. I now receive you as my Shepherd. You are my satisfaction, security and success, Amen.

Questions to Ponder

1. In what way(s) does *The Workaholic's Twenty-Third Psalm* reflect my life?
2. Have I embraced the Lord as my satisfaction?
3. Have I embraced the Lord as my security?
4. Have I embraced the Lord as my success?

CHAPTER FOURTEEN

REST, FORGIVING AS FORGIVEN

Be kind and compassionate to one another, forgiving each other, just as in Christ God forgave you.

(Ephesians 4:32)

He that demands mercy and shows none, ruins the bridge over which he himself is to pass.[131]

(Puritan saying)

H ello."

"Good morning. Is this Ramona?"

"This is Ramona." Her voice was so bright and cheerful, but that would change in a few moments.

"I'm Jim Anderson with Anderson Trucking Service."

"Oh yes, my son, Stanley, drives for your company. He really likes driving for ATS."

"I am glad to hear that." I took a long pause. "Well, I'm afraid I have some very bad news." I heard Ramona take a deep breath. "I am so sorry. There is no good way for me to tell you. Your son was killed this morning in a trucking accident." There was a long pause on the other end of the line. Like air being let out of a balloon, the cheer had been drained from her voice. I repeated, "I'm sorry. I wish I didn't have to tell you this."

Ramona was weeping. I broke the silence again, "Stanley was one of our best drivers. This is a big loss for us and a great loss for you."

Stanley was a million-mile driver, which meant he had driven a million miles without an accident. It takes about eight years of constant driving to drive a million miles. Stanley was actually well on his way to being a two million-mile driver.

In a trembling voice Ramona slowly whispered a few questions inquiring about the accident. The news had dealt her an emotional death blow, as if she had been hit by the truck. My words had drained the strength out of her. I gave Ramona a general description of what happened. She called her cousin to join her as she pondered her loss.

This was one of the hardest phone calls I have ever made. As Relationship Consultant (Chaplain) with the trucking company, I was the most likely person to make the call. I wished I could have delivered the news in person; however, I was several hundred miles away from Ramona's home at the time. Law enforcement officers and the coroner in the vicinity of the accident were a thousand miles away. They wanted the family to be contacted as soon as possible. My cell phone was the most expedient means of sharing the sad news with Ramona.

Ramona lived alone on a small pension. Stanley, Ramona's only child, was now dead at age forty-seven. He left behind no children. He had never been married. Now Ramona was more alone than ever.

Another truck had pulled out directly in front of Stanley's truck. His death was immediate. The other truck driver walked away unharmed. His company quickly offered Ramona a settlement. It was more money than she had seen at any time in her life. However, it was small compared to what she might have received had she chosen to pursue a greater amount in court. Ramona was content with the offer, expressing no desire to fight over her loss. No amount of money could bring her son back. Ramona wrote the following note to the other truck driver:

I hold no animosity toward you. It was an accident. We cannot fully understand God's plan, nor can we change it. Although I am completely heartbroken, I wish you God's peace. Pray for us both.

(Stan's Mom)

Ramona lives about a three-hour drive from me. Once in a while I make a point of stopping by to have coffee with Ramona. Her hardships have been great, as has been her freedom. She smiles and laughs freely without regret or thoughts of retaliation. Ramona is a picture of forgiveness.

Forgiveness is rest. Apart from forgiveness there is no real rest. There is hardly a relationship on earth that doesn't at some point require forgiveness. Even if a person works for himself, the day will come when he will have to forgive himself for some ridiculous or wrongful act.

After years of providing pastoral counseling in church and community situations, I have boiled counseling down to two questions: *Has the person in front of me sinned? Has the person in front of me been sinned against?*

Obviously there is much more to counseling than two questions. But those two questions provide beginning points. If the person has sinned, I must lead him or her to a response of repentance, no matter how convincing his or her rationalization or pathetic the circumstances. In the event that he or she has been the victim of someone else's sin, I must gently lead this person down the path to forgiveness, no matter how disgusting the abuse.

> *No one truly rests until they know they are forgiven by God and forgive others as God has forgiven them.*

Several years ago a woman Lois and I knew became anxious as she grew aware of abuse in her life. As a child she had been sexually abused by her brother and one of his friends, and it was all coming back to her. The woman had an eating disorder and was experiencing a wide range of emotions from sorrow to rage. Lois and I empathized with her childhood losses and adult misery as she worked through the memories and tarnished relationships. She had reason for anger but choosing a vindictive mode was unhealthy. She had watched a talk show which encouraged anger and getting even. When I suggested she move toward forgiveness she responded, "Forgive? No, get angry!" Being confident that she had neither the means nor the intentions to carry out vengeance, I said, "Let us know when you are ready to talk about forgiveness." After three weeks of bitter anguish she approached us willing and ready to learn about forgiveness. She wanted to be free, not only from the sin others had brought on her, but the anger toward those who had abused her. Unforgiveness tormented her.

FORGIVENESS IS ESSENTIAL FOR HEALTH

Recent research reinforces what has been the truth of Scripture for thousands of years: forgiveness is essential for health! Dr. Frederic Luskin,

Ph.D. in Counseling and Health Psychology from Stanford University, is the Co-Director of the Stanford-Northern Ireland HOPE Project, an ongoing series of workshops and research projects that investigate the effectiveness of his forgiveness methods on the victims of political violence.[132] He states: "The practice of forgiveness has been shown to reduce anger, hurt, depression and stress and leads to greater feelings of hope, peace, compassion and self confidence. Practicing forgiveness leads to healthy relationships as well as physical health. It also influences our attitude which opens the heart to kindness, beauty, and love."[133]

Just as the official Christian response to personal sin is repentance, the official Christian response to abuse is forgiveness. We cannot rest until we learn to forgive as God in Christ forgave us. We may engage in restful vacations, relaxing hobbies, fine fellowship, annual retreats, and periodic sabbaticals. We may even establish a weekly Sabbath-rest. However, if you and I are not convinced of God's forgiveness toward us and have not learned to forgive as God in Christ has forgiven us, we remain restless.

If you have not forgiven someone, you cannot stand to be in the same room with the person. If you happen to see someone who reminds you of that person, your blood pressure rises as you subconsciously tense up. If this person is at work, conversations are guarded and communication is limited. By the end of the day fatigue has you weary. If the person is at church, tuning in God is like attempting to listen to AM radio while going through a car wash. Without admitting it, you are in bondage to your unforgiveness.

Walter A. Henrichsen has written a daily devotional book which in my evaluation is worthy to stand on the shelf next to Oswald Chamber's *My Utmost for His Highest*. In *Thoughts from the Diary of a Desperate Man*, Henrichsen makes a case that is applicable to any life situation: "Your readiness to forgive is essential for a life of love and ministry. If you cannot forgive because of hurt inflicted by others, you will be unwilling to be vulnerable for fear of being hurt again. Because people are sinners, you cannot love and you cannot minister without getting hurt."[134]

As we mix with church members, fellow employees, neighbors, and strangers, there will be ample opportunity to forgive. We all have our personal horror stories of being used, abused, or betrayed. The question is not how often or severely we have been wronged, but how often we have forgiven as God in Christ has forgiven us.

Forgiveness is a premeditated condition of the heart based on the fact that God in Christ has already forgiven me.

If I have any hope of forgiving, I must have an accurate definition of forgiveness. After studying forgiveness as demonstrated throughout the Scriptures for years, I have settled on the following definition of forgiveness: Forgiveness is a premeditated condition of the heart based on the fact that God in Christ has already forgiven me. This definition proceeds from two similar verses of Scripture: "Be kind and compassionate to one another, forgiving each other, just as in Christ God forgave you" (Ephesians 4:32). "Bear with each other and forgive whatever grievances you may have against one another. Forgive as the Lord forgave you" (Colossians 3:13).

As I ponder forgiving as God in Christ has forgiven me, I cannot help but ask *how does God forgive?* And more specifically, *how has God forgiven me?* If I cannot answer these questions, there is little chance that I will be able to forgive others as God has forgiven me.

GOD TAKES THE INITIATIVE FOR OUR FORGIVENESS

First of all, when God forgives he takes the initiative. Figuratively speaking he doesn't stand there with his arms folded and nose in the air waiting for offenders to come crawling and begging his forgiveness. Notice who makes the first move after Adam and Eve commit the first sin: "But the LORD God called to the man, 'Where are you?' He answered, 'I heard you in the garden, and I was afraid because I was naked; so I hid.' And he said, 'Who told you that you were naked? Have you eaten from the tree that I commanded you not to eat from?'" (Genesis 3:9-11).

God took the initiative, calling to Adam and Eve while they hid in shame. God, the Righteous, made the first move toward man, the fallen. Forgiving as God forgives means you and I make the first move toward offenders when offended. Unlike God, my tendency is to leave fellow sinners to cower in their own garden of shame. Worse than avoiding, I tend to turn away from those who offend me. Instead of enhancing forgiveness, walking away makes forgiveness more awkward. God, the Righteous, builds bridges to the offenders. We, the sinners, tend to burn bridges of forgiveness toward fellow sinners.

God took the initiative by providing a solution to man's sin problem. The multitude of consequences sinful man brought upon himself belonged to man. Sin was man's problem. God could have folded his arms in disgust and responded, "You got yourself into this mess. You can get yourself out." He could have let humans squirm in their consequences for a few hundred years before giving the slightest hope that he would help them. Not God! He gave them hope by immediately taking the initiative. In the midst of the curses resulting from the fall, God gives the battle plan for defeating sin. God cursed the serpent for instigating the fall of man; with the curse came the announcement of Satan's ultimate defeat at the foot of the Messiah.

> So the LORD God said to the serpent, "Because you have done this, "Cursed are you above all the livestock and all the wild animals! You will crawl on your belly and you will eat dust all the days of your life. And I will put enmity between you and the woman, and between your offspring and hers; he will crush your head, and you will strike his heel."
>
> (Genesis 3:14, 15)

I cannot imagine that Adam and Eve understood all that there was to know about the coming Messiah by this pronouncement. But they had to get the message that God would send someone extraordinary to defeat the serpent, Satan, reverse the deadly consequences of sin, and lead them to the tree of life. This was their hope and the hope of their descendents for ages to come.

God's initiative to forgive pre-existed the fall of man. Under inspiration of the Holy Spirit, the Apostle Paul provides insight into God's kind intentions: "Praise be to the God and Father of our Lord Jesus Christ, who has blessed us in the heavenly realms with every spiritual blessing in Christ. For he chose us in him before the creation of the world to be holy and blameless in his sight" (Ephesians 1:3, 4).

Did God scramble to conjure up some response to man's twisted behavior? *Oh my! What am I to do now that man has fallen into sin?* No. His disposition was to forgive. When man sinned, God's plan to send his Son was engaged, first as a promise, then as a sacrifice.

That initial nugget of hope given by God to the first man and woman would come to fruition in the coming of Jesus Christ the Messiah. The author of Hebrews discloses many promises which in times past were mysteries: "Since the children have flesh and blood, he too shared in their humanity so that by his death he might destroy him who holds the power of death—that is, the devil—[15] and free those who all their lives were held in slavery by their fear of death" (Hebrews 2:14-15).

From the beginning God took the initiative, bringing forth a plan to forgive man—a plan that was impossible for sinful man to perform and probably beyond the imagination of his darkened mind.

God's initiatives surge forth from his love, love that precedes the fall of man. That love pre-dates all creation. It is a love that always was, is, and forever will be. God is love (I John 4:16). The love of God will not be denied. No human condition can stop it, not even the grotesque sinful condition of man. It continues to demonstrate itself in the most profound way: "But God demonstrates his own love for us in this: While we were still sinners, Christ died for us" (Romans 5:8).

God's taking the initiative to forgive was consistent in his teachings. One of the many examples in the Gospels where Jesus took the initiative to forgive is featured in Mark chapter two:

> A few days later, when Jesus again entered Capernaum, the people heard that he had come home. [2] So many gathered that there was no room left, not even outside the door, and he preached the word to them. [3] Some men came, bringing to him a paralytic, carried by four of them. [4] Since they could not get him to Jesus because of the crowd, they made an opening in the roof above Jesus and, after digging through it, lowered the mat the paralyzed man was lying on. [5] When Jesus saw their faith, he said to the paralytic, "Son, your sins are forgiven." [6] Now some teachers of the law were sitting there, thinking to themselves, [7] "Why does this fellow talk like that? He's blaspheming! Who can forgive sins but God alone?" [8] Immediately Jesus knew in his spirit that this was what they were thinking in their hearts, and he said to them, "Why are you thinking these things? [9] Which is easier: to say to the paralytic, 'Your sins are forgiven,' or to say, 'Get up, take your mat and walk'? [10] But that you may know that the Son of Man has authority on earth to forgive sins...." He said to the paralytic, "I tell you, get up, take your mat and go home." [12] He got up, took his mat and walked out in full view of them all. This amazed everyone and they praised God, saying, "We have never seen anything like this!"
>
> (Mark 2:1-12)

The paralytic was brought in because he needed to be healed. Jesus did better than heal the man. He took the initiative to forgive him despite the unbridled criticism of the teachers of the law. This narrative communicates not only Jesus' willingness to forgive but his authority to do so.

God's initiative to forgive was evident in the life as well as the death of Christ. Among the most hideous sins committed against the one who came to forgive were the scoffing rude taunts from those who so desperately needed his forgiveness. Bleeding and bruised, Christ took the initiative to express forgiveness: "Jesus said, 'Father, forgive them, for they do not know what they are doing.' And they divided up his clothes by casting lots" (Luke 23:34).

I cannot help but question, *did anyone in the New Testament actually take forgiveness as far as Jesus did? Is there any example of anyone taking the initiative to forgive as Jesus demonstrated?* The answer is found in Acts chapter seven. As Stephen was being stoned for speaking while full of the Holy Spirit, others added sins to their accounts by stoning him. Full of divine initiative to forgive in the pattern of Jesus, Stephen cried out, "Lord, do not hold this sin against them" (Acts 7:60).

Stephen's example leaves me with no excuse for failing to take the initiative when I'm sinned against. I cannot say *that's impossible. Only God has the strength to take the initiative and forgive such sin.* God gives the strength to forgive with such an initiative if we are willing to forgive as forgiven. John Ensor is president and executive director of *A Woman's Concern* (pregnancy resource centers), a ministry that cares for unwed mothers and teaches them to forgive. The following excerpt comes from his book, *Experiencing God's Forgiveness:*

> There are many people who have blocked the flow of mercy in their own lives with huge grudges. Stephen knew somehow that his own ability to receive mercy was dependent on letting go of his grudges—no matter how justified they felt. A wise Puritan once said, "He that demands mercy and shows none, ruins the bridge over which he himself is to pass." So Stephen forgave his worst enemy and in so doing received mercy from God.[135]

Every Sunday the Lord's Prayer is recited from memory by millions of parishioners in a myriad of languages. The Lord's Prayer assumes a willingness on our part to take the initiative in forgiving other sinners as God has taken the initiative in forgiving our sins: "Forgive us our debts, as we also have forgiven our debtors" (Matthew 6:12).

Forgiving as God in Christ has forgiven me requires that I, the offended, make the first move toward my offenders. Running, hiding, and avoiding my offenders are no longer options. I must take the initiative, not with passive-aggressive intentions smearing them with shame but by building a bridge to God which we can walk together.

GOD PAYS THE PRICE FOR OUR FORGIVENESS

Second, when God forgives he pays the price for forgiveness. Forgiveness, which is free to the sinner, costs the sinless his Son. Nothing is truly free. Regardless of the product or service, every free offer is a line item in a budget. Someone is paying for any free gift. What may be free to me costs someone something. We cherish our freedom as Americans, boasting about how free we are to one another and the rest of the world. However, one trip to the Vietnam Veteran's Memorial in Washington D.C., or any military graveyard is a sobering reminder that our freedom is not free.

The Hebrew word for forgiveness conveys the idea of carrying or bearing a heavy burden. This word to forgive is used repeatedly in Psalm thirty-two and provides a vivid picture of forgiveness in Isaiah chapter fifty-three:

> Surely he took up our infirmities and carried our sorrows, yet we considered him stricken by God, smitten by him, and afflicted. [5] But he was pierced for our transgressions, he was crushed for our iniquities; the punishment that brought us peace was upon him, and by his wounds we are healed. [6] We all, like sheep, have gone astray, each of us has turned to his own way; and the LORD has laid on him the iniquity of us all.
>
> (Isaiah 53:4-6)

The forgiveness that is free to me, a sinner, is not free to God or his Son. The price is very heavy. However, the weight is not measured in pounds or dollars. The price is measured in blood, the substance of life.

> How much more, then, will the blood of Christ, who through the eternal Spirit offered himself unblemished to God, cleanse our consciences from acts that lead to death, so that we may serve the living God!
>
> (Hebrews 9:14)

> For you know that it was not with perishable things such as silver or gold that you were redeemed from the empty way of life handed down to you from your forefathers, but with the precious blood of Christ, a lamb without blemish or defect.
>
> (I Peter 1:18-19)

In him we have redemption through his blood, the forgiveness of sins, in accordance with the riches of God's grace.

(Ephesians 1:7)

The forgiveness that is free to me and you was purchased with Christ's blood. His blood was one-of-a-kind, sin-forgiving, and life-giving plasma. It was the maximum price paid by God. No other human specimen would do, for he alone was sinless, satisfying the price of sin on man's behalf. As the Son of God, Jesus Christ satisfied forever the righteous demands of God. As man, Christ died on behalf of man. Grace is defined by God's paying the price for the forgiveness of our sins. It is a free gift that can never be earned or deserved: "For it is by grace you have been saved, through faith—and this not from yourselves, it is the gift of God—not by works, so that no one can boast" (Ephesians 2:8-9).

There is one cost to the recipient of free forgiveness. It will cost you and me our pride. Pride tends to think it is worthy of forgiveness. Pride wants to claim *I figured it out on my own. I worked hard enough to deserve forgiveness.* Pride sees no need for grace and no problem with sin. Pride is the price of forgiveness. It must be left at the door of forgiveness.

Brothers, think of what you were when you were called. Not many of you were wise by human standards; not many were influential; not many were of noble birth. [27] But God chose the foolish things of the world to shame the wise; God chose the weak things of the world to shame the strong. [28] He chose the lowly things of this world and the despised things—and the things that are not—to nullify the things that are, [29] so that no one may boast before him. [30] It is because of him that you are in Christ Jesus, who has become for us wisdom from God—that is, our righteousness, holiness and redemption. [31] Therefore, as it is written: "Let him who boasts boast in the Lord."

(I Corinthians 1:26-31)

May I never boast except in the cross of our Lord Jesus Christ, through which the world has been crucified to me, and I to the world.

(Galatians 6:14)

Corrie ten Boom provides this description of the prideful, self-possessed heart that at one time or another describes all of us: "Self is a tight lock. I saw many decent sinners who were in a kind of spiritual prison because self was on the throne of their hearts and Jesus was on the cross. What a liberation came when Jesus cleansed the heart with His blood. Then He came to the throne, and self went on the cross."[136]

If I am going to forgive as God in Christ has forgiven me, I must be prepared to pay some price as I offer forgiveness. This price is not to be confused with or compared to Christ's substitutionary death on the cross for the sins of the world. I am, however, likely to suffer some consequence for my offender's wrongdoing. Take, for instance, the example of Stephen who was stoned to death by jealous men. Stephen's life was shortened because of the sin of his murderers. The difference between Stephen's death and Christ's death is that Stephen died *because of* their sins, Jesus died *for* their sins. Stephen's death was a consequence of their sins. Jesus' death was a payment for their sins. "He himself bore our sins in his body on the tree, so that we might die to sins and live for righteousness; by his wounds you have been healed" (I Peter 2:24).

FORGIVENESS AND CONSEQUENCES

Forgiveness means that I am willing to accept the consequences of someone else's sin. Forgiveness does not automatically remove or reverse the consequences imposed by a careless or evil act. If that were the case, forgiving would be easy. Forgiving without consequences would be light duty. Living with one leg because a drunk driver swerved into your lane is hard to forgive. Enduring third-degree burns and scores of skin grafting procedures because some arsonist set your apartment on fire require a big, forgiving heart. Unfortunately, children are often the brunt of adult abuse.

My grandfather on my mother's side lived to be ninety-five years of age. At age eighty-seven he set out to write down his life story. He was not well educated and struggled to put it all on paper. The final copy was only sixteen double-spaced typed pages. I have wondered, *how can a person manage to cover eighty-seven years in sixteen pages?* Whatever finds its way into print must have had great impact on the autobiographer.

Peering back to when he was seven, Grandpa Joe, as he was known, remembered enduring several painful procedures to save his leg from osteomyelitis, an inflammation of the bone and bone marrow. A team of doctors would come to the house. One would hold the chloroform pad over his nose to keep him from moving while the other cut his leg open from knee to ankle. Then they proceeded to chip away the decayed bone from his leg with a hammer and chisel. It was reported that his mother had to leave the house because she couldn't bear the intensity of his screams.

He was on crutches for six months and out of school for one and one-half years. He was now well behind the children in his class, bigger than those in his stage of learning and practically illiterate. Since his immigrant parents only spoke Swedish, he didn't know much English. In his own words, "I didn't understand the teacher and she didn't understand me."

It became necessary for him to attend summer school. The teacher told the children, if they did not miss one day during the term, she would give each a football. He reported: "Ed Shafer and I made it. The last day the teacher came to me holding two toothpicks in her hand. One toothpick was higher than the other. I pulled on the lower one and she pinched her fingers tight, then I had to pull the other one and that was the short one. She then said that I should go to Ed and see who had the longest and she handed the football to Ed. Then the kids laughed. We should have both had a football."[137]

To his death Grandpa Joe always had two legs. He lived with a very thin layer of skin on his shin. If he bruised that leg his shin bone became exposed. He also lived with a very thin layer of self-respect. I don't know how my Grandpa Joe processed that belittling moment arranged by the one room school teacher. Obviously, the event influenced him enough so that he recalled it eighty years later. He forgave and learned to live with being slighted more than once. However, as a child it may have weakened his self-respect as much as osteomyelitis weakened his leg.

I was thirty when Grandpa Joe died. He had been retired my whole life and was available to spend time with his grandchildren; we loved him. Grandpa Joe left me with a wealth of memories and always encouraged good self-respect. Unfortunately, he had to fight for what little he possessed.

Forgiveness is about forgiving the sinner so you are not bound by the sin of unforgiveness, and its bitter results.

Consequences don't disappear because we forgive, bitterness does. In a discussion of forgiveness versus bitterness Neil Anderson explains how to live with consequences without becoming bitter: "Forgiveness is agreeing to live with the consequences of another person's sin. Forgiveness is costly. You pay the price of the evil you forgive. You're going to live with those consequences whether you want to or not; your only choice is whether you will do so in the bitterness of unforgiveness or the freedom of forgiveness."[138]

THE CONSEQUENCES OF UNFORGIVENESS

Painful as bearing the consequences of someone else's sin may be, failure to forgive can be far worse. In the same chapter where Paul tells us to forgive one another as God in Christ has forgiven us, he warns: "In your anger do not sin: Do not let the sun go down while you are still angry, and do not give the devil a foothold" (Ephesians 4:26-27).

Anger is not necessarily sin. However, the longer anger remains unresolved the greater the likelihood that anger will turn into sin. Stuffing anger may appear to be a safe option compared to going to jail for acting it out on someone or something. On the other hand, seething, unexpressed anger can result in another kind of imprisonment.

It is no accident that these two verses appear together. Unresolved anger gives the Devil a foothold, and literally ground in our lives. He uses anger as a beachhead from which he can further disturb a person's peace. The person becomes preoccupied with the disabling unrest and distracted from his or her awareness of God. I don't believe Satan or demons actually possess believers, since they don't really possess anything. Possession is not an accurate description of demonization. The literal meaning of demonization is "demon caused passivity."[139] Satan and his cohorts are squatters, not owners; however, as squatters they can certainly create a disturbance. No case of unresolved anger is worth coddling, given the likes of Satan's schemes (II Corinthians 2:11, Ephesians 6:11).

There is another reason to dread the consequences of unforgiveness—it easily turns into bitterness, causing us to miss out on the fullness of God's grace. Hebrews 12:15 warns: "See to it that no one misses the grace of God and that no bitter root grows up to cause trouble and defile many." Failure to give or receive forgiveness yields ground to bitter roots. Like roots of Bermuda grass these bitter roots occupy one location from which shoots of grass spread out in many directions.

I was first introduced to Bermuda grass after moving to Overland Park, Kansas. Bermuda grass soccer fields or lawns are ideal in southern climates, a nuisance in the central states. Every summer this strange grass kept springing up in my lawn. I was surprised to find that the roots did not grow directly beneath the grass. As I pulled the vine-like grass hand over hand I eventually came to roots anchored in the ground. When I tugged on the root I seldom got it all. The unwanted Bermuda grass returned to my lawn season after season. One day a lawn care specialist told me that I would need to kill the lawn in those areas if I want to get that creepy grass off my lawn. So I ended up with big brown spots of dead grass that required reseeding.

Unfortunately many communities, work environments, and churches are like that lawn. Bitter roots of unforgiveness have been sown by unforgiving people. Roots of bitterness spread poisoning attitudes decades later. It is hard to identify the true sources of bitterness; some have died, others have moved away but the bitterness remains. I am afraid that many churches are missing God's gracious blessing because of people with bitter roots. It is so severe in some churches that closing them down probably remains the best option.

VENGEANCE

I have wrestled with the question, *how can anyone rest when he or she has suffered such wounds and feels such vengeance toward those who have tortured them?* Romans chapter twelve reminds us that we can rest in the fact that God is just and vengeance belongs to him: "Do not repay anyone evil for evil. Be careful to do what is right in the eyes of everybody. [18] If it is possible, as far as it depends on you, live at peace with everyone. [19] Do not take revenge, my friends, but leave room for God's wrath, for it is written: 'It is mine to avenge; I will repay' says the Lord" (Romans 12:17, Deuteronomy 32:35).

Vengeance is God's responsibility, not yours or mine; and he carries a bigger stick than we can fathom. Imagine that you have been picked on by bullies after walking home from school. You could retaliate, which would result in getting beat up far worse than being picked on. Or you could tell your big brother what's been happening. God is your big brother who cannot be beaten. God keeps perfect records of what goes on down here. You don't have to tell him a thing; he already knows about your suffering and has a plan for executing justice. There will be no need for witnesses. He has seen it all. There will be no jury. His wisdom is perfect and without prejudice. You can rest in the fact that he will set all things right.

Jesus Christ provided the most powerful example of enduring suffering without retaliating. The Apostle Peter wrote the following to believers who were suffering for their faith: "To this you were called, because Christ suffered for you, leaving you an example, that you should follow in his steps. 'He committed no sin, and no deceit was found in his mouth.' [23] When they hurled their insults at him, he did not retaliate; when he suffered, he made no threats. Instead, he entrusted himself to him who judges justly" (I Peter 2:21-23).

I can tell you personally that entrusting my body, soul, mind, and circumstances to God who judges justly has brought great rest into my life. I have not trusted consistently; but when I have, trust has allowed me to sleep like a baby in his mother's arms.

Paul assured the suffering believers in Thessalonica that God would punish those who had wronged them:

> God is just: He will pay back trouble to those who trouble you [7] and give relief to you who are troubled, and to us as well. This will happen when the Lord Jesus is revealed from heaven in blazing fire with his powerful angels. [8] He will punish those who do not know God and do not obey the gospel of our Lord Jesus. [9] They will be punished with everlasting destruction and shut out from the presence of the Lord and from the majesty of his power [10] on the day he comes to be glorified in his holy people and to be marveled at among all those who have believed. This includes you, because you believed our testimony to you.
>
> (II Thessalonians 1:6-10)

As my awareness of God's righteous power expands, I become convinced that it is an awful thing to fall into the hands of an angry God (Luke 12:5). My attitude toward offenders has changed from fear *of* them to fear *for* them. I pray for offenders and will urge them to plead for mercy and forgiveness from Almighty God before it is too late.

GOD FORGIVES COMPLETELY

Third, it must be noted that forgiving as God forgives covers all of our sins. Paul makes a specific point of mentioning that God *forgave us all of our sins.* "When you were dead in your sins and in the uncircumcision of your sinful nature, God made you alive with Christ. He forgave us all our sins, having canceled the written code, with its regulations, that was against us and that stood opposed to us; he took it away, nailing it to the cross" (Colossians 2:13, 14).

Unlike a child who separates his vegetables at the dinner table eating carrots and corn and leaving peas and beans, God does not sort out sins, forgiving some and not others. The word *canceled* means to blot out or wipe away. When a scribe needed to remove what was written, he blotted it out with a liquid substance similar to ink. In more recent history typists used whiteout to cover mistakes. In the age of computers we highlight and press the delete key. God highlights our past sins and presses the delete key. That's forgiveness! On the topic of justification, Warren Wiersbe has provided a vivid illustration that has stayed with me for years:

> My friend Dr. Roy Gustafson has the finest illustration of justification I have ever heard. It seems that there was a man in England who put his Rolls-Royce on a boat and went across to the Continent to go on a holiday. While he was driving around Europe, something happened to the motor of his car. He cabled the Rolls-Royce people back in England and asked, "I'm having trouble with my car; what do you suggest I do?" Well, the Rolls-Royce people flew a mechanic over! The mechanic repaired the car and flew back to England and left the man to continue his holiday. As you can imagine, the fellow wondered, "How much is this going to cost me?" So when he got back to England, he wrote the people a letter and asked how much he owed them. He received a letter from the office that read, "Dear Sir: There is no record anywhere in our files that anything ever went wrong with a Rolls-Royce." Now that's justification.[140]

That's not all. So complete is God's forgiveness that he cancels the written code that was against us. Not only our sins went on the cross, but everything that identified and exposed our sins. That which made us feel guilty was nailed to the cross with the sin. When God purchased our forgiveness he did not fit us into something just good enough, He gave us a Rolls-Royce model of forgiveness. Forgiving as God in Christ has forgiven means that I turn around and forgive others with the finest forgiveness, forgiveness from heaven.

If I am going to forgive as God forgives me, I must not only release the sin of the offender from my mind, I must relinquish scorekeeping. I must ignore how many times they have hurt me versus how many times *I may have* hurt them. I must surrender record keeping all together. I am to throw away the evidence of the sin, refusing to reapply the written code that exposed the sin in the first place.   Such comprehensive forgiveness is also mine to claim for myself. Some personalities have a harder time forgiving themselves than forgiving those who have offended them. Believe me, I have been there. If I have asked for God's forgiveness in Christ, I am to treat my sin as completely forgiven. Being forgiven by God puts an end to replaying in my mind sins I have committed.

> God buries our sins in the deepest sea and puts up a sign, "No fishing."
>
> (Corrie ten Boom)

Fourth, forgiving as God in Christ has forgiven you will probably mean you will have to do it again. Peter asked the question others have hesitated to ask for fear that they may have to do the hard work of forgiving all over again: "Then Peter came to Jesus and asked, "Lord, how many times shall I forgive my brother when he sins against me? Up to seven times?" [22] Jesus answered, "I tell you, not seven times, but seventy-seven times" (Matthew 18:21-22).

Translators debate whether the Greek phrase should be rendered *seventy-seven times* (NIV) *or seventy times seven* (NASB). "You are to forgive an unending number of times" was probably the intent of Jesus' comment. That is an astonishing answer to Peter who no doubt thought he was being quite generous by suggesting he forgive an offender seven times. It is an outrageous answer to any of us who think we are being quite big after forgiving once.

"I Would Forgive You, Even if You Did it Again"

When I was young enough to be an asset to a church softball team our entire family got in the church bus with other ballplayers and their families. We were on our way to an away game. After the game we shook hands with the other team, the winners, and began loading the bus gathering chairs, blankets, balls, bats, and youngsters. Suddenly we all heard a blood-curdling scream. Nate, our seven-year-old son, had picked up and swung an aluminum bat, striking four-year-old Landon above the eye. The cut bled as freely as he cried. Realizing what he had done, our son joined the parade of tears. Landon would require a few stitches but was going to be all right. Before leaving the field I instructed Nate that he needed to say "I'm sorry" and ask Landon to forgive him.

Still whimpering, Nate walked up to Landon, "I'm sorry, Landon. Will you forgive me?"

Without prompting Landon immediately replied, "I'd forgive you even if you did it again."

Following Peter's question pertaining to the frequency of forgiveness, Jesus provided a parable stressing the importance of forgiving as God in Christ has forgiven. The punch of the parable warns all that unforgiveness has a tragic result. Anyone who does not forgive as God in Christ has forgiven him should not expect to be forgiven.

> Therefore, the kingdom of heaven is like a king who wanted to settle accounts with his servants. [24] As he began the settlement, a man who owed him ten thousand talents was brought to him. [25] Since he was not able to pay, the master ordered that he and his wife and his children and all that he had be sold to repay the debt. [26] "The servant fell on his knees before him. 'Be patient with me,' he begged, 'and I will pay back everything.' [27] The servant's master took pity on him, canceled the debt and let him go. [28] "But when that servant went out, he found one of his fellow servants who owed him a hundred denarii. He grabbed him and began to choke him. 'Pay back what you owe me!' he demanded. [29] "His fellow servant fell to his knees and begged him, 'Be patient with me, and I will pay you back.' [30] "But he refused. Instead, he went off and had the man thrown into prison until he could pay the debt. [31] When the other servants saw what had happened, they were greatly distressed and went and told their master everything that had happened. [32] "Then the master called the servant in. 'You wicked servant,' he said, 'I canceled all that debt of yours because you begged me to. [33] Shouldn't you have had mercy on your fellow servant just as I had on you?' [34] In anger his master turned him over to the jailers to be tortured, until he should pay back all he owed. [35] "This is how my heavenly Father will treat each of you unless you forgive your brother from your heart."
>
> (Matthew 18: 21-35)

FORGIVING WITHOUT PROMOTING SIN

By now you may be wondering whether or not forgiveness has any exceptions or limitations. *Can a person forgive to a fault?* I have wrestled with such questions. *If I continue to forgive am I inviting offenders to offend me and others again? How can businesses continue that simply forgive employees who shoplift, fail to show up on time, cheat on their timecards, or fail to do their work? Aren't churches that perpetually forgive actually promoting sin?*

The context of Matthew eighteen speaks otherwise. While Jesus' conversation with Peter teaches believers to forgive offenders repeatedly, in context Jesus has just instructed his disciples to repeatedly confront sinners who will not acknowledge their offenses and repent of their sins:

> If your brother sins against you, go and show him his fault, just between the two of you. If he listens to you, you have won your brother over. [16] But if he will not listen, take one or two others along, so that "every matter may be established by the testimony of two or three witnesses." [17] If he refuses to listen to them, tell it to the church; and if he refuses to listen even to the church, treat him as you would a pagan or a tax collector. [18] I tell you the truth, whatever you bind on earth will be bound in heaven, and whatever you loose on earth will be loosed in heaven. [19] Again, I tell you that if two of you on earth agree about anything you ask for, it will be done for you by my Father in heaven. [20] For where two or three come together in my name, there am I with them."
>
> (Matthew 18:15-20)

This passage challenges me to confront those who wrong me in significant ways. Just as it is my responsibility to confront, it is my local church's responsibility to see that I follow through with the process. The context teaches me to forgive in my heart as I confront my offender, always ready to express forgiveness as the person admits his or her wrong. In that same attitude of forgiveness, the church—beginning with its leaders—carries out consequences in the event that the offender refuses to admit any wrongdoing. My readiness to forgive indicates that I do not desire vengeance after I have suffered loss or injury. The individual or church that forgives without confronting may be as wrong as the individual or church that confronts without forgiving. Matthew eighteen teaches that forgiveness and confrontation go hand in hand.

Jesus and Stephen both confronted and forgave their offenders with their final words before death. They clearly voiced forgiveness while recognizing they were being put to death by those who sinned against them: "Father, forgive them, for they do not know what they are doing" (Luke 23:34) and "Lord, do not hold this sin against them" (Acts 7:60). Hopefully precious few of us will face martyrdom. If we have any hope of generating the same selfless responses at the point of death, that same blend of confrontation and forgiveness will need to be adopted in everyday life.

Failure to confront persists as one of the unhealthiest trends in twenty-first century churches. Seldom do individuals confront as prescribed in Matthew eighteen. It is even harder to find church leaders who will back them if they do confront. The ranks of churches that follow through with consequences when offenders fail to respond are even scarcer. Without confrontation true forgiveness is seldom expressed and long-term grudges produce conditions frigid as icebergs ready to fragment. Thanks to the emphasis of organizations like Peacemaker Ministries, many churches are waking up to the fallacies of *"peace-faking,"* a phrase coined by founder Ken Sande: "People who use escape responses are usually intent on 'peace-faking,' or making things look good even when they are not. (This is especially common in the church, where people are often more concerned about the appearance of peace than the reality of peace)."[141]

GRACE CONFRONTS

One of the Greek words for *forgive* shares the same root as the word grace, *Charis*. Grace has a firm side to it which confronts that which is ungodly and harmful. Grace teaches us the proper use of the word we first learned at age two: "No!"

> For the grace of God that brings salvation has appeared to all men. [12] It teaches us to say "No" to ungodliness and worldly passions, and to live self-controlled, upright and godly lives in this present age, [13] while we wait for the blessed hope—the glorious appearing of our great God and Savior, Jesus Christ, who gave himself for us to redeem us from all wickedness and to purify for himself a people that are his very own, eager to do what is good.
>
> (Titus 2:11-14)

Grace that forgives confronts! Forgiving grace is not a license to sin perpetually. Grace was granted to save us from the consequences of sin but also from perpetual sin. Paul addressed the faulty logic which says, *I can increase grace by sinning more.*

> What shall we say, then? Shall we go on sinning so that grace may increase? [2] By no means! We died to sin; how can we live in it any longer? [3] Or don't you know that all of us who were baptized into Christ Jesus were baptized into his death? [4] We were therefore buried with him through baptism into death in order that, just as Christ was raised from the dead through the glory of the Father, we too may live a new life. [5] If we have been united with him like this in his death, we will certainly also be united with him in his resurrection. [6] For we know that our old self was crucified with him so that the body of sin might be done away with, that we should no longer be slaves to sin.
>
> (Romans 6:1-6)

Grace breaks the chains of sin so we are no longer slaves to sin. Forgiveness sets me free from the perpetual cycles of sin. True followers of Christ have died to their sin just as Christ died for their sin. Perpetual sin and a life in Christ are incompatible. It is not unforgiving to confront sin that persists. The forgiving and loving response is to confront cyclical sin patterns. When confrontation does not change someone's behavior, consequences are sure to follow.

Forgiveness is not foolishness. Forgiveness is not foolish trust by which a person continues to trust the untrustworthy. Foolish trust actually sets a person up to fail again so they have to be forgiven again. Forgiveness does not pop the cork on a bottle of alcoholic beverage and set it on the table in front of an alcoholic. Forgiveness does not leave car keys available where a fourteen-year-old with a habit of driving illegally can find them. Forgiveness does not put a pedophile in a position where children are jeopardized and forgiveness marginalized. Forgiveness does not place employees in situations where they are sure to fail, so they are at the mercy of the employer's forgiveness.

Jesus did not trust contrary to what he knew. He saw through those who showed up for a handout with no intention of following Him: "Now while he was in Jerusalem at the Passover Feast, many people saw the miraculous signs he was doing and believed in his name. [24] But Jesus would not entrust himself to them, for he knew all men. [25] He did not need man's testimony about man, for he knew what was in a man" (John 2:23-25).

FORGIVENESS DOES NOT DISMISS ALL CONSEQUENCES FOR OFFENDERS

While God's forgiveness in Christ sets believing sinners free from the eternal penalty of sin, temporal consequences often follow. Ken Sande of Peace Maker Ministries provides examples of how consequences followed the sins of Bible characters:

> Forgiveness does not automatically release a wrongdoer from all their consequences of sin. Although God forgave the Israelites who rebelled against him in the wilderness, he decreed that they would die without entering the Promised Land (Numbers 14:20-23). Even Moses was not shielded from this consequence (Deuteronomy 32:48-52)....
>
> There are many times when you forgive someone but cannot afford to absorb the consequences of such wrongdoing. Or, even if you could

bear the cost, doing so may not be the wisest and most loving thing for an offender, especially one caught in a pattern of irresponsibility or misconduct. As Proverbs 19:19 warns, "A hot-tempered man must pay the penalty; if you rescue him, you will have to do it again." Thus, a treasurer who secretly stole from your church may benefit from having to repay what he or she took. Likewise, a careless teenager may drive more safely in the future if he or she is made to pay for damages. An employee who repeatedly neglects his responsibilities may need to lose his job to learn needed lessons.[142]

I remember Dad being called out of bed late one night during my high school days. He went down to his office building only to be greeted by a fellow deacon from his church, an office employee, and a policeman. The policeman had driven by and thought it peculiar that certain lights were on at that hour. He entered to find the employee stealing cash from the office. Most startling was the fact that the employee was also an officer at the same church Dad and Mom attended. I probably remember this event so well because this employee had a son my age who was a high school friend and youth group buddy. It was devastating for that family and embarrassing for the church.

Dad forgave the man. I never heard him say an unkind word about the employee. Dad also fired the man. Theft was a standard reason for firing employees. He certainly could not treat this employee differently because he attended the same church. Innocent mistakes could be tolerated; dishonesty triggered immediate consequences more than once. When consequences followed, Dad expressed more pity than anger toward those who cheated him and fellow employees. He expressed an amazing grace to forgive.

Dad had witnessed both the bitter results of unforgiveness and the beautiful results of forgiveness in his own family. One example of forgiveness must have influenced him more than any residue of unforgiveness.

I wrote about my great grandparents in chapter eight. Once Victor married Mathilda, a peasant girl without a cottage, he was disinherited and banished from his parents, Anders Nilsson and his wife. Within a year of their marriage Victor and Mathilda immigrated to Minnesota from Sweden. The young couple would never see their parents on earth again. However, there is ample reason to believe that they have been reunited in heaven.

As the legend goes Victor's brothers, Isak and Anders, traveled with the newlyweds to the new country. The brothers returned to Sweden, but not until one important change had taken place in their lives. They discovered the faith in Christ they apparently had not obtained through the stoic state church of Sweden. Either they became true believers through a source in America or, like Victor, they were persuaded to trust in Christ through Mathilda's strong faith.

That is not all—Victor's parents eventually became believers. Their faith is evident by this 1926 letter from Mathilda to her cousin Ester translated from Swedish to English.

> Hello Ester,
> Victor is fine. He has written his mother twice, and never got a letter back from her, because he married me a peasant. They were angry that he married a peasant without a cottage. But I am happy that they have found God and love Jesus. Even though they don't write back, that is good.[143]

It is believed that Victor's brothers, Isak and Anders, returned to Sweden and shared with their parents the living faith in Christ they had discovered. Whether or not that is how it happened is not the point. Mathilda was happy that they had found God and loved Jesus. She could have been angry with her in-laws, considering the way they treated their son and her husband as an outcast. Given Victor's early life of comparative ease, survival in the new land must have been a rude awakening. She could have been bitter toward them for holding on to the old country's ways of social status and stratum, but there was no indication of hostility, just forgiveness. Mathilda could rest because she had learned to forgive as God in Christ had forgiven her.

RECEIVING GOD'S FORGIVENESS

Have you honestly received God's forgiveness in Christ for your sins? He has taken the initiative for your sins to be completely forgiven. He has paid the penalty for them entirely with the blood of his Son, Jesus Christ. What remains is for you to ask for his forgiveness and receive Christ and his work on the cross. Once you have received God's forgiveness through Christ into your heart you can begin to forgive your offenders from your heart.

FORGIVING AS GOD FORGIVES

Are there people you need to forgive? Make a list of those who have offended you and note the offense. Then take the time to carefully pray through the list. Example: "Lord God, I forgive (name) for (what the person did) just as you have forgiven me in Christ Jesus."

Review the list again. Are there individuals in the list that you need to humbly confront, for God's sake? Are these individuals bringing shame to the name of Christ and his Church?

ASKING FORGIVENESS OF OTHERS

Has the Lord brought to mind the faces of individuals you have wronged? Make a list of those individuals and develop a plan to ask for their forgiveness wherever and whenever it is possible.

Prayer

My Lord and my God, thank you for taking the initiative making it possible for me to be forgiven completely and eternally through the blood of your Son and my Savior, Jesus Christ. Forgive me for all my sins. I receive your forgiveness into my heart that I may forgive others from my heart. I now begin a life of forgiving others as you have forgiven me. In Jesus' name and for his sake I pray, Amen.

Questions to Ponder

1. Could I write a note like Ramona wrote to the other truck driver?
2. Am I "peace-faking" in any of my relationships?
3. Do I need to take the initiative toward forgiveness in any of my relationships?

CHAPTER FIFTEEN

FROM REST TO REVIVAL

This is what the Sovereign LORD, the Holy One of Israel, says: "In repentance and rest is your salvation, in quietness and trust is your strength, but you would have none of it."

(Isaiah 30:15)

As a follower of Christ, you know that self-reformation is futile. Having declared spiritual bankruptcy, you came to Christ asking Him to live His life through you. He is your life; you live day-by-day in dependence upon His strength and presence.[144]

(Walter A. Henrichsen)

Church plants are notorious for picking up an assortment of people. Ours was no exception. Having never planted or pastored a congregation before, I wasn't sure exactly what to expect. I just knew that I was to love the people God brought into the flock and serve them the Word of God the best I knew how.

One parishioner comes to mind. He was a young man named Dan. Dan came to the fledgling group by invitation of a charter member. He was a new believer and fresh out of high school. One middle-aged couple took particular interest in Dan because he reminded them of the college-age son they lost in a construction accident.

Dan announced that he was going to be attending college in another community. The new congregation wanted to put on a farewell party for him before he left. Dan and the congregation agreed on a time and place for the party. Food was purchased and prepared, decorations were hung and tables were set. Everyone anticipated a delightful evening. There was only one problem. Everyone looked around and asked, *where's Dan?* Dan was nowhere to be found. We waited for Dan until the food was cold, then decided to eat without the honored guest.

A few days later Dan showed up. He apologized for having forgotten his own farewell party. After apologies were accepted the same group of people made arrangements for another farewell party for Dan. Once again food was purchased and prepared, tables were set and decorations hung. Everything was in order for the honored guest. There was only one problem. You guessed it. Dan had failed to show up to his own farewell party for a second time.

Dan's youthfulness, singleness, and limited life experience made his absence excusable. As the years have gone by and my experiences with people have accumulated, I attribute Dan's lack of response to another cause. Dan came from a broken home. I doubt that he was a special guest on very many occasions. I don't think he knew how to respond to being the center of attention. Being honored had escaped him. No one suspected the slightest tinge of guile in Dan's failure to remember those who sought to honor him.

Had this been a deliberate act of neglect by someone who knew better, his absence would have been hard to excuse. Had the honored guest intentionally stayed away to embarrass or even insult those who prepared the event, it may have been called *rebellion.*

SIN'S DELIGHTFUL FLAVORS

Sin has at least four delightful flavors which taste good going down but create severe spiritual illness and multiple consequences. The Hebrew language provides a vivid description of the different categories of sin. The general word for sin is *chataah.* It portrays a person shooting an arrow and *missing the mark.* Paul captured the idea in Romans chapter three when he wrote, "For all have sinned and fall short of the glory of God" (Romans 3:23). Guilt and punishment which accompany sin are attached to the Hebrew word *avon.* Deceit and falsehood are represented by the Hebrew word *remiyyah.* This would include treachery and perversion, twisting what is good into something evil. Rebellion is represented by the Hebrew word *pasha,* and is typically translated *transgression.* Transgressions are deliberate and often blatant sins.

Imagine not only going through a stop sign, but running it over because you don't think the sign should be there. Transgressions typically come with an attitude which the person expresses without hesitation, fueled by rage. The Boston Tea Party demonstrated defiance toward British oppression. The colonists communicated, *not only are we refusing to pay taxes on your tea, we are throwing your tea out into the sea.*

King David owned up to all of these types of sin in conjunction with receiving God's forgiveness after committing adultery and attempting to cover it up:

> How blessed is he whose *transgression* is forgiven,
> Whose *sin* is covered
> How blessed is the man to whom the Lord does not impute *iniquity*,
> And in whose spirit there is no *deceit!*
>
> (Psalm 32:1-2 NASB, italics mine)

REBEL, WHO ME?

The Prophet Isaiah was called by God (Isaiah 6:8-13) to address the rebellion of Israel's Southern Kingdom, Judah, and specifically the city of Jerusalem (Isaiah 1:1). Israel knew better than to reject God's acts of kindness toward them. The Prophet wasted no time reciting flowery introductions. He immediately calls them *rebels.*

> Hear, O heavens! Listen, O earth!
> For the LORD has spoken:
> I reared children and brought them up,
> but they have rebelled against me.
>
> (Isaiah 1:2)

> Woe to the rebellious children, declares the Lord,
> Who execute a plan, but not Mine.
> And make an alliance, but not of My Spirit,
> In order to add to their sin.
>
> (Isaiah 30:1, NASB)

> These are a rebellious people, deceitful children,
> children unwilling to listen to the Lord's instruction.
>
> (Isaiah 30:9)

Isaiah continues to confront the nation's rebellion. Chapter thirty describes their rebellion. It is not as overt as the kind that deliberately disobeys by doing the opposite from what God has commanded. Edward J. Young describes Israel's rebellion as a general attitude versus a specific action:

> The present prophecy, however, relates not so much to one particular act as to an attitude of mind, which in the face of danger turns to man rather than God; it is this attitude wherever manifested that the prophet condemns....

> Earlier Isaiah had characterized the nation's princes as rebellious, but now he applies the epithet to all the people (cf. 1:23). The root idea of the adjective is "turning aside." The people turned aside from Yahweh; they did not wish to hear His Word. Instead they turned unto their own desires and devices, and in so doing revealed their rebelliousness.[145]

Rebellious attitudes seep in long before actions have become overtly rebellious. Attitudes change as we exchange confidence in one resource for another. Judah was being threatened from the east by the Assyrians. They could either trust God who had delivered them numerous times in their history or turn to a nearby nation. They were leaning toward Egypt, ironically the nation from which they had once been delivered by God's mighty hand.

Judah's attitude refuses God's tailor-made provision. Like saying, "No thank you!" after someone has gone to the trouble of preparing a special meal specific to your tastes.

REBELLION HAPPENS AS WE EXCHANGE THE PROMISES OF GOD FOR THE PLANS OF MAN

> "Woe to the obstinate children," declares the LORD, "to those who carry out plans that are not mine, forming an alliance, but not by my Spirit, heaping sin upon sin."
>
> (Isaiah 30:1)

God had promised to protect and prosper his people (Isaiah 1:18-20). He had also promised to "crush the Assyrians" (Isaiah 14:24-27). Through Isaiah's prophecy Judah had already heard some of the clearest predictions regarding the coming Messiah (Isaiah 7:14; 9:6-7). The rebellious children chose instead to spin their own plans. They thought themselves to be more intelligent than God. They had a *better* idea, *trust Egypt.* Trust the gods of

Egypt. The Egyptians worshiped many gods and treated their Pharaohs like gods. In essence the Israelites were exchanging the Living and True God for the gods of Egypt. Impressed with the apparent strength of Egypt they made an alliance with that idolatrous nation. Resting on the promises of God who never failed them was not their choice. They had forgotten God's mighty deliverance and victory over Egypt through Moses. They didn't even consult him. Perhaps consulting God didn't even cross their minds.

Trends in the U.S. are rather disturbing, rebellious I would say. As the United States becomes increasingly secular, divine providence and promise are no longer revered. The prevailing attitude is expressed by the phrase, *we did it all by ourselves!* Battles over long-standing religious memorial symbols and the removal of the Ten Commandments are clear signs of rebellion and refusal to make God our refuge and strength. Given that the U.S. remains as the world's number one superpower, Americans are less apt to make alliances with other nations than ancient Israel. However, like Judah the U.S. continues to exchange its spiritual foundations for totally secular self-trust. Until recent years the Ten Commandments hung in courtrooms, "America the Beautiful" was sung in classrooms, and religious symbols such as the cross or the Star of David were not controversial.

Now the words "One Nation under God" in the Pledge Allegiance are contested. Never mind that the nation was founded on freedom of religion and freedom of religious expression. Anti-Christian and Jewish sentiment has turned the statement from freedom of religious to freedom from religion. Thomas Jefferson's statements on separation of church and state were intended to protect the nation from ever endorsing a single denomination as The State Church of the United States. Now this wall of separation has been twisted to mean no religion in the state or public sector.[146] Abraham Lincoln foresaw like a prophet these dangerous trends approximately one hundred and fifty years ago:

> We have been the recipients of the choicest of bounties of heaven; we have grown in numbers, wealth and power as no other nation has ever grown. But we have forgotten God. We have forgotten the gracious hand which preserved us in peace and multiplied and enriched and strengthened us, and we have vainly imagined, in the deceitfulness of our hearts, that all these blessings were produced by some superior wisdom of our own. Intoxicated with unbroken success, we have become too self-sufficient to feel the necessity of redeeming and preserving grace, too proud to pray to the God that made us.[147]

There is an old slang remark that goes something like this: "Dance with the one who brung yah." God has brought America to a dance on top of the world, and now we are exchanging partners for someone or something far inferior. I fear the dance is about to end.

I also fear that a similar exchange is permeating churches in the United States. Church leaders, including ministers, are more excited about stimulating church growth through methodology and the latest technology than prayerful dependence on the Almighty. Eugene Peterson expresses his disappointment in this growing trend:

> I am in conversation right now with a dozen or so men and women who are prepared to be pastors and who are waiting to be called to a congregation. And I am having the depressing experience of reading congregational descriptions of what these churches want in a pastor. With hardly an exception they don't want pastors at all–they want managers of their religious company. They want a pastor they can follow so they won't have to bother with following Jesus anymore.[148]

Management, improved methodology, and technology have their place as long as they are mere tools of service. I design PowerPoint presentations to enhance my sermons and seminars. I have a desktop and a laptop computer. Communication by e-mail is fast and global. Websites provide quick access to information which makes research a breeze. I utilize advanced communication systems so that I can keep up with the changes. Every once in a while there are glitches, gaps, and breakdowns to remind me that technology is a great servant and a terrible master.

Many of the fastest growing churches in the world are in places void of our management, methods, and technology. They have discovered the promises of God are more precious than the plans of man. Saying, "No thank you!" to God's promises in exchange for methods of growth is a growing rebellion. Subtle beginnings become overt over time.

As the Apostle Paul taught an arrogant congregation in Corinth, "Neither he who plants nor he who waters is anything, but only God, who makes things grow"(I Corinthians 3:7), so it is ours to humbly plant and water and it is God's to grow. From God's creation to God's Kingdom, you and I don't grow a thing. We can plant and we can water but growth is a gift of God that is promised. I find that quite humbling.

Saying, "No thank you!" to God's promises and opting for trust in human strategies is subtle rebellion. Subtle beginnings become overt over time.

REBELLION HAPPENS AS WE EXCHANGE THE POWER OF GOD FOR THE PROTECTION OF MAN

Historical Israel knew the power of God. The Pentateuch, the Poets, and now the Prophets all spoke of God's mighty acts in history. But they were out of touch with this history because they were out of touch with the God who acted in history and was on the edge of his throne ready to act again on their behalf. Instead of calling on the God of History, they passed up Divine power for whatever protection Pharaoh had to offer. They didn't even consult his opinion: "Woe to the obstinate children, ... who go down to Egypt without consulting me; who look for help to Pharaoh's protection, to Egypt's shade for refuge"(Isaiah 30:2).

How out of touch they were with the Living God. They went through the motions of worship, attending festivals and making sacrifices (Isaiah 1:11-17), but refused to trust in God's power to protect them from their oppressors.

Rebellion does that to a person. Rebellion erodes away the trail that was once a familiar path to power. Sin, especially rebellion, refuses to utilize the familiar source of power. It is just too embarrassing to return to the one whom we have sinned against. We would have to repent, renounce our belligerent ways, and humble ourselves to ask for help after having wandered from him. Shame causes us to turn away from the reliable Helper. At the moment it is easier to clear a new path than remove the shame by facing the one whom we have slapped in the face. Failure to face God is a recipe for more shame: "But Pharaoh's protection will be to your shame, Egypt's shade will bring you disgrace. Though they have officials in Zoan and their envoys have arrived in Hanes, everyone will be put to shame because of a people useless to them, who bring neither help nor advantage, but only shame and disgrace"(Isaiah 30:3-5).

INSURANCE, SECURITY, AND SOCIAL SECURITY

Far from the battle lines of war in the heartland of a vast and prosperous country, I can live in fear of catastrophe. Natural disasters, accidents, terminal illnesses, and murder happen in all areas of the country. No place is totally immune to these and other threats to life.

Most Americans do their best to cushion the fall when tragedy strikes. Insurance can be purchased to prevent physical and financial harm for most everything imaginable. Security systems are available to protect both person and property. Social Security was established years ago to protect the elderly and the impaired from abject poverty. I still wonder, *are these measures enough? When do I have enough insurance, security and retirement savings to guard against the unforeseen catastrophe?*

I have trusted insurance policies only to discover that we didn't have coverage for specific *acts of God*. We put our home on the market and failed to sell it before our moving date. Eight months later it still had not sold and our sump pump did not respond to the inflow of water during a storm. The carpet was soaked and the drywall damp. All had to be removed to eliminate mold. When we called the insurance agent he said the damage was not covered. We did not have coverage because a little box followed by the words *sump pump* did not have a check mark in it. The pump worked fine when we left. No one had suggested that we needed sump pump insurance coverage after we finished the basement several years earlier.

Americans trust all levels of government to come to their rescue when disaster strikes. Victims of Hurricane Katrina assumed that local and state governments would organize an evacuation plan if *the big one* hit. When the levees gave way local levels of government had not arranged for an evacuation. After the fact, Federal assistance could not get there fast enough to meet all the needs.

It is also assumed that Social Security will be able to provide for the retirement of all employees. Disappointment is predictable given the baby boomer bulge that is about to retire. Insurance, security, Social Security, etc., are not foolproof. Try to trust as we may, human agencies are no guarantee against disaster.

As I watch the evening news and communicate with friends and relatives, every week I hear of someone's sudden unexpected death. I wonder *who is with us this week that will be gone next week? Who is living their last day? Who is taking their last breath?* Deaths are frequent enough so that I no longer take a single day of life for granted. I am increasingly aware that God protects beyond what doctors cure or precautionary measures provide. He is able to protect and deliver all who trust in his power.

VISION, VALUES, AND POLICY MANUALS

After a church has survived a crisis, extraordinary effort goes into making sure that it won't happen again. If the problem arose because of lack of vision, a new vision statement is written or the old one revised. If values were askew, they are visited and clarified. If a job description failed to cover some vital area of responsibility, it is rewritten. Finally if policies are nil or negligent, they will certainly be revised to avoid everything from lawsuits to larceny. There is a compulsion about making sure that crises do not recur.

Compulsive reaction to every crisis that pains a congregation is itself a danger. When avoiding pain becomes the focus of a church, it builds a box for itself. For example a church decides that it will not have small groups any longer so that no small group leader will ever *cut and run* with the group again. A church makes a policy against certain displays of emotion during worship, because some visitors were offended and left. The youth groups will not invite any other youth groups to take part in activities again, because two kids got in a fight. There will be no more weddings of non-members in the church, because the last wedding party left the church building a mess. Such a church builds a box for itself better known as a coffin. It has nailed down everything to perfection until the lid is nailed shut. The final last words of churches on this path are *that will never happen again!*

How much better it is to exist for a cause than to avoid a crisis. I have spent hours writing vision statements, clarifying core values, and developing policy manuals for the churches I served as a pastor. I am not saying that such documents are not necessary. I am saying that such documents are no guarantee against problems in the future. Too many churches spend an inordinate amount of time producing written documents to protect them from past or future crises. Policies produced out of fear and self-preservation are no substitute for the power of God. One will always wonder if his or her church has locked out every potential threat to tranquility behind its doors. Policies are not the ultimate protection. God gives his powerful protection when he is the focus and cause of the organization. It is safer to put divine cause before crisis management.

Saying "No thank you!" to God's power in exchange for endless protection policies is a subtle rebellion. Subtle beginnings become overt over time.

REBELLION HAPPENS AS WE EXCHANGE THE TRUTH OF GOD FOR THE TALENT OF MAN

Go now, write it on a tablet for them, inscribe it on a scroll, that for the days to come it may be an everlasting witness. These are rebellious people, deceitful children, children unwilling to listen to the LORD's instruction.

They say to the seers, "See no more visions!" and to the prophets, "Give us no more visions of what is right! Tell us pleasant things, prophesy illusions. Leave this way, get off this path, and stop confronting us with the Holy One of Israel!"

(Isaiah 30:8-11)

This time the children of Israel are called a rebellious people for saying "No thank you!" to the seers and prophets sent from God to tell them the truth. I imagine the tone was more like *Shut up! We have heard enough of your pessimistic rumors of disaster if we don't obey. We don't care if what we want to hear isn't true. If it makes us feel good, we will listen.*

This disdain for truth continues to be the channel of choice. Entertaining lies bring big profits. In the spring of 2006 Dan Brown's best selling *The Da Vinci Code* became a movie. People flocked to the box office to view the novel that became a movie. Both the book and the movie present a perversion of the life of Christ and a distortion of Leonardo da Vinci's painting, The Last Supper. If possible, da Vinci would have turned in his grave many times. People believed it because it was on the big screen. If you want to get rich, write a novel or make a movie laced with lies about Jesus. The Apostle Paul predicted this is how it would be in the last days:

For the time will come when men will not put up with sound doctrine. Instead, to suit their own desires, they will gather around them a great number of teachers to say what their itching ears want to hear. They will turn their ears away from the truth and turn aside to myths.

(II Timothy 4:3-4)

God loves truth. He is called the God of truth (Isaiah 65:16). He speaks truth (Isaiah 45:19) and cannot lie (Titus 1:2). Jesus is the Truth (John 14:6) and came in grace and truth (John 1:17). The Holy Spirit is the Spirit of Truth (John 16:13). No person can knowingly accept a lie and at the same time draw near to God (I John 1:6). We must ruthlessly eliminate lies from our lives and desire truth in the inner person (Psalm 51:6).

The Israelites were attracted to the Egyptians in part because of their talent. They were skilled horsemen and able to refine a swift breed of stags known to this day as the Arabians.

An Egyptian soldier knew how to handle a horse. It didn't matter whether the beast was beneath him or hitched to a chariot. Pity the troops that fled from them. Judah assumed all would flee from them. That was a big assumption: "Woe to those who go down to Egypt for help, who rely on horses, who trust in the multitude of their chariots and in the great strength of their horsemen, but do not look to the Holy One of Israel, or seek help from the LORD" (Isaiah 31:1).

Good looks never hurt. The Egyptians were "a people tall and smoothed-skinned, to a people feared far and wide, an aggressive nation of strange speech, whose land is divided by rivers" (Isaiah 18:2).

Years ago Dad and I toured the Middle East together. Our minds were quickly filled with first impressions. As we crossed over into Egypt, Dad commented on the good looks of the Egyptian people. He never lost his eye for good-looking people. Good looks both attract and intimidate. While Judah found the Egyptians attractive, they hoped the Assyrians would find them intimidating. Such hopes were vain.

Judah's misplaced trust was not only rebellion, it was fatal. Returning to Egypt was forbidden as stated in Deuteronomy 17:16. They had definitely rebelled. Now they would face the consequences of exchanging truth for talent. Judah and Egypt would fall together as the Assyrians would defeat both: "But the Egyptians are men and not God; their horses are flesh and not spirit. When the LORD stretches out his hand, he who helps will stumble, he who is helped will fall; both will perish together" (Isaiah 31:3).

If exchanging divine truth for human talent is rebellion, we are a rebellious nation. Americans as a whole are intoxicated with talent and good looks. We have traded truth for talent.

Our highest-paid people are not those who protect us but those who entertain us. Financial rewards for highly talented athletes, actors, actresses, and recording artists are escalating at an unprecedented rate. In 2004 *Forbes Magazine* compared the incomes of the fifty highest-paid athletes with those of the previous ten years: "Overall, the 50 highest earners pulled in a combined $1.1 billion, 40% of which came from endorsements. The minimum to make the list was $15 million versus less than $5 million in 1994."[149]

The fault lies not with talented people for making money; I blame Americans for our addiction to them. We not only pay talented people disproportionately more than they are worth, we worship them.

American Idol rules as a reality television show. I remember the first time I heard the title "American Idol." I was filled with mixed emotions. *How pagan to call any human being an idol, an object of worship.* I also thought *how honest to actually admit that we have succumbed to worshipping people.*

I do not fault the show. I do grieve about the idea of idolizing human beings and talent. I admire talented athletes, skilled musicians, good actors and actresses, and highly intelligent people. I praise God for them since he made them and encourages the development of their innate abilities. However, without God we are nothing; we are not worthy of worship. To worship people is idolatry and the heinous sin of rebellion.

Many congregations are too easily mesmerized by ability to the neglect of character. I have seen where very gifted pastors and laymen were given latitude regarding character because it was believed that *you can't argue with success.*

Unfortunately, bad character goes sour at the worst possible time and in the most public manner. The ecclesiastical empires that such powerful leaders build typically become public embarrassments. Congregations that fail to confront questionable character because they have subtly exchanged truth for talent usually suffer the loss of people, funding, and divine favor.

Isaiah's warning and Judah's defeat warns me to never elevate any person, creature, or thing above God. To compromise truth for human ability or beauty is a dangerous proposition. The subtle exchange of divine truth for human talent is rebellion.

REVIVAL, REPENTING OF OUR REBELLION

> *Jesus cannot cleanse an excuse, so I confessed my sin...*
> *(Corrie ten Boom)*[150]

I have asked myself; *why doesn't revival happen more frequently and in more places?* I have heard various answers like: *Revival doesn't happen because Christians don't witness more, work harder, or pray more, etc.* Typical answers focus on human shortcomings. I believe the real human shortcoming is failure to own up to personal sin. Repentance, more than goodness or hard work, is the human component in revival. Oswald Chambers said it well: "What our Lord wants us to present to Him is not goodness, nor honesty, nor endeavor, but real solid sin; that is all He can take from us. And what does He give in exchange for our sin? Real solid righteousness. But we must relinquish all pretence of being anything, all claim of being worthy of God's consideration."[151]

Revival happens in individuals as they declare themselves spiritually bankrupt, unable to think, work, or plan their way out of their spiritual poverty. As we repent of our sin and spiritual bankruptcy God does his part by sending his Spirit to embrace and regenerate us. Revival happens in any heart that sincerely repents of his or her sins. Isaiah 30:15 is a powerful reminder that repentance is essential for revival: "In repentance and rest is your salvation."

When the Holy Spirit comes upon masses of people, convincing them of their sin, the righteousness of God and the reality of God's judgment (John 16:8), Christian historians recognize that a revival has taken place, declaring it an act of God.

My call to ministry took place in such a setting and time when God was moving powerfully on college campuses in the early seventies. Student after student had life-changing encounters with Christ the spring semester of 1970. It was not a single event but a series of encounters on the campus of Bethel College in St. Paul, Minnesota, and similar colleges.

I personally came to see myself as spiritually bankrupt, unable to change myself and live up to God's expectations. For six years I had been trying to please God in my own strength without total surrender to him. I declared myself *unfit* for God. There was only one thing I could do and that was to give him my life without reservation. What occurred in the months that followed stirred like a wave of the Holy Spirit that changed my life and many others.

I returned from college on weekends and began to share every old and new scriptural insight I knew with my college and high school friends. During the summer months a few of us started a Bible study. One night of the week we studied the Bible and another night of the week we prayed that our believing friends would be revived by the Holy Spirit and our unbelieving acquaintances would come to Christ.

When I returned home from college on weekends the next fall, I discovered that the Bible study had expanded. I clearly remember asking, *who is that person sitting over there? What about those three kids over there?* Consistently the replay was: *These are the kids who repented and received Christ this week.* This went on for months until we crowded many teens and adults in my parent's basement. After that we rented a facility downtown.

Some of those in attendance came from Bible-believing churches, others from not so Bible-believing churches. Many of those new believers had rejected true Christianity altogether, some were delivered from drug and alcohol addictions. The most rebellious found it easier to own up to their sins, since they were so undeniably overt. As the saying goes, *when we are at our worst, grace is at its best.*

A reliable source living in Indonesia witnessed a televised special report shortly after the tsunami had devastated so much of the islands in January of 2004. For four hours Indonesian television showed Muslims repenting of their sins. They were convinced that Allah was judging them for their disobedience. They openly confessed such sins as receiving bribes. The person watching the coverage was grieved that he never heard anyone thank God for forgiving their sins. Accepting forgiveness was not compatible with their belief system. However, repentance prepared many of them for what would occur.

There were reports of visions among Muslims. One man saw a Bible reference on the wall of a mosque, Acts 4:12. When he exited the mosque he asked about Acts 4:12 and someone handed him a Bible. He read the following reference to Jesus Christ: "Salvation is found in no one else, for there is no other name under heaven given to men by which we must be saved" (Acts 4:12).

God has ways of bringing repentance followed by massive revivals on cultures formerly thought to be impossible to penetrate with the Gospel. For decades Muslims have been moved toward Christ by dreams and visions. The following is an excerpt from The National & International Religion Report:

> More and more Muslims are having dreams and visions of Christ, Christian ministries say. There is increasing evidence that the supernatural is playing a role in drawing Muslims to Christ.
>
> Campus Crusade for Christ has received thousands of letters from Muslims, many of whom claim to have had a similar dream of Christ, according to the ministry's radio broadcast office in northern Africa. In the dream, Jesus appears and tells people, "I am the way," Campus Crusade founder and President Bill Bright said. Moved by the dreams, they contact the radio ministry and "freely respond" to the gospel message, he said. In Algeria, an imprisoned Muslim political radical said Jesus appeared to her in her cell. The woman now is a Christian and works with Campus Crusade ministering to Muslims.
>
> In one African Muslim country, a young man violently tore up a Bible tract and threatened the life of the Every Home For Christ worker going door-to-door with the literature, Dick Eastman of Colorado Springs-based EHFC told NIRR. The next afternoon as the worker sat in his home, he was shocked to see the man knock at his door. "I must have another booklet," the Muslim told him. He explained that the previous night two

hands awakened him, and when he turned on the light and asked who was there, a voice said, "You have torn up the truth." The voice instructed him to acquire another booklet, directing him to the EHFC worker's home, the young man said. There, the Muslim read the booklet and became a believer. He has since been expelled from his wealthy family, lives with EHFC's Africa director, and is preparing for ministry to Muslims.[152]

Revival is recognized by man when numbers of people repent. Revival is recognized by God when one person repents. That one person needs to be me. That one person needs to be you. Then you and I can take revival to the next person we meet.

REVIVAL, RESTING IN GOD'S PROVISION

Judah's failure to truly rest on the Sabbath bled into all of life. No wonder rest eluded them amidst threats from a militant Assyria. They had underestimated the role of rest in invoking God's protection, "In repentance and rest is your salvation."

Salvation (*yasha*) in this context has a wider application than salvation from sin. Judah's obsession with deliverance from the impending threats of Assyria drove them to consider every human option for survival. After engaging their problem-solving skills, turning to Egypt got the most votes. Their plan rested on Egypt's military power for survival. Whatever rest they experienced through this plan evaporated like fog under the midday sun.

Assyria was not Judah's biggest problem. A more devastating enemy had already infiltrated Judah's ranks. Like a virus attacking an immune system, this enemy had turned the people against their true and powerful Protector. Their perspective was now poisoned so that the Protector looked like the enemy and false help appeared as the tangible solution. As a biological virus invades the body and a computer virus raids a hard drive, this intruder assaults souls. Sin is a ravaging terrorist.

Sin was the real reason for defeat at the hand of the Assyrians. Sin had to be conquered before Judah could defeat any other enemy. This enemy refuses to bow to human plans and efforts. The sinner must rest in God's plan and power to defeat sin. This is the ultimate salvation.

Revival happens as we rest in the power of God for salvation. God has endowed man with tremendous problem-solving abilities. Sin, however, lurks beyond human ability. Try as we may to solve the problem of sin with money, education, or planning, sin prevails. God gave mankind amazing abilities, but we cannot save ourselves. Walter Henrichsen points out the irony of being an able, self-reliant, self-made, self-sufficient person in light of eternity:

> The worse thing that can happen to the non-Christian is for him to be able to solve his own problems. Nothing is more deadly than self-reformation. The great Physician heals those who cannot heal themselves. If people conclude that they can solve their own problems, or at least learn to accommodate them in their lives, they lose their incentive to turn to Christ for help, and that is a short path to hell.[153]

Appalled as some may be at the thought of man's inability to save himself, there is no recourse but to trust in God's plan. The gospel about Christ's death for sin remains forever as the only answer to the problem of sin: "I am not ashamed of the gospel, because it is the power of God for the salvation of everyone who believes: first for the Jew, then for the Gentile" (Romans 1:16).

> For the message of the cross is foolishness to those who are perishing, but to us who are being saved it is the power of God. [19] For it is written: "I will destroy the wisdom of the wise; the intelligence of the intelligent I will frustrate." [20] Where is the wise man? Where is the scholar? Where is the philosopher of this age? Has not God made foolish the wisdom of the world? [21] For since in the wisdom of God the world through its wisdom did not know him, God was pleased through the foolishness of what was preached to save those who believe.
>
> (I Corinthians 1:18-21)

> For it is by grace you have been saved, through faith–and this not from yourselves, it is the gift of God—[9] not by works, so that no one can boast.
>
> (Ephesians 2:8)

If salvation were achieved by bloodline, education, ability, or determination, the Apostle Paul had a huge advantage over the rest of us. Paul trashed all attempts to save himself by human advantage once he accepted the saving power of Christ.

But whatever was to my profit I now consider loss for the sake of Christ. What is more, I consider everything a loss compared to the surpassing greatness of knowing Christ Jesus my Lord, for whose sake I have lost all things. I consider them rubbish, that I may gain Christ and be found in him, not having a righteousness of my own that comes from the law, but that which is through faith in Christ—the righteousness that comes from God and is by faith.

(Philippians 3:7-9)

If you want to be saved, don't do something, stand there! Receive God's provision of salvation through Christ. Rest in what God has done for you. Saying "No thank you!" to God's provision for salvation and opting for trust in human strategies is rebellion.

If our greatest need had been information,
    God would have sent us an educator.
If our greatest need had been technology,
    God would have sent us a scientist.
If our greatest need had been money,
    God would have sent us an economist.
If our greatest need had been pleasure,
    God would have sent us an entertainer.
But our greatest need was forgiveness,
    So God sent us a Savior!

(Source Unknown)

QUIETNESS AND TRUST

Lois and I learned to enjoy soccer through our sons, Scott and Nate. Soccer was a sport we knew little about in our own childhoods. Both boys started at age five. Nate played through college and continues to play, coach, and referee the game. We have spent many vacations following soccer tournaments over the years.

Once while traveling with a load of boys to a tournament, we began to talk about behavior on the field. One player volunteered that some opposing players attempt to intimidate with chatter. Such players may talk about how many goals they have scored, or their team's superior record. They may challenge, "Bet yah can't get around me." Another volunteered that some players talk a lot of *trash* to intimidate you. *Sometimes it's racial; some of it's about your ancestry.* The lads agree that the players that got under their skin the most were the ones who said nothing; *they just stare at you with a somber look of confidence. They look you in the eye and say nothing. They're the most intimidating.* Quietness does not necessarily communicate timidity. It can be a sign of strength.

In contrast, constant chatter, profanity, and macho behavior reflect insecurity. Such mannerisms camouflage discomfort. They operate like an alarm system warning all challengers to back off while hinting that there is something fragile inside. The hair on the back of a small dog rises when in the presence of larger dogs. Anxiety works in the small dog to make it look bigger than its actual size. Threatened people also have ways of making themselves look bigger than reality.

We, today, know everything but ourselves. We never really come to know ourselves because we cannot get quiet enough.

(A.W. Tozer)[154]

Anxiety attempts to hide in a blizzard of activity. I met a girl in high school who competed in everything. She strove to be the best in music competitions, gymnastics, and horsemanship. I asked her why she chose so many activities. She replied, "When I am quiet and have time to think about myself I get depressed." Rather than face the pain within her, she smothered it with activity. Her perpetual motion hid her insecurities, so she thought.

The only horse races I have ever watched have been on television, but my general observation is that the horses that walk to the gates without getting lathered up usually rank better than those that stomp around, resisting their trainers and jockeys when entering the gates.

An inability to be still and quiet on the outside may indicate a disturbance on the inside. This disturbance may reflect anxiety generated by a lack of trust in objects or persons worthy of trust. Trust is as good as the object or person in which it is placed.

Judah had been busy making alliances with countries that were not trustworthy. The Lord through Isaiah had this to say about Egypt: "Look now, you are depending on Egypt that splintered reed of a staff, which pierces a man's hand and wounds him if he leans on it! Such is Pharaoh, King of Egypt, to all who depend on him" (Isaiah 36:6).

Isaiah had warned Judah not to trust the nation the Lord once defeated through Moses. Now that they had trusted Egypt, there was still time to transfer their trust to the Lord. He was willing to meet them more than halfway. Calmness would come as they trusted him. The Lord intended that quietness and trust be their strength. He made it clear that trusting in him would provide a life of grace through the verses that followed.

> Yet the LORD longs to be gracious to you; he rises to show you compassion. For the LORD is a God of justice. Blessed are all who wait for him! O people of Zion, who live in Jerusalem, you will weep no more. How gracious he will be when you cry for help! As soon as he hears, he will answer you. Although the Lord gives you the bread of adversity and the water of affliction, your teachers will be hidden no more; with your own eyes you will see them. Whether you turn to the right or to the left, your ears will hear a voice behind you, saying, "This is the way; walk in it."
>
> (Isaiah 30:18-21)

QUIETNESS AND TRUST SPEAK VOLUMES

Today many occupations encourage verbosity. If you can talk louder, faster, and over the voices of others you are a lead candidate for a job as a lawyer, teacher, talk show host, politician or preacher. Obviously many careers require verbal skills. They also require listening. Talking without listening produces answers to questions that have not been asked.

I have a couple of seminary degrees and work with pastors who have attended seminary. A seminary education focuses on verbal skills as applied to preaching and teaching. Seminaries would do students and churches a favor by enhancing the seminarians' listening skills. Christian education teaches students how to do ministry through activity better than they teach how to be ministers by listening and being quiet. Quietness and trust speak volumes.

Trusting God in major areas of life has been a long journey. One painful step after another God has expanded my trust in him. The pain was what I experienced as I trusted myself and those unworthy of trust. Pleasure followed as I found him trustworthy. It has been a long process of getting free from insecurities. I only regret that I didn't learn to trust God in more areas earlier in life.

Today I thank God for the freedom to relax and laugh because the big tickets are paid for—the biggest of all being forgiveness of my sins through the death of Christ, my Savior. If this temporal life should end without warning, I know where I will spend eternity. I could not relax on earth without assurance of my heavenward destiny.

King David had many troubles. Some were induced by God's special calling on his life, such as Saul's sin of envy against him. Saul was enraged by God's powerful anointing on David. Some troubles were the consequences of David's own sin, such as his adultery with Bathsheba and prideful act of numbering the people. But David found rest in his eternal hope. He proclaimed, "My soul finds rest in God alone; my salvation comes from him" (Psalm 62:1). Within the Psalm David reminds himself where he can find deep rest. I find that I need to remind myself as well that the Lord is the source of rest because he is trustworthy. David called God his "Mighty Rock," a figure of speech communicating security and trustworthiness.

> Find rest, O my soul, in God alone;
> my hope comes from him.
> He alone is my rock and my salvation;
> he is my fortress, I will not be shaken.
> My salvation and my honor depend on God;
> he is my mighty rock, my refuge.
> Trust in him at all times, O people;
> pour out your hearts to him,
> for God is our refuge. Selah.
>
> (Psalm 62:5-8)

I was about nine years old the first time I went duck hunting with my grandfather, father, and older brother. Since I was too young to legally hunt, I was the only one not carrying a gun. My senses were on overload just taking in the pre-dawn experience. I remember walking on a snow fence that had been laid down to make a path on the swampy bog. Without the fence one would sink deep into the mud. Even with the fence one could get stuck if he didn't watch his step. I had to be very careful since my legs were short and my boots only went up to my knees; everyone else wore hip boots.

The object was to walk out on the snow fence a half mile into the bog to our hunting positions. The law permitted hunters to start shooting one-half hour before sunrise. Since the best opportunities were before sunrise, all hunters wanted to be at their positions on time.

That morning the air was crisp and cool. Reeds overhead swayed back and forth with the gentle breeze. The eastern sky was beginning to glow with first light and the sky was beginning to hum from the sound of duck wings in flight overhead. It was a stimulating experience. However, one thing made me uneasy. Every time I took a step on the submerged snow fence my foot sank down three or four inches and sometimes more. Furthermore it was pretty dark. It was like reading Braille with my feet. On occasion the person ahead of me pointed out a hole in the snow fence that I should avoid if I wanted to stay dry. The water temperature was not very inviting in Minnesota during October. If I got wet on the walk out, it might be five or six hours before I was able to put on a dry set of clothes.

The morning hunt had been enough of a success that I immediately longed for the day I turned twelve and could carry a gun like the rest of our hunting party. The entire experience deserved a return trip as soon as possible. The only thing I wasn't sure about was the walk on the snow fence in the dark. Now that the hunt was over, it felt so good to be back on hard ground. The gravel road was packed with rock. It did not sink when I drove my foot into it. I felt my body relax. I could rest now that my feet were on solid ground. I took a deep breath and a sigh of relief. I trusted the hard ground.

Trust is as good as the object of trust. Churning up greater trust in a slippery soggy snow fence wouldn't turn it into a slab of granite. The Lord God is a Mighty Rock.

> *The secret of Christian quietness is not indifference, but the knowledge that God is my Father, He loves me, I shall never think of anything He will forget, and worry becomes an impossibility*
>
> *(Oswald Chambers)*

David's advice was available for all of Judah to read. Unfortunately their trust had shifted from rest in God alone to a tenuous relationship with Egypt. God sent Isaiah with the same plea, find rest in the Almighty alone. Isaiah 30:15 ends with a sobering bottom line, "But you would have none of it."

Is that your bottom line—"But you would have none of it?" Providing that you have read *For God's Sake, Rest!* from the beginning, you have seen the value of rest from my personal experiences, the references of others, and above all, the Word of God. Will it be said of you, "But you would have none of it," or will you "For God's sake, rest"?

I am afraid that Voltaire knew something that we have forgotten when he said, "I can never hope to destroy Christianity until I first destroy the Christian Sabbath."[155]

Rest as God intends invigorates his people to rise and serve with a refreshed perspective and renewed obedience. Rest remains a key to revival!

Prayer

Dear Lord God, forgive my rebellious ways. I admit that I have rebelled overtly by consciously disobeying your commands. I admit that I have rebelled subconsciously by responding with a "No thank you!" after you have offered what is best for me and pleasing to you. Lord, I repent of my rebellion and enter your rest as my deliverance in keeping with your salvation. I quiet myself as I trust in you as my strength now and forever. I want all of it, Lord. In Jesus' name and for his sake I pray, Amen.

Questions to Ponder

1. Am I rebelling overtly or passively against the Lord in any way?
2. Have I identified in my life any of the forms of rebellion mentioned in this chapter?
   List which ones:
3. Am I repentant about my rebellion?
4. Do I need to be revived through the key words of Isaiah 30:15: repentance, rest, quietness and trust?

CONCLUSION:
REST, A CORE VALUE

Much emphasis has been placed on values in recent years. Corporations, educational institutions, churches, and charities have been identifying and defining their core values. In his book, *Values Driven Leadership*, Aubrey Malphurs defines a church's core values as "its constant, passionate, sacred core beliefs that drive its ministry."[156] Malphurs makes reference to two other definitions of values. A more general definition by Charles O'Reilly, et al, reads as follows: "Basic values may be thought of as internalized normative beliefs that can guide behavior."[157] Malphurs makes reference to another definition by Patrick Lencioni that is fitting for corporations: "deeply ingrained principles that guide all of a company's actions."[158] After years of studying the theme of rest in the Scriptures, I have come to believe that *rest is a core value with God.* In my mind that is the statement that best summarizes *For God's Sake, Rest!*

Rest is a core value with God, so much so that he modeled it for us at the completion of Creation (Genesis 2:1-3).

Rest is a core value with God, so much so that he blessed rest (Genesis 2:3).

Rest is a core value with God, so much so that a day of rest was the first thing he called holy (Genesis 2:3).

Rest is a core value with God, so much so that he named a day after it (Exodus 16:29).

Rest is a core value with God, so much so that he included a commandment about rest, declaring one day a week be devoted to rest and not work (Exodus 20:9-11).

Rest is a core value with God, so much so that he granted rest to all including servants, animals, and aliens (Exodus 20:10-11).

Rest is a core value with God, so much so that he made it a sign between himself and his people (Exodus 31:17).

Rest is a core value with God, so much so that he gave his people land in which they could rest (Joshua 1:13-15).

Rest is a core value with God, so much so that he grants his people sleep (Psalm 127:2).

Rest is a core value with God, so much so that he connected rest with salvation (Isaiah 30:15).

Rest is a core value with God, so much so that the land was given a Sabbath year every seven years (Leviticus 25:4).

Rest is a core value with God, so much so that he made a day of rest as a gift to man (Mark 2:27).

Rest is a core value with God, so much so that he continues to offer rest to all who are weary and burdened (Matthew 11:28-30).

Rest is a core value with God, so much so that he used the word rest when referring to heaven (Hebrews 4:9, 10).

If rest is a core value with God, rest ought to be a core value with us. We can't function well for him without it.

I hope that all who read *For God's Sake Rest! Discovering the Pleasure of His Rest* will enter the rest intended for the pleasure of God and man. It is also my prayer that millions more will find his rest apart from the persuasion of this contribution.

APPENDIX

APPENDIX A: A SABBATH-REST EXPERIENCE

This exercise is a suggested means of beginning an extended weekly time with God. It is not intended as a rigid formula prohibiting variation. Like training wheels designed to help a person learn to ride a bike, a Sabbath exercise encourages a person to begin. With practice the training wheels may be removed. There is, however, always a need for some structure. It is my conviction that the release of concerns, the review of one's life, and the remembrance of the living Lord are vital to a relationship with God.

PART I: SABBATH
A TIME TO RELEASE

Cast all your anxiety on him because he cares for you.

(I Peter 5:7)

Do not be anxious about anything, but in everything, by prayer and petition, with thanksgiving, present your requests to God. And the peace of God, which transcends all understanding, will guard your hearts and your minds in Christ Jesus.

(Philippians 4:6-7)

Praise be to the Lord, to God our Savior, who daily bears our burdens. Selah

(Psalm 68:19)

Then he said to them, "The Sabbath was made for man, not man for the Sabbath. So the Son of Man is Lord even of the Sabbath."

(Mark 2:27-28)

On a Sabbath Jesus was teaching in one of the synagogues, [11] and a woman was there who had been crippled by a spirit for eighteen years. She was bent over and could not straighten up at all. [12] When Jesus saw her, he called her forward and said to her, "Woman, you are set free from your infirmity." [13] Then he put his hands on her, and immediately she straightened up and praised God. Indignant because Jesus had healed on the Sabbath, the synagogue ruler said to the people, "There are six days for work. So come and be healed on those days, not on the Sabbath." [15] The Lord answered him, "You hypocrites! Doesn't each of you on the Sabbath untie his ox or donkey from the stall and lead it out to give it water? [16] Then should not this woman, a daughter of Abraham, whom Satan has kept bound for eighteen long years, be set free on the Sabbath day from what bound her?" [17] When he said this, all his opponents were humiliated, but the people were delighted with all the wonderful things he was doing.

(Luke 13: 10-17)

EXERCISE FOR RELEASING CONCERNS

1. List your concerns in your journal.
2. From that list make a second list of actions you might take for given situations.
3. Make another list concerning what only God can do. This becomes a prayer list.

(Plan to spend an hour on this portion of the weekly exercise.)

SERENITY PRAYER

God grant me the serenity to accept the things I cannot change; courage to change the things I can; and the wisdom to know the difference.

(Reinhold Niebuhr)

PART II: SABBATH
A TIME TO REVIEW

Let us examine our ways and test them, and let us return to the LORD.

(Lamentations 3:40)

Search me, O God, and know my heart; test me and know my anxious thoughts. [24] See if there is any offensive way in me, and lead me in the way everlasting.

(Psalm 139:23-24)

"How can you say to your brother, 'Let me take the speck out of your eye,' when all the time there is a plank in your own eye? [5] You hypocrite, first take the plank out of your own eye, and then you will see clearly to remove the speck from your brother's eye."

(Matthew 7:4-5)

"Woe to you, teachers of the law and Pharisees, you hypocrites! You clean the outside of the cup and dish, but inside they are full of greed and self-indulgence. [26] Blind Pharisee! First clean the inside of the cup and dish, and then the outside also will be clean."

(Matthew 23:25-26)

EXERCISE FOR REVIEWING ONE'S LIFE

1. Read over passages of Scripture which call for self-examination. Make them your prayer.
2. Read any Scripture passage which comes to mind that pertains to you. Remember, this is not a time to analyze others; you are the subject at hand. Record your thoughts and prayers.
3. Review your past week of activity, accomplishments, and frustrations. Pay particular attention to any feelings or emotions.
4. Study any passages of Scripture which speak to your situation and record any discoveries regarding yourself (i.e., actions, attitudes).
5. Take careful notes and do not be surprised if you find yourself incorporating many of your insights into devotionals to share with others.

(Plan to spend an hour on this portion of the weekly exercise.)

Part III: Sabbath
A Time to Remember

But remember the LORD your God, for it is he who gives you the ability to produce wealth, and so confirms his covenant, which he swore to your forefathers, as it is today.

(Deuteronomy 8:18)

When my life was ebbing away, I remembered you, LORD, and my prayer rose to you, to your holy temple.

(Jonah 2:7)

Remember the wonders he has done, his miracles, and the judgments he pronounced.

(I Chronicles 16:12)

Remember your Creator in the days of your youth, before the days of trouble come and the years approach when you will say, "I find no pleasure in them."

(Ecclesiastes 12:1)

Remember Jesus Christ, raised from the dead, descended from David. This is my gospel.

(II Timothy 2:8)

He is not here; he has risen! Remember how he told you, while he was still with you in Galilee:

(Luke 24:6)

Remember that you were slaves in Egypt and that the LORD your God brought you out of there with a mighty hand and an outstretched arm. Therefore the LORD your God has commanded you to observe the Sabbath day.

(Deuteronomy 5:15)

Exercise for Remembering the Lord

1. Read passages of Scripture which bring to mind both the work and person of God. Record your thoughts and prayers.
2. Praise God with words, songs, and prayers, etc. Find a place where you will not be inhibited.
3. Do an activity which is an expression of your appreciation of God.

(Plan to spend an hour on this portion of the weekly exercise.)

APPENDIX B: EXERCISE FOR LOOKING FORWARD

There remains, then, a Sabbath-rest for the people of God.

(Hebrews 4:9)

This exercise may be approached as an advanced Sabbath-rest exercise. As one progresses in the practice of rest, the aging process, or endures suffering, a heavenward focus becomes more appealing. Every believer needs to develop a heavenly mindset in the midst of earthly pressures and pleasures. Sabbath-rest provides a viable means of doing so.

Search the Scriptures for verses and passages which express the believer's hope. This may be done by using a concordance or simply by identifying hope as expressed by biblical authors and characters. Two lists have been provided. One list has been formed by looking up the word "hope" in a concordance. The other represents selected statements of hope from several Bible characters.

"HOPE" IN SCRIPTURE

Then Paul, knowing that some of them were Sadducees and the others Pharisees, called out in the Sanhedrin, "My brothers, I am a Pharisee, the son of a Pharisee. I stand on trial because of my hope in the resurrection of the dead."

(Acts 23:6)

And I have the same hope in God as these men, that there will be a resurrection of both the righteous and the wicked.

(Acts 24:15)

Be joyful in hope, patient in affliction, faithful in prayer.

(Romans 12:12)

May the God of hope fill you with all joy and peace as you trust in him, so that you may overflow with hope by the power of the Holy Spirit.

(Romans 15:13)

Therefore, since we have such a hope, we are very bold.

(II Corinthians 3:12)

But by faith we eagerly await through the Spirit the righteousness for which we hope.

(Galatians 5:5)

Brothers, we do not want you to be ignorant about those who fall asleep, or to grieve like the rest of men, who have no hope. We believe that Jesus died and rose again and so we believe that God will bring with Jesus those who have fallen asleep in him.

(I Thessalonians 4:13-14)

May our Lord Jesus Christ himself and God our Father, who loved us and by his grace gave us eternal encouragement and good hope, encourage your hearts and strengthen you in every good deed and word.

(II Thessalonians 2:16)

Paul, an apostle of Christ Jesus by the command of God our Savior and of Christ Jesus our hope.

(I Timothy 1:1)

Command those who are rich in this present world not to be arrogant nor to put their hope in wealth, which is so uncertain, but to put their hope in God, who richly provides us with everything for our enjoyment.

(I Timothy 6:17)

In this way they will lay up treasure for themselves as a firm foundation for the coming age, so that they may take hold of the life that is truly life.

(I Timothy 6:19)

A faith and knowledge resting on the hope of eternal life, which God, who does not lie, promised before the beginning of time...

(Titus 1:2)

So that, having been justified by his grace, we might become heirs having the hope of eternal life.

(Titus 3:7)

STATEMENTS OF HOPE FROM BIBLE CHARACTERS

Job

I know that my Redeemer lives, and that in the end he will stand upon the earth. And after my skin has been destroyed, yet in my flesh I will see God; I myself will see him with my own eyes—I, and not another. How my heart yearns within me!

(Job 19:25-27)

Abraham

By faith Abraham, when called to go to a place he would later receive as his inheritance, obeyed and went, even though he did not know where he was going. By faith he made his home in the promised land like a stranger in a foreign country; he lived in tents, as did Isaac and Jacob, who were heirs with him of the same promise. For he was looking forward to the city with foundations, whose architect and builder is God.

(Hebrews 11:8-10)

Instead, they were longing for a better country—a heavenly one. Therefore God is not ashamed to be called their God, for he has prepared a city for them.

(Hebrews 11:16)

Moses

By faith Moses, when he had grown up, refused to be known as the son of Pharaoh's daughter. ^{25} He chose to be mistreated along with the people of God rather than to enjoy the pleasures of sin for a short time. ^{26} He regarded disgrace for the sake of Christ as of greater value than the treasures of Egypt, because he was looking ahead to his reward.

(Hebrews 11:24-26)

Jesus

After taking the cup, he gave thanks and said, "Take this and divide it among you. ^{18} For I tell you I will not drink again of the fruit of the vine until the kingdom of God comes." ^{19} And he took bread, gave thanks and broke it, and gave it to them, saying, "This is my body given for you; do this in remembrance of me." ^{20} In the same way, after the supper he took the cup, saying, "This cup is the new covenant in my blood, which is poured out for you."

(Luke 22:17-20)

I have brought you glory on earth by completing the work you gave me to do. ^{5}And now, Father, glorify me in your presence with the glory I had with you before the world began.

(John 17:4-5)

Paul

And if what was fading away came with glory, how much greater is the glory of that which lasts!

(II Corinthians 3:11)

I pray also that the eyes of your heart may be enlightened in order that you may know the hope to which he has called you, the riches of his glorious inheritance in the saints.

(Ephesians 1:18)

The faith and love that spring from the hope that is stored up for you in heaven and that you have already heard about in the word of truth, the gospel that has come to you. All over the world this gospel is bearing fruit and growing, just as it has been doing among you since the day you heard it and understood God's grace in all its truth.

(Colossians 1:5-6)

If only for this life we have in hope Christ, we are to be pitied more than all men.
But Christ has indeed been raised from the dead, the firstfruits of those who have fallen asleep.

(I Corinthians 15:19-20)

Now there is in store for me the crown of righteousness, which the Lord, the righteous Judge, will award to me on that day—and not only to me, but also to all who have longed for his appearing.

(II Timothy 4:8)

While we wait for the blessed hope—the glorious appearing of our great God and Savior, Jesus Christ, who gave himself for us to redeem us from all wickedness and to purify for himself a people that are his very own, eager to do what is good.

(Titus 2:13, 14)

To him who is able to keep you from falling and to present you before his glorious presence without fault and with great joy—to the only God our Savior be glory, majesty, power and authority, through Jesus Christ our Lord, before all ages, now and forevermore! Amen.

(Jude 1:24-25)

John

How great is the love the Father has lavished on us, that we should be called children of God! And that is what we are! The reason the world does not know us is that it did not know him. [2] Dear friends, now we are children of God, and what we will be has not yet been made known. But we know that when he appears, we shall be like him, for we shall see him as he is.

(I John 3:1-3)

Do not be afraid of what you are about to suffer. I tell you, the devil will put some of you in prison to test you, and you will suffer persecution for ten days. Be faithful, even to the point of death, and I will give you the crown of life.

(Revelation 2:10)

Then the angel said to me, "Write: 'Blessed are those who are invited to the wedding supper of the Lamb!'" And he added, "These are the true words of God."

(Revelation 19:9)

And I heard a loud voice from the throne saying, "Now the dwelling of God is with men, and he will live with them. They will be his people, and God himself will be with them and be their God. He will wipe every tear from their eyes. There will be no more death or mourning or crying or pain, for the old order of things has passed away." He who was seated on the throne said, "I am making everything new!" Then he said, "Write this down, for these words are trustworthy and true."

(Revelation 21:4-5)

I did not see a temple in the city, because the Lord God Almighty and the Lamb are its temple. [23] The city does not need the sun or the moon to shine on it, for the glory of God gives it light, and the Lamb is its lamp. The nations will walk by its light, and the kings of the earth will bring their splendor into it.

(Revelation 21:22-23)

Then the angel showed me the river of the water of life, as clear as crystal, flowing from the throne of God and of the Lamb [2] down the middle of the great street of the city. On each side of the river stood the tree of life, bearing twelve crops of fruit, yielding its fruit every month. And the leaves of the tree are for the healing of the nations. [3] No longer will there be any curse. The throne of God and of the Lamb will be in the city, and his servants will serve him. [4] They will see his face, and his name will be on their foreheads. [5] There will be no more night. They will not need the light of a lamp or the light of the sun, for the Lord God will give them light. And they will reign for ever and ever.

(Revelation 22:1-5)

Reading the biographies of Christians whose hopes were fixed on heaven and the return of Christ will also refine your forward look. Keep your eyes open for contemporary authors who write about heaven and your ears open for conversations about the believer's future hope.

At least once a month focus on heaven during your Sabbath-rest. Read verses about heaven and visualize what you have read. Remember to guide your visualization by Scripture. Imagine the beauty of a perfect world where there is no injustice, arguing, suffering, or aging. Above all imagine yourself praising God forever with all other believers from all of time.

[9]And they sang a new song:
> "You are worthy to take the scroll
> and to open its seals,
> because you were slain,
> and with your blood you purchased men for God
> from every tribe and language and people and nation.

[10] You have made them to be a kingdom and priests to serve
> our God,
> and they will reign on the earth."

[11] Then I looked and heard the voice of many angels, numbering thousands upon thousands, and ten thousand times ten thousand. They encircled the throne and the living creatures and the elders. [12] In a loud voice they sang:
> "Worthy is the Lamb, who was slain,
> to receive power and wealth and wisdom and strength
> and honor and glory and praise!"

[13] Then I heard every creature in heaven and on earth and under the earth and on the sea, and all that is in them, singing:
> "To him who sits on the throne and to the Lamb
> be praise and honor and glory and power,
> for ever and ever!"

[14] The four living creatures said, "Amen," and the elders fell down and worshiped.

(Revelation 5:9-14)

ENDNOTES

CHAPTER 1

1. John H. Sailhamer, "Genesis," vol. 2, *The Expositor's Bible Commentary* (Grand Rapids: Zondervan, 1990), 39.
2. James G. Murphy, "Genesis" vol. 1, *Barnes' Notes* (Grand Rapids: Baker, 1983), 70.
3. Gordon MacDonald, *Ordering Your Private World* (Nashville: Oliver Nelson, 1984), 174-175.
4. C.F. Keil and F. Delitzsch, "The Pentateuch," vol. 1, *Commentary on the Old Testament in Ten Volumes* (Grand Rapids: Eerdmans, 1978), 68.
5. Sailhamer, "Genesis," 35.
6. W. Zimmerli, "Der Sabbath ist das Vorrecht" [The Sabbath Belongs to Israel] (Zurich: 1943), quoted by Harold H. P. Dressler, *The Sabbath in the Old Testament,* in D. A. Carson, ed., *From Sabbath to the Lord's Day* (Grand Rapids: Zondervan, 1982), 39.
7. Abraham Joshua Heschel, *The Sabbath, Its Meaning for Modern Man* (New York: Noonday, 1951), 83.
8. Ibid, 9.
9. James Montgomery Boice, "Genesis," Vol. 1, *An Expositional Commentary* (Grand Rapids: Zondervan, 1982), 87.
10. Heschel, *The Sabbath*, 29.

CHAPTER 2

11. Oswald Chambers, *My Utmost for His Highest* (New York: Dodd, Mead & Company, 1935), 297.

12. Sue Halena, "Anderson Trucking Founder Dies at 85," *St. Cloud Times*, Thursday, Nov. 29, 2001.

13. Marva J. Dawn, *Keeping the Sabbath Wholly* (Grand Rapids: Eerdmans, 1989), 65-66.

14. Howard Dayton, "Give it a Rest," *Money Matters* (Crown Financial Ministries, Issue No. 328: June 2005 Gainesville), 7.

15. Walter C. Kaiser, "Exodus," *The Expositor's Bible Commentary*, Frank E. Gaebelein General Editor, Vol II (Grand Rapids: Zondervan, 1990), 402-403.

16. Ibid.

CHAPTER 3

17. David Hansen, *Long Wandering Prayer* (Downers Grove: InterVarsity Press, 2001), 118.

18. Martin Luther King, Jr. *The Peaceful Warrior* (New York: Pocket Books, 1968).

19. Tilten Edwards, *Sabbath Time* (Nashville: Upper Room Books, 2003), 16.

20. Alan Loy McGinnis, *Confidence: How to Succeed at Being Yourself* (Minneapolis: Augsburg, 1987), 53.

21. Peter Scazzero, *The Emotionally Healthy Church* (Grand Rapids: Zondervan, 2003), 34.

22. Charles H. Spurgeon, *The Treasury of David* (Mclean, Virginia: MacDonald Publishing Company), Vol. I, 340.

23. Erwin W. Lutzer, *Failure: The Back Door to Success* (Chicago: Moody Press, 1975), 113-114.

CHAPTER 4

24. Mark McCloskey, *Tell It Often, Tell it Well: Making the Most of Witnessing Opportunities* (San Bernardino: Here's Life Publishers, 1989), 128.

25. Larry Crabb, *The Safest Place on Earth: Where People Connect and are Forever Changed* (Nashville: Word Publishing, 1999), 178.

26. The World Book Dictionary, "Perspective," (Chicago: Doubleday Co., 1982 edition).
27. Ibid.
28. Ibid.
29. Oswald Chambers, *My Utmost for His Highest*, 316.
30. John Eldredge, *Wild at Heart* (Nashville: Thomas Nelson, 2001), 207.
31. Martin Lloyd Jones, *Out of the Depths* (Evangelical Press of Wales, Bethan Loyd Jones, 1987), 35.

CHAPTER 5

32. Mark Buchanan, *The Rest of God: Restoring Your Soul by Restoring Sabbath* (Nashville: Word Publishing, 2006), 35.
33. Gordon Dahl, *Work, Play, and Worship in a Leisure-Oriented Society* (Minneapolis: Augsburg, 1972), 12.
34. Men of Leisure Limited Website, 1999.
35. Randy Alcorn, *Money, Possessions and Eternity* (Wheaton: Tyndale House, 1989), 78.
36. David Mckenna, "Financing the Great Commission," *Christianity Today* (May 15, 1987), 28.
37. Leland Ryken, *Worldly Saint* (Grand Rapids: Zondervan Publishing House, 1986), 62.
38. David Hansen, *The Art of Pastoring* (Downers Grove: Intervarsity Press, 1994), 99.
39. J. Alex Kirk, "Learning to Rest," *Christianity Today*.
40. John Piper, *The Dangerous Duty of Delight* (Sisters, OR: Multnomah, 2001), 20.
41. Steven McVey, *Grace Walk* (Eugene: Harvest House, 1995), 133.
42. CCLI Song No. 2697066 © 1998 New Spring Publishing, Inc. (Admin. by Brentwood-Benson Music Publishing, Inc., 741 Cool Springs Blvd., Franklin TN 37067).

CHAPTER 6

43. Voltaire quoted in *Encyclopedia of 7700 Illustrations*, Paul Lee Tan, ed. (Rockville: Assurance, 1979), 1387.
44. Scazzero, *The Emotionally Healthy Church*, 55.
45. Lyle E. Schaller, *The Middle Sized Church* (Nashville: Abingdon, 1985), 8.

46. MacDonald, *Ordering Your Private World*, 174.

CHAPTER 7

47. Henry T. Blackaby & Henry Brandt, *The Power of the Call* (Nashville: Broadman & Holman, 1997), 192.
48. Eugene Peterson, telephone interview with James Anderson, May 8, 1990.
49. John A. Lavender, "Person of the Year," *Bakersfield Lifestyle Magazine*, December 1986, 9.
50. J. Oswald Sanders, *Spiritual Leadership* (Chicago: Moody, 1980), 67-68.
51. Marva J. Dawn, *Keeping the Sabbath Wholly* (Grand Rapids: Eerdmans, 1989), 23.

CHAPTER 8

52. Peter Scazzero, *The Emotionally Healthy Church* (Grand Rapids: Zondervan, 2003), 100.
53. William P. Farley, "The Indispensable Virtue," *Discipleship Journal*, Issue 125, 2001)
54. Larry Crabb, *Inside Out* (Colorado Springs: NavPress, 1988), 33-34.
55. Scazzero, *The Emotionally Healthy Church*, 102.
56. Ibid., 102-103.
57. Anderson, *Victory over the Darkness: Realizing the Power of Your Identity in Christ* (Ventura, CA: Regal, 1990), 126.
58. Scazzero, *The Emotionally Healthy Church*, 78.
59. Stephen Kingsley, *PreachingToday.com*, & *Christianity Today International*, 2005.
60. Buchanan, *The Rest of God*, 5.
61. Nancy Stark Muyskens, *The Curtain is Torn* (Xulon Press, 2006), 172.
62. Scazzero, *The Emotionally Healthy Church*, 83.
63. James Bryan Smith, *Rich Mullins: An Arrow Pointing to Heaven* (Nashville: Broadman & Holman, Publications, 2000), 53.

CHAPTER 9

64. Chambers, *My Utmost for His Highest,* 366.
65. Bob Cook, Midwinter Institute for Evangelical Free Church Pastors, Hershey, PA, January 1979.
66. Gary Collins, *The Magnificent Mind* (Waco: Word, 1985), 113-114.
67. Ibid, 114.
68. John Piper, *The Reconciled Life,* (2006 Peacemaker Conference, Minneapolis, MN, September 22, 2006).
69. Eugene H. Peterson, *Working the Angles* (Grand Rapids: Eerdmans, 1987), 52-53.
70. Andrew Murray, *Waiting on God* (Chicago: Moody, 1986), 25, 29.
71. John Piper, *The Supremacy of God in Preaching* (Grand Rapids: Baker, 1990), 70.
72. Piper, *Preaching,* 70.
73. Jonathan Edwards, *Selections*, eds., C.H. Faust and T. Johnson (New York: Hill and Wang, 1935), 69.
74. David Hansen, *Long Wandering Prayer* (Downers Grove: InterVarsity Press, 2001), 40.
75. Tim Hansel, *When I Relax, I Feel Guilty* (Elgin: David C. Cook, 1979), 67.

CHAPTER 10

76. Buchanan, *The Rest of God,* 215.
77. Vicktor E. Frankl, *Man's Search for Meaning* (New York: Touchstone Books Third Edition, 1984), 79.
78. Frankel, *Man's Search for Meaning,* 85.
79. Sailhamer, *Genesis,* 14.
80. A.T. Lincoln, "Sabbath, Rest, and Eschatology in the New Testament," in *From Sabbath to Lord's Day*, ed. D. A. Carson (Grand Rapids: Zondervan, 1982), 208.
81. Boice, *Genesis*, vol. 1, 86.
82. Lincoln, *From Sabbath to Lord's Day,* 212.
83. Heschel, *The Sabbath,* 29.
84. A.T. Lincoln, *From Sabbath to Lord's Day,* 209.
85. Sailhamer, *Genesis,* 39.
86. Keil and Delitzsch, *The Pentateuch*, vol. 1, 69.

87. Ben Patterson, *The Grand Essentials* (Waco: Word, 1987), 118.
88. Erwin W. Lutzer, *One Minute After You Die* (Chicago: Moody,1997), 75.
89. Joni Eareckson Tada, *Heaven Your Real Home* (Grand Rapids: Zondervan, 1996), 124-125.

CHAPTER 11

90. Chambers, *Utmost*, 193.
91. Corrie ten Boom, *Clippings from My Notebook* (Nashville: Thomas Nelson, 1982), 64.
92. Chambers, *Utmost*, 282.
93. Corrie ten Boom, *Clippings,* 64.
94. Hansen, *The Art of Pastoring*, 131.
95. Ibid.
96. Alan Loy McGinnis, *Confidence: How to Succeed at Being Yourself*, 150.
97. Francis A. Schaeffer, *No Little People* (Wheaton: Crossways Original InterVarsity, 1974), 25.
98. Schaeffer, *No Little People*, 29, 31.
99. Gregg Bell, AP Sports Writer | **January 12, 2006.**
100. Howard G. Hendricks, "Definition and Myths of Leadership," *In Search of the Excellent Leader* (Dallas: Dallas Seminary Video Ministry, 1987).
101. Os Guinness, *The Call* (Nashville: Word, 1998), 74-75.

CHAPTER 12

102. Henri Nouwen, *Reaching Out* (New York: Double Day, 1986), 38-39.
103. Parker J. Palmer, *The Active Life* (New York: Harper & Row, 1990), 16.
104. Ibid., 25.
105. Ibid., 5.
106. Ibid., 2.
107. Jean Fleming, *Between Walden and the Whirlwind* (Colorado Springs: NavPress, 1986), 83.
108. Parker J. Palmer, *The Active Life*, 11.
109. MacDonald, *Ordering Your Private World*, 13.